THE WEALTH OF
CHINA

THE WEALTH OF
CHINA

Untangling the Mystery of the World's Second-Largest Economy

Gao Qiang
Yu Yi

DiPietro Library
Franklin Pierce University
Rindge, NH 03461

BEIJING MEDIATIME BOOKS CO., LTD.
CN Times Books, Inc.
501 Fifth Avenue
New York, NY 10017
cntimesbooks.com

ORDERING INFORMATION
Quantity sales: Special discounts are available on quantity purchases by corporations, associations, and others. For details, contact the publisher at the address above. Orders by U.S. trade bookstores and wholesalers: Please contact Ingram Publisher Services: Tel: (866) 400-5351; Fax: (800) 838-1149; or customer.service@ingrampublisherservices.com.

Originally published as 中国之谜: 财富大爆发背后的真相
(The mystery of China: the truth behind the explosion of wealth).
Nanjing: Jiangsu Literature and Art Publishing House, 2012.

TRANSLATORS: Mabel Low, Katie Xiao, Julian Lee
COPY EDITOR: Andrea Koprowicz
PROOFREADER: Michael Eric Stein

ISBN 978-1-62774-005-0

Printed in the United States of America

CONTENTS

The Chinese Model of the Mystery of China

THE THICK AND HEAVY ink of the golden age is splashed about, the colors running together to paint a diverse world with a mix of joys and sorrows.

Many of the scenes currently playing out leave people dazzled, yet sad at being coerced by smoke and mirrors. It is *déjà vu* all over again, and we are trapped, trancelike, in the wheel of fate. A variety of time fragments both familiar and strange are mixed together and rearranged, as if in a theatrical show that has not been previously rehearsed.

On stage, the romantic dream-in-the-garden scene of *The Peony Pavilion* is being played. The audience is mesmerized, enveloped by fog, and sometimes it is difficult for them to discern the truth. There are all manner of mysteries—from those made by conjuring, to the accumulation of obscuring layers, to the truth's being gently wiped away by the hand of time—and there are always new tricks. The old questions have not been answered, yet the story has come to an abrupt end, and new questions have been raised. With a certain kind of phenomenon, a certain story, a certain outcome, there has not been enough time for last night's drizzle to wash away the protagonist's footprints, no matter how faint—even if the protagonist of the story was just the familiar Tom, Dick, or Harry from next door. In such close proximity or from a distance of only a few dozen yards away, yet separated by what seems like a thousand years in time—it cannot be severed and is entangled.

A China that once was known for extreme poverty and weakness has compressed more than two hundred years of the Western economic miracle into just over thirty years. Why is the rapid growth of a large country framed as "ruining prospects for success by hurrying along the process" rather than "bucking convention"? And amid the funeral bells tolling for the "collapse of great powers," why is China thriving? There has been an enormous surge of currency, yet inflation remains moderate. Has a benevolent god really bestowed the industrious and brave Chinese people with a miraculous reservoir to absorb and issue currency day and night? Traditional economists sell a package consisting of economic and stock trends. China's stock market is a caper-cutting clown: it goes up and down like a seesaw and will temporarily soar depending entirely on its mood. It has completely failed to get onto a good economic track. There has been a clean break from the country's impoverished past. But then, when one looks at the account ledger for one's own life, sadness emerges over a faltering pace that makes the pursuit of national wealth difficult. Real estate has been labeled market oriented in a manner resembling a wild horse prancing out a farcical scene on the national stage about how difficult people's livelihoods are. Macroeconomic controls have increased, but they have only further fueled the rise of property. "The more controls are placed on housing prices, the higher they go" has become a profoundly meaningful curse.

There are many mysteries, both good and bad. Some of the mystery is prosperity, and some of it is untold desolation that is difficult to speak of. This is the mark that more than thirty years of reforms has left on every single person in the country.

In *Wanqing qishinian* (Seventy years in the late Qing dynasty), United States–based historian Tang Degang once predicted that 2040 would be the year for China's tumultuous and great transformation:

> Regardless of how long it will take, there will come a day in history when the Three Gorges will finally be built. This is a historical inevitability. When that day arrives, Qinchuan will clearly have Hanyang trees, and there will be a lush growth of grass on Parrot Island. Amid our cheering, we will be able to sail straight down along the mighty eastward-flowing river, and we will enter a boundless sky over the Pacific Ocean.[1]

This nation is immersed in thousands of years of culture, but it also has a good digestion and appetite, and has continually absorbed foreign culture. It constantly accepts new challenges as it steps up to one historical turning point after another. Whether "standing in the shallow end of the water feeling stones to cross the river" or "wading into the deep water and crossing the river while carrying stones," has there never been a tale told of completing the historical Three Gorges and accomplishing everything else once and for all? If one makes the slightest mistake, the evanescent happiness will last only a few moments.

Today, we are deep inside the riddle, and it is difficult to glimpse the truth of the "China model." To find a way out of the maze, capture what is obscured behind appearances, and, at the end of our winding path, distinguish the true silhouette from the haze, we must step carefully, as if on thin ice, and trek through the vast secrets of complex affairs.

In the context of reality, there are no purely economic issues. Once all the issues that have been dressed up as economic ones reveal their true nature, none of them can be relieved by economic laws. Western economists who examine China are mystified, and the crux of the problem is probably in this: they try to conceive of China in a purely sterile environment, severed from politics and culture, and thus their pondering does not bear any fruit. China has become the counterexample of economics.

How eager people are to appeal to the market, hoping it can enter China and occupy the streets and back lanes, provide armor for people's brains and teeth, and bring about a rebirth that shakes China even more. However, it is very easy for mere idealism to be strangled in a China overgrown with brambles. After the initial rush forward that is based on wishful thinking, idealism runs itself to death in the complex games and negotiations of reality.

Sometimes, and especially when an economic issue ascends to the height of politics, the market cannot be left to solve problems on its own. It needs the support of political and administrative decrees. However, it is hoped that the broad trend toward marketization will leave the market with unfinished business and more flexibility in the use of political and administrative solutions to tackle difficult problems, so that more space can be freed up for economic laws to take effect.

Who is performing on stage, and who is in the audience? Whose joys and sorrows are being enacted—yours, mine, or his?

Under the China model, there is freedom and there is commotion, there is firm control and there is also a state of unbridled abandon. We are happy to be in it, and we are also aloof. It is hard to discern whether we are beneficiaries, victims, onlookers, or a combination of the three. However, we can never forget Liang Shuming's question of the century—"Will this world be well again?" The answer is undoubtedly yes. Fortunately, we have an unprecedented situation of opening up. Amid happiness, anxiety, and confusion, we have inherited the wealth that tradition has left to us, and we continue to innovate. We travel a road that our predecessors were never on; we keep going without looking back; and we simply wait for everything to become clear.

CHAPTER ONE

Why Are People Unable to Read the Chinese Economy?

China Is a Mystery

A traveler walked into the study of a retired and wealthy high-level official and saw many expensive ink slabs, from which he concluded that China is a learned civilization. Another tourist visited Shanghai briefly and bought several obscene books and drawings. He then went looking for oddities and bizarre things, and he concluded that China is a country of pornography. One could even view feasting on bamboo shoots in Jiangsu and Zhejiang as evidence of a lecherous culture; but if the observer visited places such as Guangdong and Beijing, where there are few bamboo plants, he would not see many being eaten. Had the first traveler gone to the house of a poor scholar, not only would there have been no so-called study, but he would have found the fellow using only a twenty-cent ink slab. Looked at from this angle, the previous conclusions do not hold up, so the observers become embarrassed and are forced to draw other conclusions. Thus, they proclaim that China is difficult to understand, China is a nation shrouded in "mystery."

—LU XUN[1]

THE NEW WESTERN RHETORIC: THE MYSTERY OF CHINA

China—this nation with vast lands and rich and profound culture—has always exuded a certain mysterious and alluring air in the eyes of Westerners.

In 1942, Joseph Needham was a biochemist at the University of Cambridge. When he finally had the chance to set foot in the Far East, it was at a time when the entire nation was spread out in all directions to protect the its sovereignty. The question that he thus raised was:

Why did modern science, the mathematization of hypotheses about Nature, with all its implications for advanced technology, take its meteoric rise *only* in the West at the time of Galileo? . . . Why was it that between the second century B.C. and the sixteenth century A.D., East Asian culture was much *more* efficient than the European West in applying human natural knowledge to practical human needs?[2]

Even though these words contain criticism as well as praise, people naturally are less attentive to the latter segment, though it may be heartfelt. They linger on the first question, which cuts straight to the point, because the absence of modern science was precisely the reason for that era's sense of displacement. Also, mentioning past glories in terrible times seems rather ill-timed and presumptuous.

Liang Shuming's question "Will this world be well again?" echoed Needham's questions about China. For Chinese and Westerners alike, emotions waver between disappointment, dismay, and doubts over prospects for the future. China, why did you fall behind? China, will you turn out well?

Today, almost seventy years have passed since Needham asked his question, and the land he stumbled across has undergone far-reaching changes, particularly in the more than thirty years since its reform and opening up. People are astonished by the speed of China's rise. However, that so-called rise is an interpretation mainly derived from the economic dimension. A sustained sprint-style growth of GDP; the presence of "made in China" throughout every corner of the world; the world's creditor; and a dynamic wealth creator. . . . Any words can be used—tasteful or vulgar, straightforward or subtle—as long as they are rousing and invoke the miraculous in order to describe the metamorphosis of this country that endured so many years of suffering and growing pains.

When China's role changed, the West remained full of wonder. They had no time to ponder the puzzle that gripped Needham earlier. They were more interested in knowing how China was able to engineer an economic miracle in the short span of just over thirty years though it took the West two hundred years to reach similar milestones. What was even more baffling to them was how a country such as China—with insufficient per capita resources, a lack of technological innovation, undefined property rights, a planned economy in place, and the prelude of not being completely open to the outside world—was able to lift the curtain on reform and opening up. With disbelief, skepticism, and even ridicule, the West looked on helplessly as China, the sleeping lion, awoke, began to run at a faster pace, and with just one leap managed to surpass their home countries.

There is a vast array of Western economic theories, yet no theory can be found that can explain China's rise. Any Western economic theories that are arbitrarily applied are neither here nor there (i.e., hardly seem to make any sense). Thus, new rhetoric appeared—the mystery of China.

In 1993, Ronald McKinnon proposed the "Chinese puzzle." What perplexed him was China's peculiar financial state: when China's fiscal situation deteriorates, the Chinese government fires up the printing press, but the rapid growth in money supply has not led to serious inflation. In his view, this phenomenon of high fiscal deficits and high money supply with concurrent maintenance of price stability is a "Chinese puzzle."[3]

Harvard University professor Martin Weitzman's doubts were based on the reform experience of Eastern European and former Soviet Union countries, where Western mainstream economists believed that a great depression would follow after socialist countries enacted reforms. But the parallel reform and rapid economic growth that appeared in China stands as a counterexample to this belief.

University of Cambridge economist Peter Nolan shared the view that in accordance with the logic of mainstream economic theories, it would not have been thought possible for China to obtain the success it has today. The Nobel Prize–winning economist James M. Buchanan believed that the beauty of the "Chinese mystery" lies in that "it seems to defy reason, and yet it works." Moreover, Thomas L. Friedman, an economist who has a soft spot for the Chinese economy and has brought the interpretation of the Chinese mystery to new heights, said that he who can provide feasible plans for China's economic reforms should be awarded the Nobel Prize in economics.[4]

This is China, which has been blessed with prosperity in a short period of time by displaying unprecedented courage and strength. It also has an appetite for adversity, tackling issues that many Western countries have found difficult to digest, and creating a mystery in its rise that the Western world just cannot comprehend.

WE ARE ALSO A MYSTERY TO OURSELVES

We are a mystery to the West, and we are also a mystery to ourselves.

The speed of China's rise is indisputable. Whenever we think of this, the delight we take in such a "rise," and the pride of being a world power, wells up and will be inadvertently revealed. It is true that in the abstract GDP growth figures, there is simply no way for us to clearly identify the scope of our own contributions. Even though GDP is only a generic symbol for the progress of 1.3 billion people, we still cannot help but revel in the pride of a prosperous world power.

At the same time, we also have new mixed feelings. Standing in the limelight, we find it strange yet familiar. The country is currently wealthy, yet some people still "self-identify as poor." They express their emotion, but cannot discover its origin.

In addition to the mystery of its rise, there are many other unsolved mysteries in China. These Chinese mysteries mostly flow from the collision of the country's ascent and that of the people. Following the trajectory of the country's rise, people have ascended. Some take delight in going with the current, while others stumble and go against the flow. A number of contradictions and issues have appeared against the backdrop of national wealth.

Reform and opening up introduced the market economy, yet politics still hover over the territory of the market. From time to time, the feet of political power tread on the market's "invisible hand." At the policy level, the market is already open. It has endured the embarrassment of strutting in through the front door only to sneak out the rear window. The national wealth has a palette of colors and hues, but it is difficult to hastily portray the people's prosperity in vivid detail, and the rate at which individual wallets fatten up cannot be compared to the climbing GDP. Real estate, which remains close to people's hearts, has carried the banner of high prices all along, even as prices continue to skyrocket. And the stronger the regulations, the more freely housing prices have risen. The entire nation's wealth has increased to the great satisfaction of the people. Average living conditions have transitioned from merely adequate food and clothing supply to relatively well-off. Nonetheless, outside the walls of riches, the pulse of the people beats with a mixture of confusion, anxiety, and dismay.

During a period overflowing with unmatched beauty, magnificence, and splendor, there remain many subtle fluctuations, from the macronational to the microscopic level of personal gestures. The past looms over us, but the present is more closely tied to the future. A bewildering variety of mysteries never ceases to appear, driving us to continually search for the truth. The chase for the truth is quite a mixed bag. A braggart carrying a modern camera with romantic sentiments of world salvation turns out to only be a tabloid "paparazzi" trying to support his family. No matter what, the truth is closer to us than ever, and will not be completely engulfed in the clamor of history.

No One Can Fathom the Mystery of China

A nation's mental outlook, cultural attainment, social structure, and policies may shape its behavior. All of this and even more are recorded in its financial history. Those who understand how to read the information contained in this history can more clearly predict earth-shaking surprises than from anywhere else.
— JOSEPH SCHUMPETER[5]

THE GRIEVANCES OF WESTERN SCHOLARS

A person or a country that has the desire and passion to try to control the path of fate and reverse the cycle of reincarnation is helplessly swept along by fate.

Regardless of whether they are the domestic "us" or the foreign "them," they all debate incessantly and look China up and down in order to size it up. From China's time as a traditionally prosperous center of the world to its era of desolation and depression, and finally to today's prosperity, the pundits have tried to find holes in an airtight argument. They cut through the song and dance extolling peace in order to search for the secret keys to the mystery. Yet, they have also involuntarily been swept along by the truth itself.

It is not easy for a country with a large population, complex national conditions, and an astounding length and continuity of culture and history to diffuse the heavy fog surrounding it.

Many Western economic theorists have a deep and unwavering faith in the Western market economic system, and have affixed it with the label of "universal." If China's rise, which seems to be a contrary case, is put inside the framework of the Western market economic system at just the right angle, there probably would exist no better proof of the achievements of their economic theories. However, the self-fulfilling prophecy, "first there was the chicken of Western economics, and then there was the egg of Chinese economic development" will become their "tinted glasses" and cloud their theoretical field of vision. With busting debate at the conference table, and heated arguments even in academic journals, it is difficult for them to provide a relatively convincing answer to the "mystery of China."

Renowned expert on global development issues Jeffrey Sachs believes that the reason why China's economic success surpassed that of the Soviet Union and Eastern Europe is due to China's unique economic structure. In China, there is a massive economic entity: the countryside, which became the source of China's labor. Before the negative effects produced by the state sector reached the bottom line of what the overall economy could withstand, the implementation of progressive changes and the transfer to industry of a powerful labor force promoted economic growth.

However, some economists, such as Thomas Rawski, do not believe that the labor force transfer can explain the Chinese economy's overall growth. In fact, the significant improvement in productivity of China's industrial economy—which included state-owned enterprises—was the lever that promoted rapid growth of China's economy.

Some economists even believe that China's economy is not a mystery at all and can be interpreted using neoclassical theory. Paul Krugman, winner of the Nobel Prize in economics, believes that China's high economic growth stems from China's high levels of savings and investment.

In the eyes of Westerners, the mystery of China is getting more and more difficult to solve. They rack their brains, hoping to put China, this no longer sleeping giant, in a Western economic theory framework. However, regardless of whether it is neoliberalism or Keynesianism, because the national conditions of China are too mysterious and complex, those theories are often useless. Thus, some scholars have developed new methods of their own.

Time and time again, some Western scholars have looked contemptuously upon systems with Chinese characteristics. Under all manner of guises (including humanitarianism, human rights, democracy, and freedom), they have ridiculed this ancient East Asian country for staggering behind modern civilization, especially modern political civilization, and for losing its direction in its chaotic pace. However, there is still a group of scholars who are kind and gentle, or filled with enthusiasm, or insightful and forward-looking, who profusely praise the Chinese system, and define it as an institutional advantage.

China has a surprisingly hearty appetite and has calmly digested many of the challenges faced by a nation. The government-initiated "top-down" instruction, and the people's participation from the "bottom-up," have successfully maintained the stability of Chinese society and spurred reforms on the economic level. John Naisbitt calls this type of change "China's vertical democracy."[6] The government mapped out a plan for the forests, and the Chinese people created the trees. For example, in the case of the market economy, the government mapped out a plan for the market economy, and the masses applied their creativity to establish a market economy.

Many bestselling Western authors have echoed John Naisbitt's praise and show of appreciation. Érik Izraelewicz, a Frenchman with nearly thirty years of media experience, published a book with the somewhat deceptive title "When China changes the world" (*Quand la Chine change le monde*), in which he was unsparing in his praise for the advantages of China's system:

China under the leadership of Deng Xiaoping and his successors is in fact more like the American West of the nineteenth century. The building of the legal system is still in an embryonic stage and the forces for checks and balances are nearly everywhere. However, unlike the American West of that time, China has a very large and strong government. Through various measures, the country is currently attracting all forms of capital, whether it is large amounts of capital or small amounts of capital, private capital or public capital, local capital or foreign capital. Some people have said that the central empire is currently under the control of "super-capitalism." To borrow the words of thinker Karl Marx who helped usher in communism, a favorable environment for the extraction of "surplus value" very rarely seen in history has emerged.[7]

However, many people do not believe that these economists have deciphered the mystery of China.

Henry Kissinger is the international statesman who has had the most concern for China's national conditions. As someone who represents one of the first in the West to open the door to China, this elderly gentleman has been closely watching every subtle change in China for many decades. He used a catchphrase of Western politicians to judge the changes happening in China, "It is still too early to draw a conclusion."

But even the protagonists of this research, the Chinese people, do not think that the keys to China devised by these "enthusiastic" Western economists are terribly impressive. The cold state of mind left by Western economists is similar to the legacy of grievances that Italian film master Michelangelo Antonioni left in China.

In 1972, at the Chinese government's invitation, Michelangelo Antonioni came to China to film the documentary *Chung Kuo, Cina*.[8] In December 1972, *Chung Kuo* premiered in Rome, and at the premiere, he said with great enthusiasm: "I went to China first of all because I wanted to understand this country that is showing its new face with respect to the political and social structures and history."[9] After the movie screening, he met with an avalanche of criticism from China: he had slandered Chinese children, lowered the height of the Nanjing Yangtze River Bridge, and masked China's real colors and scenery with "cool hues" inspired by ulterior motives. Faced with these angry accusations, Antonioni professed his innocence but was helpless. "People insulting me were everywhere, and I could not find anyone to defend me."[10]

Perhaps the injustices they suffered were not entirely unjust. After all, it is not easy to forge a key to unlock the mystery of China. Moreover, when the foreign perspective struggles to bridge cultural differences, there will inevitably be crude and unwelcome assumptions. More often, they are exhausted by creating a key to show China to the world. And while they can open the door to insight, they cannot make expectant onlookers suddenly see the light.

THE EASTERN PERSPECTIVE

As with a path winding along mountain ridges, all the particulars are hidden in the broad outlines of China's spiraling rise, and choose to show themselves on different occasions. Western scholars mixing rationality with irrationality will again and again create confusion from the details of this mixed picture. Of course, China's various coalitions—be they onlookers or authority figures—also will not be outdone in their interpretation of the mystery of China.

Tall and slim with a head full of untamed curly white hair and sharp features, the economics genius Zhang Wuchang has refused to save Western economics any face. He has bluntly pointed out that China's experience belies many points in economic theory. So-called macroeconomics has gotten things completely and utterly wrong. China experienced a clean eradication of private property rights, followed by decentralized power and the formation of a system of intense interregional competition. This system is unprecedented, and is the best economic system ever witnessed.

Because Huang Yasheng published books such as *Selling China* and *Capitalism with Chinese Characteristics*, which were shocking and appeared to display qualities of sensationalism, he instantly became a star in the field of economic research. He did not buy into the reforms of state-owned enterprises in the least, and he had a soft spot for grassroots and private enterprises. "The greatest success of the reforms was to allow flexibility to exist in a strictly static and statist economy. This flexibility created opportunities for hardworking entrepreneurs to pursue entrepreneurship and expansion."[11]

Zhou Qiren, a seasoned huntsman who once spent seven and a half years hunting in the Wanda Mountains, attributed China's rapid economic development to the reduction of institutional costs:

> Reform aroused the desire of Chinese people to acquire knowledge while opening up lowered the cost of learning for Chinese people. Put them together, and the already existing cost advantages and the institutional fees visibly lowered by reform and opening up, along with the rapid accumulation of labor costs in China, jointly resulted in the achievement of China's economic competitiveness. Among these was the real secret of the Chinese experience: a signification reduction in institutional costs."[12]

In 2011, following the publication of two books with diametrically opposed viewpoints, the mystery of China, and especially the mystery of China's development, once again set off a fresh wave of controversy.

Zhang Weiwei's *The China Wave: Rise of a Civilizational State*[13] was representative of the emotional experience and perspective of fans of the "China model." The book's author considers China's economic growth to have benefited from a continuously open market, but also concedes that it is inseparable from the government's control of important industries. Market liberalization and government promotion have formed a unique China model that has overturned the conventional view that sees public enterprises as inefficient. Moreover, "China's current ruling party is also a ruling group that is fulfilling its destiny. Its destiny is to restore the world status of the Chinese nation and its status as a world power."[14]

In contrast, Huang Yasheng's "Just how unique is the 'China model'?" (*"Zhongguo mo shi" dao di you duo du te?*) attempted to debunk the "China model": "In my opinion, China's economic development model is not unique. What China practiced was price liberalization and the growth of private enterprise. This is, in fact, just the market economy model, and China is also taking the path of a market economy."[15] Economists Zhang Weiying and Huang Yasheng echo one another's views in that both believe we should not take the China model on blind faith alone.

Disputes founded in diametrically opposed attitudes toward the model are manifesting more and more as ideological divisions. These impassioned debates are characterized by positions that are distinctly black or white, and exude a strong air of idealism. It is difficult for any of these ideas to fit seamlessly with reality, no matter which side of the debate they fall under. Some people jokingly said that Professor Zhang Weiwei's book may be given to more ordinary people to read in order to strengthen the self-confidence of the nation.

Huang Yasheng and his colleagues are particularly concerned that if we excessively deify the "China model," it may result in a rejection of deep-seated reforms, and an incontestable opposition to the mainstream view that "China's highly centralized political system, the high rate of economic growth, and the Confucian cultural tradition, together constitute important characteristics of the China model."[16] However, even those gold-plated "universal values" and "fundamental principles" of Western economic theory are still wavering and evolving amid a continuous cycle of negation. At the same time, our cultural roots are entirely different from those of the Western world, and copying Western economics and regarding them as the golden rule for China's economic transformation must be done with discretion.

Whether the Chinese economy's "high jump" will strictly conform to Western essentials of exercise is not the most important consideration. The most important thing is that we are now jumping very high (even if our flying style of jumping is seen by some people as strange or awkward), but also question the "legacy" of this time, and exactly how high we will be able to jump in the future.

China Uses Both the "Plow" and the "Sword"

Exactly what types of values or what types of culture have interacted with historical experience and common ethnic origins to bring the Chinese People close together?
  —JERRY DENNERLINE (in translation)[17]

"THE WORKER'S PLOW" AND "THE SOLDIER'S SWORD"
The young French writer Alexis de Tocqueville discussed two types of models for the rise of great powers in his work *Democracy in America*:

> There are at the present time two great nations in the world, which started from different points, but seem to tend towards the same end. I allude to the Russians and the Americans. . . .
>
> . . . The American struggles against the obstacles which nature opposes to him; the adversaries of the Russian are men. The former combats the wilderness and savage life; the latter, civilization with all its arms. The conquests of the American are therefore gained by the ploughshare; those of the Russian by the sword. The Anglo-American relies upon personal interest to accomplish his ends, and gives free scope to the unguided strength and common sense of the people; the Russian centers all the authority of society in a single arm. The principal instrument of the former is freedom; of the latter, servitude.[18]

Unlike the United States, China does not allow the individual to exert their "unguided strength and common sense." Nor is it an exact reproduction of the model of concentrating "all the authority of society in a single arm." Rather, it is more like something in between the worker's ploughshare and the soldier's sword. And it is closer to the direction of letting the individual use their own "strength and common sense," which has a more positive significance. Since the continued prosperity of the United States and the collapse of the Soviet Union after its period of tremendous splendor, this exactly proves that the model of

America's rise is more viable and reasonable than the model of Russia's rise. The rise of the United States is the rise of a country resulting from the rise of the people, while the rise of Russia is only the rise of a country. A distinctly different model of a country's rise extends to a different outcome of success or failure.

On one hand, people find time-honored philosophies insightful—undoubtedly "no two leaves in the world are the same." On the other hand, they continue to explore a linear development model and believe that the prosperity of latecomers is only following and perfecting the road of forerunners. But the real fact is that economic development has never been separated from the insights of time-honored philosophies.

Under the same economic principles, the space for policy choices is very large. The principles of economics are also described in very general terms, so it is no wonder that the marketplace, property rights, contracts, and incentives give people more freedom to create wealth.

The views of Harvard economist Dani Rodrik may be able to provide us with some reminders:

first-order economic principles—protection of property rights, contract enforcement, market-based competition, appropriate incentives, sound money, debt sustainability—do not map into unique policy packages. Good institutions are those that deliver these first-order principles effectively. There is no unique correspondence between the *functions* that good institutions perform and the *form* that such institutions take. Reformers have substantial room for creatively packaging these principles into institutional designs that are sensitive to local constraints and take advantage of local opportunities. Successful countries are those that have used this room wisely.[19]

SHADOWS CAST BY GLORY

Dragging behind glory will always be a sort of twisting tail—"but." Expect, once and for all, a happy "utopia," "an ideal country," whether it is local or foreign; once it was only a stone's throw away from the instigator's "encouragement," however, despite liking it to be within reach, only a romantic passing vision is left.

The dry humor of "even the landlord does not have any surplus grain" is just right for insinuating that Shangri-la is only an illusive dream. Even if many people regard America as a place where the streets are paved with gold and even the leaves on trees on the roadside of Wall Street give off an air of prosperity, there are untold difficulties, and a financial crisis has brought disgrace on the "economic hegemon."

China, which has bid farewell to the red revolution and is stepping on stones while crossing the river of reforms, has also had undercurrents and whirlpools spring up. In 2003, Ren Zhongyi said that China's reforms had still not passed the critical point, noting, "The revolution has not yet been succeessful; comrades must persevere."[20] Efficient integration of the advantages of social resources should not cover the shadows in the background as if one has "one eye open and one eye closed"—a prosperous nation and strong people versus corruption, the affliction of state ownership, and polarization . . .

Rapid social change has also brought an unprecedented cultural crisis. The traditional value system has fallen apart with lightning-fast speed. Dressed in trendy new clothes, democracy and freedom are showing up at the conference table, dining table, bar counter, the dance floor, between the lines, and even by the bedside. They are running wild and intractable, and a new tone has even appeared: "natural selection." . . . "I am certain I am that wolf in sheep's clothing, and you are my prey. You are the lamb in my mouth. I have sworn off companions and am wandering alone because I do not want others to share you."[21]

In 2007, a popular Internet song with mediocre lyrics and a flat melody, "Siqin Gaoli's Sadness," suddenly became a hit sensation because it had stumbled upon the consciousness of the times:

> One is soaked by the rain; no one cares when you get sick
> Love arrives, after it leaves one will be alone again
> Dad and mom make a solemn pledge to each other, in the
>   end they will still divorce
> This is the sadness of Siqin Gaoli
>
> . . .
>
> Like brothers, yet even they will disown their relatives for
>   shares of stocks
> Buy a lottery ticket, win the jackpot, and [have] too many
>   distant relatives at your door
> This is the sadness of Siqin Gaoli[22]

The rise of a new commercial order and a technological revolution have swept society and formed a more powerful ecosystem. Dispersed throughout this are freedoms mixed with clamor, and confusingly firm control mixed with unconstrained indulgence. People involuntarily get involved, and are confused about their identity. They cannot tell whether they are beneficiaries, participants, victims, or a combination of the second and third. In the end, they cannot clearly see their own true appearance.

Today, we have witnessed the glory of the rise, and we have also experienced the accompanying worries and ordeals. They are like a coin with two sides, spinning faster, and reflecting an equivocal light. We must try to discern the secret order and assignment hidden behind the spinning that coincides with heaven's will. We must work hard during this time in order to find the unfolding visible and invisible clues in the flow of time.

Is Freedom to Create Wealth the Answer?

On the background of the monotonously grey sky, there towered
in the east a huge cloud of an amazingly beautiful rose colour; it
was so detached from its surroundings that it looked like a smile,
like a greeting from afar.
    —ROSA LUXEMBURG[23]

THE ULTIMATE ANSWER TO THE MYSTERY OF CHINA: FREEDOM

No matter how hard the exterior casing of national wealth, there are still fragile and sensitive individuals hidden inside. They are full of longing and hopes for a better life in the future. This is the ultimate goal of national wealth, which is wealth that can be possessed by the people.

There are countless paths to the "possession of wealth by the people," including institutional changes, the construction of rule of law, the construction of morality, cultural reunification, and opening to the outside world. These all allow the concept of the possession of wealth by the people to move beyond what is on paper at the policy level to reach the practical level. In the end, all of these elements are nothing more than freedom. This is precisely the ultimate answer to the mystery of China.

The long stem of time endlessly continues to divide, growing longer and sprouting. There are choices, inheritances, and betrayals. The yardstick for all of time cannot escape the two characters that form the word "freedom." Regardless of whether a country and its people are wealthy, regardless of whether there is development at the economic level or the political level, these all have their basis in the freedom of people to create.

The sudden relaxing of the system brings development and freedom. Within the suddenly liberated space, people can more easily exercise their abilities. The silenced or confined resources of the various parties are mobilized. People can start their own businesses, they're no longer doing things surreptitiously, they do not need to hide or conceal when they scale up, and they do not need to be secretive about revealing their own brand.

At the same time, the degree of freedom people have in career mobility has also gradually increased from a contracted state to an open state. "Allocation," a word that previously affected the rice bowls of countless families, has entered a state of dormancy or has ceased to exist. Hopping between jobs is more commonplace now. The factors that previously impacted the multidirectional workflow—such as class and composition—have gradually been withdrawn from the social arena and have been replaced by academic credentials, qualifications, and skills.

ANTICIPATING THE OPENING UP OF MORE SPACE
The greatest consequence of advocating for freedom is that all kinds of physical thresholds are getting lower and lower, and more and more people are nominally obtaining admittance tickets. But these freedoms are still far from sufficient.

Some freedoms to create wealth, despite already existing, once even subtly turned into the consensus. However, when they touch on certain interests or emotions, there will still be some relapses. Some freedoms to create wealth will still be held captive by power, such as the emergence of crony capitalism. Some freedoms remain mere "meals of illusions"—"sandcastles in the sky." While policy has trended toward rationality, the reality is that one ends up firmly pressed against a glass door.

The expansion of the freedom to create wealth in China has met with all manner of problems. The government should create a wider opening in the bag of freedoms: it needs to provide validation and encouragement at the policy level at a more heightened and robust pace. What has been acknowledged at the policy level should have its materialization and implementation strengthened at the level of reality, and officials should stay the course in order to avoid policy reversals. Policy reversals will only dampen people's optimistic expectations for the future and sap people's confidence and enthusiasm for wealth creation. Even though political reform is extremely challenging, we must be determined to carry on. The improper alliance of capital and power should be severed, and power should be returned to its normal role. A market economy with rule of law should be established and operate in accordance with the law.

A foreigner wrote after experiencing a trip to China:

For only a few cents, a street hooligan pierces a wrist with a dagger; the massage parlors are run by blind persons; severed heads are exhibited in the underground palace; the countryside, the polluted cities, the crowded train station that can crush people into pieces . . . so ancient, so chaotic, and so strange . . . the memory of it is like a dream. . . . I can see clearly hundreds of millions of ordinary Chinese people currently on their way to a better life . . . this chaotic place has given birth to a kind of firm sense of purpose . . .[24]

"Reddened cherries, green plantains." We very confidently fill the future up with sap and make a shining impression on people precisely because we believe that the strong current of time will eventually uncover the translucent true nature of freedom. It all becomes incredibly clear, like a moonlit city.

Why Is It Possible to Concentrate the Economic Miracles of Two Hundred Years into Just over Thirty Years?

China's Rise Is a Counterexample to Economics

I myself have been surprised by the speed of change that followed. Nearly thirty years of continuous and rapid economic growth have surpassed the Meiji Restoration era in Japan, and occurring in a country as large, as populous, and as complex as China, it is almost beyond belief.

— Economist ZHANG WUCHANG (aka Steven N. S. Cheung)[1]

THE RISE OF GREAT POWERS AFFECTS THE GLOBAL MOOD

The China of today has changed beyond recognition. In particular, after more than thirty years of respectable and dignified reform and opening up, the huge political, economic, and cultural changes have delivered a shock to circumstances that had remained unchanged for a thousand years. It has pushed people to make a clean break with poverty and conservatism. The current economic situation is like an unbridled horse that has galloped straight to the summit of prosperity.

China's GDP is currently growing at a pace that has stunned Western scholars and is racing toward the finish line at a rate of around 10 percent. This has been referred to as "the fastest growth among the major economies in history." Approximately 400 million people have been lifted out of poverty, and per capita income has also been increased nearly sevenfold. Economist Jeffrey Sachs went straight to the heart of the matter and pointed out, "China is the most successful development story in world history."[2]

In 2000, China's total economic output ranked eighth in the world with a per capita GDP of $849, achieving "the preliminary stages of a moderately prosperous society." A new target was established—the total economic output would quadruple by 2020, per capita GDP would reach $3,000, and a "comprehensive, moderately prosperous" society would be achieved. However, the galloping speed of China's economic growth has surpassed the dreams in the blueprints, and in only eight years, the goal of $3,000 has been left in the dust.

China's rise is not the sole example. Japan has already risen, and the "Four Asian Tigers" also created the mythology of the rise of Asian nations. At the same time, India is also rising, and Africa is also rising. However, no other country's rise has had a broad trajectory that affected the global mood in this way.

When the nation is in a precarious state, people repeatedly mention a brighter vision—*"smash all shackles, destroy the entire old world, and create a new world."* After reform and opening, their attitude is aimed at restoring the present map, making it three-dimensional, true to life, and abundantly dazzling, more eye-catching and brilliant.

A CAPTIVATING "REBEL"

Economists are buried under a broad array of economic theories. Desperate to find an economic theory that matches China's development track, they often fail to do so, and perplexities that run counter to theory and reality have even appeared.

> It has been almost three decades of sustained, rapid economic growth, surpassing Japan's Meiji Restoration. Also, it is nearly unbelievable that it has occurred in as vast, densely populated, and complex a country as China. Furthermore, during the development of this miracle, China has had to face corruption, had to face an incompetent judicial system, and control the freedom of speech and religion. Education and health care are public and nonpublic, private and nonprivate. There are foreign exchange controls, and there are conflicting policies . . .[3]

The environment that our economic development faced was more complex than the starting point for Western economies.

When England started the Industrial Revolution in the eighteenth century, the native population was just over ten million people, and less than the statistical count of a single one of China's most populated provinces. When China started its industrialization, its population had exceeded one billion. This densely populated nation needed to begin industrialization within fifty years' time. Also, the large population determined the complexity of social classes. People with differences in gender, age, educational background, and/or family background will exhibit different economic and political aspirations.

China and Western countries also face differences in natural resources. Western countries walked the path of "develop first, clean up later." Their industrialization has pushed the earth's resources and the state of the environment to alarmingly low levels. Thus, Western countries have only encountered resource and environmental bottlenecks in the aftermath of industrialization. At the same time, the West does not have to suffer undue consequences for the energy consumed by industrialization or the resulting pollution, and has externalized the cost. China has lost the opportunity to externalize costs. China faced resource and environmental impediments at the outset of its industrialization. Because resources have been abundantly consumed, there is a world of difference between the price of resources for China and prices during the beginning of industrialization in Western countries. This means that China will bear the brunt of the burden regarding industrialization costs. In terms of the environment, China is much less able to take the path of "pollute first, clean up later." Environmental pollution and the waste of resources will not only threaten China's own living environment, but they will also threaten the world's resources and environment.

Cynics repeatedly use solemn words to criticize the initial development path of Chinese reforms for being too bloody, barbaric, and erratic. In the pursuit of wealth creation, people go to great lengths to encroach on limits; they violate all kinds of legal, ethical, and policy prohibitions; and they are simply arrogant and terrible to the point of lawlessness. However, this pales in significance when compared to the Machiavellian ferocity of the initial industrialization in the West. By continuously expanding, Western countries resolved various social conflicts of the time. Great Britain, for example, could "export" criminals to Australia, and could "export" the unemployed to Africa. The United States could also unscrupulously but legally use tens of millions of slaves and countless Chinese laborers. They had a strong developmental advantage: sufficient raw materials, an unlimited supply of labor, and abundant domestic and foreign markets.

China will not and cannot possibly resolve various social conflicts through expansion and will only engage in legitimate economic trade expansion. By comparison, the conditions of international competition that China faces today are exceptionally stringent. Even exporting something as small as an apple to Europe requires going through more than ten kinds of externally developed technical indicator inspections, many of which constitute outright trade protectionism.

However, in just a few decades, the world of yesterday has become strange, distant, and divided. The year 1978 has become a watershed that flew by, and the history of a withdrawn economy ends abruptly there. It seems like one side of a mirror that is rotating nonstop and suspended in air, reflecting the boom and clamor of this era, as well as the partly hidden and partly visible helplessness of Western economics. According to the formula prescribed by Western economics,

China has a weak foundation. Regardless of the strength of the "nth power" of reform and opening up, such a huge and sustained pace of development should not emerge in China. Moreover, China's economic growth, beginning with the jump-start of industrialization, has displayed the vigorous momentum of its meteoric rise. Even during their triumphant era of colonialism, Western countries did not experience such an astounding pace of growth. From 1820 to 1870, England's GDP growth rate was only 2 percent, and the growth rate of the United States in the same period only hovered slightly above 4.2 percent.

American scholar Arthur H. Smith has a way to explain the mystery: "If it be the teaching of history that the fittest survive, then surely a race with such a gift, backed by a splendid vitality, must have before it a magnificent future."[4]

All things in the world have cause and effect. What appear to be secret instructions sent from God are not the preferences of God, and our messiah is just our own self.

"Forced" into a Collective Vision: "To Get Rich"

Honor to those who in their lives
are committed and guard their Thermopylae.
Never stirring from duty;
just and upright in all their deeds . . .
    —CONSTANTINE P. CAVAFY[5]

REVELRY OF THE LITTLE PEOPLE

A period of flourishing revelry brought about by the people's thirst for material things, regardless of how shallow it has been accused of being, has brought about tangible change in China—the rise.

Martin Jacques recalled the scene of a bustling Guangzhou countryside where people were engaged in production in 1993. It remains something to marvel at today:

Played out before my eyes was the most extraordinary juxtaposition of eras: women walking with their animals and carrying their produce, farmers riding bicycles and driving pedicabs, the new urban rich speeding by in black Mercedes and Lexuses, anonymous behind darkened windows, a constant stream of vans, pick-ups, lorries and minibuses, and in the fields by the side of the road peasants working their small paddy fields with water buffalo. It was as if two hundred of years of history had been condensed into one place in this single moment of time. It was a country in motion, its people living for the present, looking for and seizing the opportunity, as if it might never be offered again. I was engulfed by an enormous torrent of energy, creativity and willpower.[6]

If you walked into the cities, it would be another bustling scene: the noise of the bulldozer persistently refuses to let up until dark. There is a cloud of dust next to the construction site. Pedestrians holding their noses as they pass by may miss the roadside real estate advertisements—"boat dwellers, you are only one hundred meters away from Venice. Developers cannot believe the opening price . . ." Messages such as these at first entice you with a taste of the petty bourgeoisie followed by an unexpected sharp turn as they take on a direct and unveiled marketing method, which can be seen everywhere, in order to fool consumers. Every yard of the city square is filled with peddlers and big stalls. The faces of the peddlers are filled with enthusiasm, as they show passersby that the commodities in their hands are of great quality for great prices. Most of these commodities are brightly adorned and always have a rough edge exposed— the spray paint on the toy gun is not applied evenly enough, the seams of the colorful Hong Kong–style T-shirt are coming apart at the shoulders, and the socks labeled with an eye-catching Adidas logo are just outright entertaining. . . . Randomly walk into an alley with many ground-floor shops on both sides where a series of store signs for supermarkets, jewelry stores, clothing stores, luxury product stores, and electronics fills the whole street with color. The loud sound of popular music floats out from the stores, and the popular songs of the ages assault the ears. There is the liveliness of "a tune every five steps, and a song every ten steps." Just when Teresa Teng's demoralizing tune "Wine and Coffee" gets to "I drank a second cup," Beyond's "Glory Years" begins to inspire: "Any time I spread my wings and fly high between the heaven and earth, who says it is a naive prophecy . . ."

Change and passion are floating in the air. The desire to get rich quickly has rapidly and unremittingly fermented so as to break any traditional mantle of "contentment with small wealth." The pendulum of status has indisputably stopped on the position of the "economic man." In different regions of China and in different generations, this type of picture continues to unfold.

THE FERMENTING DESIRE TO CREATE WEALTH

Since the time when the farmers of Xiaogang Village inked their red thumbprints on the sacred agreement to secretly divide up commune land into household plots, people have been eagerly demanding to get rich, and they have moved to the forefront of official calls for the grand narrative of reform and opening up. When one is restrained too long, the now fermented desire for wealth creation that has had no outlet will be catalyzed once there is room to maneuver. And when people have a mind-boggling ability to create wealth, they will run with lightning speed into the future.

Not all people have lofty aspirations and walk the world with the pragmatism of managing state affairs and the romanticism of preaching salvation. The majority of wealth creators do not necessarily possess faith as great as the big rivers and seas. Their desires are very simple: to be fed and dressed, to drive a nice car, to live in a luxurious house, and for their family to live a life of wealth. Simple desires are imbued with all manner of complex and ambiguous emotions and thoughts—the traditional idealism of the happy reunion of perfect conjugal bliss, the vanity of seeking to outshine others, and the enthusiastic embrace of the trend of money worship. . . . These seemingly shallow material needs precisely inspire in people an unprecedented enthusiasm for wealth creation.

During the utopian people's commune era, the party attempted to achieve the unified leadership of farmers politically by exercising coercive power, and then to achieve the blueprint of communism with the collective labor method. However, the remote communist ideology and collective system choices did not generate more enthusiasm for labor in the farmers. The moral constraints strung together in slogans and denouncements were clearly not enough to redeem the system's deficiencies. After being upheld as compulsory by the leadership and proponents for twenty years, the people's communes were eventually abandoned.

Cui Jian's rock and roll cries of "nothing to my name"—"I once asked endlessly when you would come with me, but you always laughed at me for having nothing to my name"[7]—resonated with countless people. While chanting the lyric, "I would like to face the sea during the warmth of spring when flowers bloom," it is difficult to bear the loss of one's dignity from the mundane fireworks of daily necessities. Even one's beloved laughs that one has nothing, that one has no material basis, and there is no place for one's dignity. This material sense of hunger has produced "poverty-induced insanity" followed by an economic "rising of rebellion." This has drawn the curtain on the intermingling of good and evil in large swathes of commerce. People from all walks of life wander among the unprecedented waves of quid pro quo games in a sea of commerce in order to find the wonderful "life in the cracks" on this timeless map of reforms.

Farmers who have not yet washed the mud from their feet, people within the system who once lived a leisurely life of "drinking tea and reading the paper" at an office, factory workers who have experienced the distress of being laid off, and young triumphant college students who have walked out of the ivory tower . . . they dread poverty, they never want to return to the bitter days of eating wild herbs and barely staying alive, in order to "be able to eat braised pork every day." Or, they avidly yearn for the glitzy mystique emanating from big cities such as Beijing, Shanghai, and Guangzhou, hoping one day to live a life that is stimulating and tasteful—wearing brand-name clothing, eating out in restaurants, and photographing tourist attractions around the world. Or they are "charmed" by this era and are not resigned to relinquish these great, gilded hours—in which they go into business, get jobs far from home, start small businesses, and/or become entrepreneurs . . .

Most of them have innocuous shortcomings in character, but falling tears can also bruise. One will be excited as well as apprehensive carrying a lot of people's money, all the more so when one has no ability to change the world. However, they have resolved that poverty will not be a death sentence, and they have the courage and determination to "open a roadside inn on the path to the underworld, and set up a night market at the gates of hell." Encountering blinding wind and pouring rain all along the way, they fight to make it. There is unbridled growth of commercial sprouts, which in the end will characterize the prevailing economic climate.

An American named Peter Hessler rented a car in Beijing for a driving excursion from the villages to the factories, and he published a book titled *Country Driving: A Chinese Road Trip*. In the book, he was surprised to discover that a town in the Wenzhou region could produce only a single type of commercial product, and yet the commercial products they produced accounted for most of the market share:

> Qiaotou's population was only 64,000, but the town had 380 factories that manufactured more than 70 percent of the buttons for clothes made in China. . . . Former peasants hawked buttons out of grain sacks—big twenty-five-pound bags, still labeled "Rice" and "Flour," now filled with nothing but buttons.[8]

In Zhejiang, small towns that only produce one kind of commercial product are found everywhere. The reason for this is very simple: these farmers lack formal training, and thus their best option for getting rich is products that have relatively low technical and capital requirements. Wuyi County has an annual output of one million decks of playing cards, accounting for half of the market share in China; Yiwu City's production of plastic straws accounts for a quarter of the world's market share; Yongkang's production of scales represents 95 percent of China's total production; Datang's production of socks equals one-third of world production; and Shengzhou meets the world's pervasive needs for ties.

Earthly interests as a sculptural force on people are always sharper and faster than any cutting tool. The business principle of survival of the fittest will allow people to apply more optimal logic to completing a restructuring that is well adapted to society. Of course, it is not without some coarse designs and clumsily performed commercial segments: shrewd petty traders and small business operators are ubiquitous, as are people who take delight in talking about trickery, and imitate Western business concepts in a disagreeable manner. However, these problems do not constitute an excuse to reject reform and opening up. We have taken off the hat of poverty and ignorance, and become materially richer. After long years and many months of advancing and retracting, we can provide thick material soil that is moist and rich for the flourishing of politics and civilization.

People will face birth, old age, sickness, and death as they always have. What is simply the initial sense of hunger will eventually be satisfied. The determination to survive will transcend all kinds of metaphysical idealism and nationalism. Yesterday's feelings of inferiority will be swept away. Today, the gentle hybrid of individual and national sentiments breeds self-confidence, and it will become a significant benchmark in people's daily lives. When that time comes, the collective vision that was "forced" will have become a spontaneous self-motivation—a glory much greater than that of the former dynasties will be regained.

Institutional Deregulation: Disintegration of the "Supernational Company"

Without the proper system, it is impossible to pursue a market economy. Thus, it seems that what China needs to do is to establish a similar system. If the system is established, then you do not need to worry about privatization. If I know what you can provide and you also know what my needs are, and the opposing party is well aware of this, then we don't need to have the government run everything. However, it is necessary for the government to inform all parties of their rights and obligations . . . there must be some relatively advanced methods, but it must be done slowly, do not do it too fast, and moving fast is not necessarily a good thing. I remember that the ancient Chinese have a famous saying, "When the elephants are crossing the bridge, it is wise to stop and let

them get across first." This was a famous Chinese saying several
thousands of years ago.

—Nobel Prize Laureate in Economics GARY BECKER
(in translation)[9]

COMMON CONSENSUS: ESTABLISH A SOCIETY WITH
"FEW POWERS AND MANY RESPONSIBILITIES"

People disoriented from the torment of poverty anxiously hope that, in time, the
mural of accumulated political joys and sorrows will crack, and the many blind
emotions stirred up by slogans and violence will fade from the wall together
with the shadows of antiquities. There has been a sharp turn away from frantic
political fanaticism, and a collective appeal for a new temperament and meaning.

At the same time, the modernization of the Western world is playing out
far away on the other side. Even though the details are unclear, the outline is
clearly visible, making people feel a bit restless with longing and infatuation.

The Chinese government is facing an unprecedented opening situation, and
it must face the times and answer to them—after experiencing the twists and
turns of political fanaticism, what leadership attitude will remain?

Friedrich Hayek in *Fatal Conceit* has this text:

> The biggest difference between the coercive power of the state and the
> tribal way of the past is that it is not necessary to formulate a unified target
> for the entire community and concentrate wealth to achieve this goal. It
> only needs to limit its own functions to the provision of public safety, the
> protection of property rights, and the implementation of fair rules . . .[10]

The consensus has become to establish a society with "few powers and
great responsibilities." On the one hand, government should know how to
decentralize and provide society with more autonomous space to maneuver,
thereby enabling the populace to gain more space for wealth creation and
enjoying life. Everyone has the opportunity to change their situation through
industrious labor and hardship. On the other hand, the government needs to
bear responsibility for the people's livelihoods: safeguarding social equality and
justice, providing subsistence guarantees for the underclass, and ensuring that
they enjoy certain basic rights of health, education, and housing.

Under the planned economy, the government is taking on all roles, not only
being the "player" but also the "coach" and the "referee." Political omnipotence
is a fatal conceit. China began to carry out institutional deregulation with a
gradual and orderly progression of deep-rooted reforms. The earlier phase of

reforms sowed the seeds for the latter phase, and the latter phase retained some of the splendid legacies of its predecessor. Through this constant cycle of new ideas, "supernational companies" gradually disintegrated.

A SERIES OF INSTITUTIONAL DEREGULATIONS

Since reforms surfaced in 1978, China has carried out a series of institutional deregulations. In 1978, the Third Plenary Session of the 11th Central Committee confirmed the termination of "class struggle as the guiding principle" and "continuous revolution under the dictatorship of the proletariat," in order to shift the focus to socialist modernization construction. In 1984, the Third Plenary Session of the 12th Central Committee requested the construction of a "planned commodity economy." In 1992, the 14th National Congress of the Chinese Communist Party clearly articulated the development of a "socialist market economy."[11] In 1997, the 15th National Congress took an even clearer stand and set up our country's basic economic system with "public ownership as the mainstay and diverse forms of ownership in the economy allowed to develop side by side."[12]

Institutional deregulation has broken the impasse of political omnipotence. A large number of economic organizations have become independent, and more and more resources are being optimally allocated by the hand of the market rather than by that of the government; government has gradually returned to the role of arbiter and servicer.

The central government has delegated its economic and political decision-making powers and provided more favorable conditions for economic growth. The system is invisible and intangible, but there are also costs. Institutional economics takes the ability of a system to facilitate the occurrence and consolidation of market transactions as the most important criterion for judging the strengths and weaknesses of that system. The precondition to sound economic operations is that economies with comparable conditions can be open and compete with one another along with the free flow of all kinds of products and essential factors. In the event that products and key elements encounter barriers, people's professional skills and enthusiasm will be greatly reduced. Transformations in political and economic systems eliminate barriers to product and parts market transactions, thus stimulating people's enthusiasm for work and labor.

Take for example the reduction of constraining factors or regulatory requirements on founding and expanding new businesses in an attempt to ensure as much as possible that entrepreneurs and enterprises continue to innovate. When the political risk that entrepreneurs bear is reduced, when they possess a certain freedom for entrepreneurship and getting rich, when their productive activities are encouraged, and they gain social recognition from wealth creation: this will create stable expectations for future investment growth. At the same time, the original, rigid allocation pattern has been broken, and the labor market freely flows at the command of the magic wand of the market. Thus, the stagnant water begins to flow.

In the past, even if people secretly sold just a few eggs and a few bundles of leeks, they would be publicly condemned as "capitalist tails." Building a fortune was at one time suppressed at the moral and political level. Institutional deregulation, however, was just right for awakening those "small proprietors" who had been forcibly subdued, and a flourishing economy became the natural course of things. Life and death in the economic realm is no longer dependent on how many shares of power one holds, but is instead determined by competition. Any one person and any one company—regardless of their success or failure—are free to choose to operate independently. Moreover, individual rights are respected, and individual energy has also been set free.

According to the assessment of economist Wu Jinglian, the key to China's economic achievements over the past thirty years lies in a series of flexible systems and policies adopted during the process of reform and opening up. This unlocked the shackles of administrative orders in command economies, expanded the freedoms and rights of residents to choose their professions and to be enterprising, and enabled previously suppressed potential to be brought out.

Perhaps the market economy is not the best choice, but "it is the lesser evil among the systems humankind can implement." Under such an economic system, there is a limited government, limited freedoms, limited benefits, and limited justice and conscience so that we can coexist, and our society will also show the face of progressive reform. Even though the road is not lacking in perplexity, confusion, and circuitous paths, it is always moving forward.

Incentives to Create Wealth:
From the Iron Rice Bowl to Private Chefs

Speaking in terms of reform objectives, the establishment of property rights and ownership rights must be universal. It must never be that one party is protected while the rights of another party are violated. Economic freedom also has boundaries, namely that it cannot infringe on another individual's freedom. Otherwise, it

would be impossible to have market and social order, and it would
be socially unacceptable.

—ZHOU QIREN[13]

"YOURS," "MINE," AND "OURS"

The labor scene during the people's commune period was far less busy than
media portrayals suggested. When people went down to the fields, they pro-
crastinated, they chitchatted while working, slacked off on the job, and rushed
to call it a day. Yongjia County in Zhejiang Province once had a proverb, which
was both refined and popular, and provides evidence:

> Setting off for work is like an osprey searching for snow,
> Leaving work one is as quick as a meteor running after the
>   moon,
> Li Kui said working on the land is miserable,
> Earning work points is like Wu Song beating the tiger.[14]

In the winter of 1978, when the former party secretary of Anhui Province was
taking an extended tour of the countryside, he had a chance encounter with a
young man wearing a cotton-padded jacket with nothing on underneath, and
cotton protruding out of the tattered areas. He asked this youth:

"What do you need?"
The young lad opened up his padded jacket and patted his deflated
stomach:
"To have a full stomach!"
"Your request is too simple, what other needs do you have?"
The young fellow then opened his padded jacket again and patted his
stomach a second time:
"To change the dried sweet potatoes into grain!"[15]

In reality, the desire for prosperity became like laying one's hands on scorched
earth, and the outcome turned painful. The self-interests of farmers clashed
with the political ideals of the people's communes. The enterprises in the towns
and cities similarly faced slacking off on the job and the embarrassment of being
lacking in drive and vigor. All enterprises were either state-owned enterprises or
collective enterprises, so factory managers obeyed upper-level administrative
orders, and none of them were shrewd entrepreneurs who were intent on getting
rich. Production materials were branded as publicly owned, and there was no

definition of property rights. There was a large labor force, but the pricing of human capital was not dictated according to quality.

Rights as defined under the planned economic system nearly depleted people's desire to create wealth. "Egalitarianism" and the iron rice bowl seriously undermined the socialist principle of distribution according to one's labor. The ideal incentive of "utopia" became more and more low-yield. In the final analysis, we still took the wrong path when it came to defining property rights.

As the basic element to defining all economic systems, clear property rights is a precondition to market transactions. For ordinary people, "public" and "private" have entirely different meanings. The economic purpose of defining property rights should not be underestimated. If this thing does not belong to me, how do I have the right to sell it to you? If this thing in the future will not belong to me, what reason do I have to diligently engage in its production and manufacture?

In 1981, economist Zhang Wuchang (Steven N.S. Cheung) wrote in *Will China Go "Capitalist"?*:

> The property rights structure will include various constraints and limitations. Everyone in society will become accustomed to a variety of constraints, competing with each other, and influencing each other. In the event that the system changes, the competition rules will also change accordingly. For this reason, rather than use words such as "ism" or "capital" to describe the way forward for China, we might as well discuss changes in the property rights system. China may never self-identify as a "capitalist" country or even use terms such as "private property rights." My speculation is simply that the property rights structure adopted by China in the future will by necessity be very similar to the private property rights system.[16]

AN INCREASINGLY CLEAR DEFINITION OF PROPERTY RIGHTS

To be exact, China's reform and opening up is the process of changing the system of property rights. Private contractors and private property rights are currently transitioning from agricultural to nonagricultural industries. These have spread to cities and become an important institutional basis for promoting the development of China's economy.

The initial changes in property rights emerged in the countryside. For the leadership, the picturesque scenery of the countryside was still too abstract. Production activities such as transplanting rice seedlings, harvesting wheat, picking melons, and raising fish were only transmitted to higher levels as economic minutiae. In documents, they tended to take the role of footnotes. The risk that the rural area residents took in "contracting work to households" just escaped consequences since "a tall tree catches the wind"—a person in a high position is liable to be attacked—and this was a quiet "uprising."

The coming changes found a suitable niche in the countryside. The reforms took what had been solely state-owned and collective in only an abstract sense, and refined it into a specified definition of private rights. Through a subcontracting agreement method, individuals could redefine their tasks as individual responsibilities and obligations. Some production materials, such as land and factories, the rights to their usage, the rights to profits, and the rights to transfer, were subcontracted to the individual for the long-term. Even though these remained nominally public, they were turned over to individuals to be used only according to the agreed-upon conditions.

Under the agreed-upon conditions and environment, the shared resources obtained through these contracts were very exclusive. This became the definition of property rights with Chinese characteristics; and property rights and contracts have worked together to promote the Chinese market economy's dispersion from the edge to the center.

The rural household contract responsibility system has grown by leaps and bounds. The term of land contracts has extended from one year, two years, fifteen years, and thirty years to long-term granting of land use. Enterprise contracts have also spread like wildfire. Ma Shengli, who gained the nickname *Ma Chengbao* (Contracting Ma), put under contract not only his factory, but also over a hundred other factories that had showed losses.

The year 1992 was a watershed for the transformation of property rights in China. There was a turning point in the reform thinking regarding state-owned enterprises. The transformation of the property rights system had become the center of reforms, and the previously assumed unchanged property rights system had turned into property rights that could be sold to individuals. In just five years' time between 1992 and 1997, Chen Guang, party secretary of Zhucheng, Shandong Province, sold Zhucheng's 272 state-owned and collective-owned enterprises above the town and county level to individuals through seven methods. Chen Guang's casual remarks reveal some truths about the transformation of property rights:

With ten years of reforms and all these changes, the enterprise (workers do not have any real say, factory managers have the right to not implement, and enterprises are not responsible for profits and losses) still lies within the embrace of the government. Starting today, we have changed the relationship between the two. You will sign up and I will register; you will earn money and I will collect taxes; if you make a fortune, I will be happy; if you violate the law I will investigate; and if you go bankrupt, I will sympathize.[17]

In 1993, the Third Plenary Session of the 14th Central Committee of the CCP[18] was convened. During this plenum, the Third Plenary Session proposed clear property rights, clarified powers and responsibilities, separated government functions from enterprise management, and made management scientific. China had truly lifted the curtain on official property rights reform.

The Far East Group donned and then discarded the "red hat" four times over the course of twelve years, reflecting the "love-hate" struggle and ebb and flow of the transformation of property rights for private enterprises and state-owned enterprises. In 1992, looking for more resource protection, Far East-affiliated township and village enterprises in individual sectors of the economy donned the "red hat." In 1994, with a push from local government, Far East conformed to the growing trend of shareholding system reform, and enterprise employees successively purchased stock shares. In 1997, Far East signed a joint venture and joint stock agreement with a state-owned enterprise to become China's first cross-sector, cross-industry, and cross-regional mixed ownership enterprise. Before and after 2002, the Far East Group once again cast off the "red hat," establishing a corporate governance structure that had a complete organizational framework consisting of a board of directors and a supervisory committee. This structure of corporate management became a new type of private enterprise.

After many years of property rights reform, the right to private use that was an extension of the contractor's rights has further evolved into the right to transfer. Meanwhile, production materials such as labor capacities and entrepreneurial skills have also been reacknowledged; that is, laborers can allocate their own labor as they see fit, and China has welcomed entrepreneurs back. Lastly, diverse forms of private property rights have entered the market in the meantime, economic activities are being undertaken with contracts as the basis, and public property has been formed. What's different now is that public property is privately based.

On March 16, 2007, the Fifth Meeting of the 10th National Congress overwhelmingly approved the Property Law and Enterprise Income Tax Law, which meant that the definition and protection of private property had once again been strengthened. Owners worried most about the volatility present in all levels of administrative departments. As government departments, they possessed the power to change laws and regulations at any time, as well as to introduce all kinds of regulations and documents. The Property Law and Enterprise Income Tax Law legally confirmed the institutional framework for the protection of private property owners. More scholars advocate that the protection of property rights should be confirmed as the fundamental constitutional principle, and that no subject of power may arbitrarily expropriate the property rights of citizens, so as to provide the basic conditions for the functioning of the market economy.

When property rights are protected, and the definition of property rights grows more and more clear, people's enthusiasm for wealth creation increases, and greater potential is unleashed. When the right of entrepreneurs to start a business is protected, the vitality of the market is also greatly enhanced.

During the reform of property rights, on many occasions there have been ambiguous areas, contradictions, and confusions arising from legal, ethical, and value judgments. Even to this day, there remain many loose ends, such as rural land expropriation, environmental pollution, operating rights to mountainous and forest regions, and administrative monopolies of industries—to such an extent that some people have criticized the reforms for being overly sentimental, as well as unsatisfying and incomplete.

No reform is Pareto optimal, and with any institutional evolution there is a price to pay that will touch on the vested interests of a considerable part of the population.[19] These populations are complicated and difficult to deal with, and they are dispersed throughout every corner of China, prepared at any time to defend their interests. If reforms are too thorough, a dramatic change that clears all obstacles in the way will often not take place. On the contrary, the reforms will be stonewalled, and it will be difficult to make progress, so much so that the reforms may even be aborted. Using an excessively violent manner to remold institutions and force institutional changes that bring along the spark of swift and instantaneous personal upheaval may result in even more unnerving chaos.

The detailed changes that happen quietly and secretly have become repeatedly eroded by time. Change has become more and more massive and unstoppable, resembling gathering clouds in the sky. There are no peals of thunder, yet it is enough to leave an impression on the minds of people, until one day when there comes a heavy downpour, and the whole world has a brand new look. Only then will the people be able to take the good with the bad, which they will see as being a natural occurrence. They realize this baptism is simply a matter of course and that when conditions are ripe, success is assured—because this world is ultimately changing inch by inch, and individual interests are subsumed by the aspirations of the people (individual interests are like an arm that is twisted, but the dreams of the people are the untwistable thigh).

Standing on the Shoulders of the Giants of Globalization

A closed-off country is doomed to failure, and it will be defeated
by creativity. Creativity produces competitiveness, so that people
always want to compete and want to do better. We can come
away with this reflection: an economy that has excessive national
protection cannot fully develop.

　　—PIERRE DOCKÈS, professor emeritus at
　　　the University Lumière Lyon 2[20]

THE THIRD WAVE

One hundred years ago, American missionary, Arthur H. Smith, believed that
"the face of China is always and everywhere towards the darkness of the remote
past,"[21] and so, "To attempt to reform China without 'some force from without,'
is like trying to build a ship in the sea; all the laws of air and water conspire to
make it impossible. It is a principle of mechanics that a force that begins and
ends in a machine, has no power to move it."[22]

Smith's statement is somewhat distorted, but it is not without redeeming
features.

In 1963, American meteorologist Edward Lorenz proposed the "butterfly
effect" theory in a paper submitted to the New York Academy of Sciences: a
butterfly lightly flapping its wings in Brazil can produce a tornado in Texas a
month later. The conventional knowledge that systems theory teaches people is
that for living systems to maintain their normal, balanced operations, countless
pathways that connect with the outside world must be established, so that the
energy transfer and the replacement of the old with the new can be smoothly
completed.

In the nearly thirty years after the founding of the country, China's foreign
footsteps are still hesitant and uneasy. It is worried that it will be struck by
the sugarcoated bullets of "United States imperialism and its lackeys," or be
dragged under water by "Soviet revisionism and its agents." As such, it has
hidden behind the Great Wall and maintained self-sufficiency in an attempt to
keep itself out of harm's way.

After 1978, China's internal reforms surged ahead: the institutional prison
gradually eroded like melting snow, as globalization echoed outside the walls.
Taking advantage of the tide of reform, bans on opening up were gradually lifted,
a crack of temptation emerged in the impregnable fortress, and the sunshine of
the world economy shone in.

The world during this time provided a more solid foundation for China's development. We stood on the shoulders of two "giants" as globalization and national systems converged.

With its unique logic and rules, the world has had a subtle impact on each country's politics and economics, either directly or indirectly. Under the trend of economic globalization, everyone can participate in world competition. With the reality of economic integration, the scientific and technological, political, and economic revolutions are currently eliminating all kinds of barriers, and for a long time there have been no national boundaries.

In addition, the world order has already been transformed from the ancient lawless era of barbarism and the plundering imperialist era of yesterday, into the civilized era of today with codified governance.

In *The Third Wave*, Alvin Toffler vividly describes the impact of the third wave on the world:

> The Third Wave brings with it a genuinely new way of life based on diversified, renewable energy sources; on methods of production that make most factory assembly lines obsolete; on new, non-nuclear families; on a novel institution that might be called the "electronic cottage"; and on radically changed schools and corporations of the future. The emergent civilization writes a new code of behavior for us and carries us beyond standardization, synchronization, and centralization, beyond the concentration of energy, money, and power. This new civilization, as it challenges the old, will topple bureaucracies, reduce the role of the nation-state, and give rise to semiautonomous economies in a postimperialist world, It requires governments that are simpler, more effective, yet more democratic than any we know today. It is a civilization with its own distinctive world outlook, its own ways of dealing with time, space, logic, and causality. Above all, as we shall see, Third Wave civilization begins to heal the historic breach between producer and consumer, giving rise to the "prosumer" economics of tomorrow.[23]

The trend of converging national systems has also reduced the cost of cross-border trade, and rapidly magnified the cross-border market. People have drastically increased opportunities to engage in international trade, and at the same time, international capital and technology also have the freedom to access the "legitimate portals" of different parts of the world.

STANDING ON THE SHOULDERS OF THE REGULATIONS OF WORLD CIVILIZATIONS

China has benefited a great deal during the "third wave."

The international rules of the game have developed out of more than two hundred years of back-and-forth play and mediation between developed countries. These have greatly expanded the appetite of the world market, which is like a "consumer black hole" that has no end. Still, the great quantity of products produced in Chinese factories match the appetite of the world market.

China's products are not the only ones that have been inserted kaleidoscopically into the map of the world. There are also enterprises that are actively expanding operations abroad. Expansion is a natural quality that enterprises possess, and to a certain extent, a company comes into existence precisely so that it can cross the oceans and travel far. Natural disasters, the raging fires of war, an unfathomable political divide, and cultural differences are all incapable of suppressing the impulse and eagerness of enterprises to go abroad. With globalization as the backdrop, the company's tentacles protrude into all corners of the globe.

The desire of Chinese enterprises to expand abroad is not only a farsighted strategy, it is also a choice against which these businesses feel helpless. China's wave of entrepreneurship is surging forward, and its development is in urgent need of resources. Per capita resources are scarce, and are far from enough to guarantee self-sufficiency. In the world of today, the coercive allocation of resources (through approaches such as colonial rule and warfare) is inconsistent with the demands of the times; in addition, these methods lack a moral basis. Hence, China can only engage in a peaceful rise. Moreover, China's local companies are not resigned to passively wait for rival multinational companies to arrive at their doorstep, so they have begun to "go abroad" on the long, overseas journey. On April 27, 2011, during the fifth Chinese Enterprise Outbound Investment Conference, Kong Linglong, director of the Foreign Investment Department of the National Development and Reform Commission, said that at present, the scale of China's annual foreign investment had reached nearly $60 billion, ranking fifth in the world, and first among developing countries. The number of investment regions and countries had reached 177, with the establishment of thirteen thousand overseas enterprises; and these investments extended to all sectors of the national economy. The State Council's research center had also provided such data. By the end of 2009, the foreign direct investment stock of Chinese enterprises had reached approximately $246 billion, and the total foreign assets was over $1 trillion.[24]

"ASKING FOR TROUBLE" OR WIN–WIN?

We are exporting goods, technology, labor, and even corporate brands. Furthermore, foreign enterprises and capital have long coveted China's emerging markets that are full of economic vibrancy. At this point, the Western imported goods flooding China are not only entrancing and in Technicolor, but they also leave a full-bodied and sweet taste lingering on the lips. The products, the capital, the technology, the management, the brands, and the market regulations—with international trade and outbound investment as the conduit, we come across a city that still has anxiety, and even hostility, toward the Western world.

"Why do you only discuss the introduction of technology, rather than bringing up joint venture operations?" In 1978, the United States' General Motors Company Chairman, Thomas Murphy, was invited to visit China. During this visit, he made the above inquiry of his host, Li Lanqing.[25] The Western world was full of expectations about China. China was also eager, and hoped to bring about immediate changes in the Chinese economy through the introduction of foreign investment. Deng Xiaoping once encouraged the introduction of capital thus:

> Do more business with foreign countries, go for fifty billion, take advantage of the capitalist crisis, the situation is not to be missed. Be a little bolder, and take bigger steps. Don't always be discussing; if one sees the opportunity, then do it, begin it tomorrow. Take on several hundred projects ranging from coal mines, nonferrous metals, petroleum, power stations, and electronics to military industry, transportation and shipping, and feed processing factories, and begin factory operations next year.[26]

It now appears that the target of fifty billion was slightly unrealistic, and some contracts signed with foreign countries had to be canceled or postponed, but the determination of the leadership to open to the outside world was quite evident.

The Japanese commercial legions, as well as leading world companies such as Coca-Cola and Nike, successively entered and established a presence in China. From the mid-1980s to the early 1990s, a pattern of opening up was already taking shape, and gradually spreading from the coastal areas to the hinterlands. In 1992, Deng Xiaoping took his southern tour, and made the positive aspects of bold utilization of foreign investment explicitly clear. A new wave of attracting foreign commercial investment began, and a large number of multinational companies entered China. From 1992 to 1999, the actual investment by foreign businesses in China reached $379.94 billion.

In 2001, China's accession to the WTO brought it into deeper and more expansive territory for economic development. The total average annual investment by foreign business in China reached as high as $100 billion.

In April 1981, the Coca-Cola Company finally decided to establish operations in a roast duck factory under the Beijing branch of the China National Cereals, Oils, and Foodstuffs Corporation (COFCO) located in Beijing's Wulidian district. After the factory's construction had been finished, some older comrades asked, "Why must we drink foreigners' soda? Can we not drink China's soda?"

The Coca-Cola Company's partner COFCO Group gave this reply:

1. Coca-Cola is a beverage, and it is famous because of its successful sales. Americans drink this kind of thing when they are in all parts of the world. After reform and opening up, more foreigners are coming here. It has become a necessary kind of beverage, and we should satisfy this demand.
2. Coca-Cola uses Chinese cinnamon oil and contains Chinese ingredients.
3. We have not yet mastered beverage bottling technology, and if we introduce this equipment, it will contribute to technological progress.
4. Every year we spend $300,000 on juice concentrate, but our profits are two to three times greater than $300,000.
5. We have only set up a factory in Beijing and are not setting up factories in other locations. The construction of a factory in Beijing is also being controlled, and the relevant review and approval procedures were completed before beginning construction of the factory. National policy stipulates that Coca-Cola's production will not exceed 5 percent of China's total beverages.[27]

There was a large influx of foreign capital, which provided China with commercial resources needed for development, such as capital, technology, and management. The new enterprises it generated absorbed a large amount of the labor force and became a safety valve to ease China's employment pressure. Also, this influx produced a "catfish effect" in which the sense of competition and competitiveness of domestic enterprises was greatly enhanced and provided a steady flow of labor for China's reforms.

In 1979, economist Zhang Wuchang stayed for a few days at Dongfang Hotel, the finest hotel in Guangzhou, which he found cold and miserable. In 1984, the China Hotel established as a joint venture between six Hong Kong businessmen officially opened for business, and guests had an endless supply of praise for it. Zhang Wuchang also found time to stay a few days in this hotel, which truly lived up to its reputation. The high level of care and comfort put into the hotel was reflected in its every detail. For instance, all of the granite in the lobby was of a consistent color, and the door to the large wardrobe inside the room closed perfectly. He enjoyed the breakfast dining area the most, where proper waitresses greeted them with a smile; and when guests had drunk half of the coffee in their cup, more coffee was immediately added. During the heyday of its business, the China Hotel even caused a demonstration effect in its domestic counterparts. The state-owned Dongfang Hotel also attempted to change its insolent and haughty attitude, and the quality of service significantly improved.

The seawater has swept in invisible commercial strength and busted open the gates, thereby creating a complete transformation in the inland areas. Even though the seawater impact is brimming with growing pains, through this process, China has actively integrated into the world, peacefully shared a new civilization with all the countries of the world, and brought blessings to humanity. Nor has it fulfilled the prophecies foretold by ultranationalists that China was inviting disaster by letting in invaders and would ultimately fall prey to these outside powers. These results are precisely why, in December 2006, World Trade Organization Director-General Pascal Lamy gave China's accession into the World Trade Organization a grade of "A+."

A Large Population Is Substantial Leverage for an Economic Rise

China is not just a populous country; more specifically, it is actually a populous agricultural country. Leading such a large agricultural populace to engage in transformation toward industrialization is an unparalleled act anywhere in the world. The experience of the West in its process of industrialization has never provided the wisdom on how to transform a country with such a large agricultural population. So, China has gone down its own unique path to industrialization.

—Professor ZHENG XIAOYING,
    Beijing University Population Research Institute[28]

NATURAL ENDOWMENT OF HUMAN CAPITAL

In the economically developed areas within Jiangsu, Zhejiang, and the Pearl River Delta area, there are vehicle stations, makeshift-talent exchange centers, and produce markets operating from seven o'clock in the morning until late at night. And there are fliers and wooden signs everywhere advertising for jobs. The lettering on the signs is unusually large and crooked. Much of the time, when signs have just been put up, and before the ink has even dried, a large number of migrant workers squatting on the side have already rushed up to inquire about job conditions and remuneration.

No matter how low the wages or how terrible the working conditions, these crude signs still have strong appeal. Young people in the villages, with introductions from their hometown or local talent intermediaries, drop out of school early in order to head as part of a group or on their own, luggage carried on their backs, to factories that are several hundred and even thousands of miles away. They begin simple and repetitive work for long periods of time, producing colorful clothing, toys, jewelry, and fireworks.

After the first day, their arms ache, and their legs are swollen. After a few mouthfuls of rice, they rest in the dormitories, and then continue to work the next day. This process repeats over and over again. Occasionally, the boss will "show mercy" and grant rest days. They will then come out in droves for shopping, to eat from street vendors and take walks, chasing and fighting all the way (interspersed with some flirting). The youthful and ringing laughter attracts sidelong glances from passersby. Nothing can stand in the way of the blossoming of youthful dreams far from home, and its specific breed of courage.

Such a scene could be seen everywhere thirty years ago, twenty years ago, ten years ago, and even just several years ago, when a large number of investors from Hong Kong, Macao, Taiwan, and even overseas were eager to come to the mainland to exploit the cheapness of this demographic dividend.

In addition to the farmers who are eager to leave their villages, there are factory workers that have been laid off as a result of state-owned enterprise reforms, and students who have just left school: they form a massive army reserve of labor. Because this army reserve is large in number, everyone either accepts a demotion from their previous position, or their position was originally very low. As long as they fill their stomachs and still have something left, no harsh working conditions are beneath contempt.

At one China investment opportunities symposium, an assembly plant supervisor was talking on at length. When asked by foreign scholars about the wage issue, he immediately responded scornfully, "You still worry about wages here? It has been ten years, and the wages of factory workers have not risen once, and I also think that after ten years, there is no need for a wage increase."

Low wages, meager benefits, and an absence of social security requirements have formed a cheap labor force that constitutes a demographic dividend. This has become an important competitive advantage behind the Chinese economy, particularly the rise of the private economy. The advantage of having a cheap labor force is pervasive, and to a certain extent it makes up for China's shortcomings in technology. At the same time, the price of other key factors is also very low, which reduces production costs, so that when the majority of enterprises go abroad, they can calmly rely on a fierce price war with those foreign enterprises that have long had a firm foothold on the commercial map. These companies may engage in close combat, and the Chinese enterprises will emerge victorious. Cheap Chinese manufacturing in the overseas market has proved almost invincible, which has caused panic in Western industrial sectors. Western business owners have sleepless nights over the "Eastern trouble" expanding overseas, because they will then have to reduce the cost of their products by 30 percent or risk losing customers.

A VALUABLE MARSHLAND FOR WESTERN ENTERPRISES

An enticing demographic dividend has turned China into the land of depressed values in terms of product prices, to which Western companies are flocking. At the 2004 Davos Forum in Switzerland, there was a moderate debate. One speaker predicted that "the future is in India's software and China's hardware." This prediction sounded almost "too ostentatious," and caused a professor at Tsinghua University to counter on the reasonable basis that "we are not just small handicraftsmen, we also have brains." The banquet event continued in silence, and an Indian entrepreneur trying to smooth things over said, "I closed my own factory, left my motherland, and invested in the Chinese region. People at least let us work in peace there. There aren't people often quibbling with us, and there is not too much bureaucratic interference. Furthermore, we can also find high-quality labor." I do not know: was this endearing entrepreneur in the end smoothing things over for India or for China? In any case, Western entrepreneurs responded with enthusiastic applause. These enterprises long ago made their choice, and as such, Western investment in China is several times, even more than ten times, that of India.

The figure of 1.3 billion also represents the huge market potential. Zhai Zhenwu, dean of the School of Sociology and Population Studies at Renmin University, said, "1.3 billion people need to eat and drink and have a place to live. The consumer market for them is enormous. An economy must possess a market in order to produce. In this sense, if the total population is of a certain size, it plays a strong role in boosting the economy."

Someone once said that all golden eras must come to an end. The brighter the heyday, the more miserable the end will be. The low wages of the demographic dividend will eventually bid us adieu. As the representative of "Made in China," the low wage enterprises have gradually discovered that this sharp blade has become dull and rusty. The mainstream originally had only a single color: there was only an intense shade of bright red—cheap labor, which will be replaced by human capital. There will be an increasing assortment of colors with economic implications such as health, strength, skills, knowledge, talents, and even appearance, which will allow human capital to take on a polished sheen.

Faced with China's rise, a great many people cannot help but gush forth in disdain. It is no secret whatsoever that the partial exit of the government grants space for society and individuals, which has in turn ignited the fuse of material thirst. Indeed, the secret of China's rise does not contain increasingly confounding economic principles, and there is no need to tax the discipline with coming up with a new school in order to demonstrate the impact of China's economic growth. However, an enormous country—in the broader context of countless details, clues, and deep-rooted contradictions—has created the image of prosperity in just over thirty years. The abundant content in the story of this rise makes it seem like a century. It has rapidly transformed like the elusive dream of a golden era from another lifetime. It is only this dream that firmly rests on the shoulders of reality. It is both visible and tangible.

CHAPTER THREE

Why Is There an Explosion of Monetary Wealth in China?

The Golden Age of High Growth and Low Inflation

Over all history, [money] has oppressed nearly all people in one of two ways: either it has been abundant and very unreliable, or reliable and very scarce.

    —JOHN KENNETH GALBRAITH[1]

IS THERE A BLACK HOLE IN CHINA?

The Chinese economy, after traversing a road of prolonged darkness and gloom, suddenly arrived at a courtyard gate, where its past would disappear and its fortunes reverse. Stories of wealth and prosperity, with ever changing protagonists and boundaries, would come and go in this courtyard. And the flourishing prosperity in these stories raised the people's pride and confidence to sky-high levels.

In this blooming garden, we may always find stories among the finely dressed people strolling in the night. We have pointed them out, talked about them, and delighted in their dazzling appearances. Since 2001, China's economic development had been simply incredible and mind-blowing: high-speed economic growth, the colossal injection of money, and an inflation that has remained tepid.

After going through the crests and troughs of "panic buying," "price reforms," and deflation, etc., China's CPI has been mellow since the beginning of the year 2000. With the exception of a minor peak of nearly 4 percent in 2004, the CPI at other times has been stable at less than 2 percent. Prudent but relieved experts, scholars, and officials described this as "a relatively low level of growth." This amazing growth rate continued until 2008, when a steep curve of 8.2 percent appeared in April of that year. What followed was inflation, which began a slow ascent, after gathering dust for a long time. This round of inflation also came with a particularly plausible explanation: it was affected by the international financial crisis.

Inflation was nowhere to be found for many years. Economists specializing in economic theory had to make an arduous journey—"search through hell and high water"—just to find a single piece of evidence proving its existence.

According to the laws of economics, China's CPI should not be so low that it is "only as significant as mountain dew"—i.e., cannot be observed.

Since 2000, China has witnessed runaway GDP growth, with the growth rate hovering around 10 percent. However, there was a mountain higher than this mountain—there would always be something else bigger. Compared to GDP growth, the accelerating growth of enormous amounts of money was much more generous.

In 2010, Zhong Wei, a professor from the Financial Research Center at Beijing Normal University, threw open a pension-fund Pandora's box: reserving ¥10 million in pension funds may not be adequate for retiring employees in the first-tier cities of Beijing, Shanghai, Guangzhou, and Shenzhen by the year 2027. The basis of this conclusion was that China's treasury had printed too much money:

> Between the period of 1987 and 2007, the annual growth rates of China's M2 (money in circulation outside of the banking system + current deposits of institutions and enterprises + term deposits of institutions and enterprises + savings deposits of residents), and M1 (money in circulation outside of the banking system + current deposits of institutions and enterprises), were 19.8 percent and 17 percent, respectively. In 1990, the balance of M2, M1, and currency in circulation was ¥1.53 trillion, ¥695 billion, and ¥264.4 billion, respectively. By 2007, these figures were ¥40 trillion, ¥15.2 trillion, and ¥3.1 trillion, respectively. In less than twenty years, M2, M1, and currency in circulation has grown by twenty-six times, twenty-two times, and twelve times respectively. The money a person saves when in his prime will become worthless when he is old. This is a key reason why a person who works his entire life will still be unable to live in comfort later in his life.[2]

Under the general laws of economics, once there is rapid growth of M2, inflation will appear within three to six months, and the CPI growth rate will be the difference between the growth rates of M2 and GDP. In the Chinese economy, the reverse was true: the growth rate of M2 was even higher than the combined growth rates of GDP and CPI. Economists have been cracking their brains to uncover the mysterious "black hole" that was sucking these enormous amounts of funds.

American economist Ronald McKinnon deemed the Chinese banking system a black hole for capital, continuously absorbing excess money. The large amounts of doubtful accounts and bad debts were forming whirlpools in the bottomless black hole of Chinese banks. In order to prevent these nonperforming assets from pulling down and bankrupting commercial banks, the Chinese government established a "green monetary channel" whereby the excess money issued first flowed into the banking black hole. This provided some monetary compensation to fill the holes caused by the doubtful accounts and bad debts. Some of this money was thus drawn to the bottom of the black hole, and some of it entered into the market. That is why the monetary total entering into the market has been less than the actual monetary total issued.

However, as financial reforms progressed, the nonperforming assets of banks slowly became a thing of the past and the black hole disappeared. Nevertheless, the mysterious economic phenomenon persisted, hyperinflation did not occur, and the clouds surrounding the mystery of this Eastern economy lingered on. Where did the money go? Was it submerged forever at the bottom of the sea, or was it hiding in a dark corner waiting for an opportunity to rear its head and unleash its giant waves?

From 2008 onward, inflation appeared to be fed up with its anonymity and began to make its presence felt in food, clothing, housing, and transportation. Whether it was pork, mung beans, garlic, or cotton, as long as prices reflected the application of clownishly deceptive makeup, the farce of inflation was pushed to climax after climax; as long as prices continued to increase, inflation would reach another high. In July 2011, the national consumer price index increased by 6.5 percent. Within this statistic was an increase in food prices of 14.8 percent.

Exactly how troubled is this world, where rosy commodity prices can abruptly disappear and where old debts may come knocking on the door at any time? Or perhaps this was just temporary warm weather turning back the cold, where the chilled early plum blossoms hung low on the branches and the garden of flowers waited in anticipation for the arrival of a better season?

Were the good old days really over, or were they starting from the beginning again?

State Clearly That It Is Inflation

The first panacea for a mismanaged nation is inflation of the currency; the second is war. Both bring a temporary prosperity; both bring a permanent ruin. But both are the refuge of political and economic opportunists.

—ERNEST HEMINGWAY[3]

INFLATION IS CATEGORICALLY THE MULTIPLICATION OF MONEY

Currencies protected by the authority and good credit of a government may seem unshakable, but in fact they can be extremely fragile. They can falter or even head toward destruction because of suffering a chronic illness. One of these chronic ills is inflation. Because of inflation, hope that seems assured may become a mere illusion in the twinkling of an eye.

As in a contract, money refers to bank notes that stipulate a certain face value and can be exchanged for commodities and services in the market. In market transactions, in order to obtain a certain type and quantity of a commodity, we need to offer our products, labor, or service in exchange for bank notes, and hold on to the expectation that the value on the bank note allows us to purchase products or services corresponding to that value. Once the increase in the quantity of money exceeds the increase in the quantity of commodities, the purchasing power of money decreases, meaning that the money you hold in your hand becomes less valuable. Its value is no longer equivalent to the product or service you are purchasing.

In his book *Money Mischief*, Milton Friedman describes the scourge of inflation in this manner:

> Inflation occurs when the quantity of money rises appreciably more rapidly than output, and the more rapid the rise in the quantity of money per unit of output, the greater the rate of inflation. There is probably no other proposition in economics that is as well established as this one.[4]

THE VEIL COVERING INFLATION

To understand inflation, one must first differentiate between several concepts:

Inflation is not equivalent to the price increase of all commodities and services. If the government increases the issuance of money, but the prices of all commodities double, including commodity prices, wages, and savings, then this will not affect people's lifestyle. Although the money held by the populace is no longer valuable, the total amount of money has increased, hence the total quantity of commodities purchased has not changed. Real inflation starts from the price increases in "hot" items that have poor alternatives and are in great demand—e.g., pork, eggs, grains, salt, and houses. What is sad is that although the prices of some "hot" items are soaring, the wealth in the hands of the people, such as savings, does not increase. In addition, equity investments are not doing well, and wages are stagnating. These are excellent goods at fair prices that are really "not worth the money" and conceal the plunder of people's wealth. Therefore, some people term inflation as the gangster logic of the market.

Commodity price increases caused by the easing of price controls also do not constitute inflation. Governmental price and market controls of certain commodities through administrative means exist in name only since the controlled price does not reflect the actual value of the commodity. Once the control is eased, there will be a strong reaction in the market, and commodity prices will rise freely in accordance with demand. The commodity price increase in these cases is a normal return to true value, and not a manifestation of inflation.

Inflation includes both the concept of reality and that of expectation. The concept of reality refers to the percentage increase of general commodity prices at a certain time, while the concept of expectation refers to the continued percentage increase of commodity prices until these trigger a new concept of reality. This cycle will carry on until "the fruition" of inflation.

Once there is an excessive increase of currency in the market, no matter how intricate and complex the stories are in the market, they will cause honest nervous reactions. So "small tales that become tomorrow's news" continue to grow and spread, and absurd or irrelevant gossip, stories, or rumors drive up the price of a commodity ridiculously. Just some persuasion by the *Zhang Wuben*, the town swindler, that "mung beans have health benefits" is enough to double the price of mung beans. The congestion of money supply is now a general trend and any intentional or unintentional "tip" may lead to a general expectation of inflation. Inflation means the shrinking of wealth, and even the calmest person will have some worries when that happens. The anticipation of inflation is thus passed on, and spreads rapidly.

In China, the objectivity and accuracy of the CPI, an index which reflects the degree of inflation, should also be questioned.

The CPI index has had numerous flaws as a key index reflecting inflation. For instance, it did not progress with the times: even though the Chinese economy and consumption structure were undergoing tremendous changes from 1992 onward, the system's samples and setup were still based on the regional networks and categorical weightages determined in 1992. In 1992, the real estate market was not yet developed, and the automotive market sold only a few cars, but now, both markets are soaring. There was certainly a divergence from the actual situation, which included a fundamental change in consumption, but the CPI index was still based on old consumption patterns. China's residential consumption accounted for about 13 percent of CPI, which was very low, and this resulted in a deviation whenever residential consumption was reflected in the CPI.

It was not until 2011 that the National Bureau of Statistics adjusted the aggregate of CPI, increased the significance of residential consumption by 4.22 percentage points, and reduced the value of food by 2.21 percentage points. With real estate's gradually becoming a major expense in people's lives, a proper increase in the magnitude of residential consumption would enable the CPI index to better reflect actual inflation.

The offset of commodity prices will also affect, to a certain degree, people's perception of the truth about inflation. Simplistic price analysts do not consider that commodity prices have already risen, because from an overall perspective, general commodity prices have not soared upward, and it appears to be just a hedging effect between different products and services. In actuality, the rise of commodity prices does not mean that all commodities rise at the same time. The prices of bulk commodities such as real estate, food, and energy, tend to increase easily, while consumption of these commodities is barely affected by price changes, and hence their price increases are easily detectable. Also, investment channels in China are limited: people's mentality leads them to buy when the price goes up and sell when the price goes down. There is also a tendency toward herd behavior, so capital can easily gather into a price convexity within a very short time, thus pushing the price of the commodity up further.

In general, the room for price increases in the manufacturing industry and the service industry is limited, and it can even remain in a state of recession. People thus interpret this as commodity prices not being high. Unless there is hyperinflation, there will not be a widespread increase in the prices of all commodities and services. Rather, prices will increase only gradually.

Inflation can only grow if there is excess money. To eradicate inflation, the fundamental solution is to contain the supply of excess money. Although there are a variety of solutions, they are just temporary remedies. A small movement in "price chaos," and the change will be enough to bring a painstakingly created illusion into disarray.

Who Ate Up the Excess Money?

The task of economic stabilization does not end with the achievement of full recovery. There remains the problem of keeping the economy from straying too far above or below the path of steady high employment. One way lies inflation, and the other way lies recession. Flexible and vigilant fiscal and monetary policies will allow us to hold the narrow middle course.

—JOHN F. KENNEDY[5]

A STAR POLITICIAN'S ERA OF WEALTH

"Every different stage of history has its own path, and like personalized poetry, its final value will depend on the force and abeyance gathered behind the verse."[6] Now, it seems that these words by English biographer Lytton Strachey are more than appropriate in explaining the golden era of high growth and low inflation.

The turmoil of the current period tends to be accompanied by the shadows of the past. The past, fractured into countless fragments of time which are continuously shifted and gathered, will finally reveal the clear distinctions that we see today.

Twenty years have passed since China's most serious inflation, in 1993. Since then, the might of China's inflation disappeared suddenly, to the extent that the "Zhu Rongji–type" of reforms and the currency and exchange rate mechanisms could not be overlooked.

With his exceptional vitality at work, his personal charisma, his wisdom in administrative management, and his political passion that declared "Even if a minefield or the abyss should lie before me, I will march straight ahead without looking back,"[7] Zhu Rongji was meant to be the political hero and star whom the people were seeking. Even the most cynical among them, those who would "criticize whoever they can think of"—even the Beijing cab drivers—were touched by Zhu.

In 1993, the provincial governments displayed an enthusiasm for "going all out and getting there fast" that was like a huge deluge engulfing China. The central government had to rein them in by saying "one must take note of soundness when accelerating development, and avoid losses, especially those that are huge." All the provincial governments understood it well and unanimously proclaimed "we are not hot," "even if a certain province is not hot, we are certainly less hot," "we do not even have any warmth here," ...

Rushing economic development requires huge sums of money, and the provincial governments realized that it was faster and more effective to get money from banks than from the central government. Hence, money from the major banks, like water being released from a dam, flowed like a flood tide into economic development. The People's Bank of China was nearly reduced to a decorative ornament and had little say in monetary and credit controls. Money flowed freely, and what followed was raging inflation. The situation turned perilous and the central government had no choice but to intervene.

When then vice premier Zhu Rongji issued a number of heavy-handed polices and suppressed the "head" of the inflation, the three farthest reaching initiatives were recovery of loans exceeding the bank's limit, functional reforms to the People's Bank of China, and reforms to the foreign exchange retention system.

At that time, the local banks did as they pleased. Even though the governor of the People's Bank of China issued seven consecutive directives, these big banks retained their old ways. Zhu Rongji made a "ruthless move" by taking up the post of governor of the People's Bank of China, to rectify the acts of corruption and violation in the financial system. Among others sentenced, Zhao Jinrong, head of the Hengshui branch of the Agricultural Bank of China, was placed in custody;[8] Shen Taifu, who raised a huge capital sum, was sentenced to death by firing squad;[9] and the vice-director of the State Science and Technology Commission was sentenced to twenty years of imprisonment for bribery. These punishments served as a warning to others, and the previously unrestrained bank officials were reduced to silence. In July of that year, Zhu Rongji convened a meeting with the leaders of all the major banks and demanded that they recover all of the unplanned loans and short-term loan capital within forty days. Zhu said:

You are not diligent, and do not govern honestly; you feast and drink, and approve anything at will; you practice nepotism and build for yourselves networks everywhere; but you don't give a damn about the State's assets. You still have the cheek to go on stage and give a report—how can those who are seated not reprimand you? They will certainly not do what you say. You also do not dare to discipline anyone; you only dabble in offering material benefits and giving everyone bonuses. This will result in a vulgar form of office, which will only serve to harm others.[10]

Needless to say, the rest is history: the big banks became impartial and beyond reproach, pressed their customers to repay the loans, and left no room for accommodation.

REFORM OF THE PEOPLE'S BANK OF CHINA: ANOTHER TRUMP CARD PLAYED BY ZHU RONGJI

On December 25, 1993, the State Council promulgated the *Decision Concerning the Reforms of the Financial System*, which explicitly called for "dos and don'ts" in the running of the People's Bank of China as a central bank. Prior to that, the People's Bank of China and the State's financial expenditure shared an independent-dependent relationship with each other. Whenever the national finance authority lacked cash, it would make an overdraft or borrow from the central bank. As of the end of 1993, the central finance authority had overdrawn up to ¥55.71 billion from the People's Bank of China, with many of these loans having little chance of recovery, a situation akin to what the Chinese would describe as "throwing meat buns at dogs." After the functional reforms, the People's Bank of China would cease to provide overdraft and loans to the Ministry of Finance, and if the central finance authority faced budget deficits, it could raise capital by issuing bonds. The People's Bank of China would not directly subscribe or sell treasury bonds and other government bonds. Hence, the central bank would no longer be a "money-dispensing institution" and if the national finance authority came asking for help, even if it really wanted to help, the central bank would not be able to do anything. It no longer had the authority or cash to act. In this way, the borrowing channel of local governments and officials—e.g., the senior cadres or their children, and the state enterprises—was cut off.

In addition, the link between policy-oriented fixed asset loans and the monetary base was also severed. Prior to 1993, the central bank was the capital base for fixed asset investments and enterprise capital funds; and whenever there were problems, they would seek help from the central bank. The central bank had no choice but to increase the circulation of base money, and the funds required for the enterprises' normal operations were instead diverted. From the second half of 1993, the central bank gradually cut off channels for providing policy-oriented fixed asset loans; and the growth of fixed investments has thus become effectively controlled.

With its supervisory functions becoming more focused, the central bank next set its sights on supervising the financial institutions and currency market, and using independent monetary policies to achieve macroeconomic regulations and controls. At the same time, the monetary policies were also constantly changed, shifting from direct control over loan sizes and cash issuance to a combination of direct and indirect controls using tools such as loan quota management, rediscounts, and interest rates.[11]

The impact of the foreign exchange management system reforms implemented in 1994 was similarly far-reaching. In November 1993, the Communist Party of China convened the Third Plenum of the 14th CPC Central Committee and adopted the *Decision of the CPC Central Committee on Some Issues Concerning the Establishment of the Socialist Market Economy System*, which called for reforms to the foreign exchange system and for the convertibility of the renminbi. On January 1, 1994, a single managed floating exchange rate based on market demand and supply was implemented and the exchange rate between renminbi and U.S. dollars was set at 8.72:1. Prior to this act, the official exchange rate was set at 5.7:1, thus finally putting an end to the two-tiered pricing system. Through this reform, the renminbi returned to the path of market-based pricing.

The implementation of a series of heavy-handed policies on the Chinese monetary system and framework, from "incremental reforms" to "overall reforms," helped to control the deluge of money from the source, and provided a good system prototype for the later successful control of inflation. In addition, the continuous progress in systemic reforms released a large quantity of "valuable marshland" which continuously absorbed large amounts of money, forming a positive "black hole" of money consumption.

REFORM IS A GOOD THING

Before the advancement of market-based reforms and reforms of property rights, resources such as land and minerals were held by the government. Many of these resources were of "no value" or "low value" and were transferred through administrative allocation or sold at below-market prices, hence the emergence of "valuable marshland." With deepening reforms, land and mineral resources were gradually opened to the market, and these resources generally became more valuable, and their prices returned to a reasonable level. Once isolated from market transactions, they now "ate up" a great deal of money. For instance, reforms in China's housing sector have made it one of those large customers that absorb large amounts of money. The lands held by the government can be auctioned, and commercialized housing has been trading and flowing in the market as commodities, which have helped to absorb large amounts of money.

The systemic reforms not only released the market value of some economic elements, they also created a new habitat for wealth. The joint stock reforms of state-owned enterprises established a property rights system based on a marketized allocation of resources. Some of the state-owned assets were based on market value and sold to the public in the form of considerations; this attracted a large amount of private capital, which brought about further prosperity in the capital market.

After thirty years of development, the Chinese capital market has grown from almost nothing to a market that is flourishing, attracting large amounts of individual and structured capital and becoming an important outlet for capital flow. The data released by the China Securities Regulatory Commission showed that from 2002 to August 2010, domestic financing in the Chinese securities market reached ¥2.7 trillion, and in 2007 alone, domestic financing was nearly ¥800 billion. People are getting more wealth conscious and the intangible financial market is becoming the people's choice for wealth accumulation, with large quantities of money being placed in stocks.

However, if we were to bring up the discussion on "black holes" sucking in excess money today, it would seem like something of the past that is unfamiliar, strange, and distant. As money grows with each passing day, "black holes" will become more and more a thing of the past. Money will no longer be absent and unseen, and "black holes" will no longer be the endless sponges they are made out to be. Finally, the contradictions between the strength of money and the vulnerability of "black holes" will no longer be able to be suppressed and will explode on the price labels of daily necessities.

The Bulge That Cannot Be Hidden

Lenin is said to have declared that the best way to destroy the Capitalist System was to debauch the currency. By a continuing process of inflation, governments can confiscate, secretly and unobserved, an important part of the wealth of their citizens.

—JOHN MAYNARD KEYNES[12]

THE DECLINE OF THE "BLACK HOLE EFFECT"

As a ninety-year-old woman with bound feet complaining unceasingly about moral degradation would lament, times change. Whether or not you are paying any attention, the "black hole effect" will become more and more distant from us. Once considered a bottomless abyss, the black hole will eventually become old and no longer enjoy applause and accolades from others over its steadfast pace with the "economic miracle."

In the early phase of market reforms, there were stories of heavy-handedness, fickle-mindedness, and difficulties, but the economic transitions and upheavals, combined with all kinds of complicated and convoluted business tales, slowly created a "money-consuming" black hole that resolved the problem of excessive monetary liquidity.

We are treading in the deep water of reforms. The resources left over from the "planned economy era" of more than thirty years ago are shrinking, and the separate resource bonuses are slowly disappearing. Their values are being subjected to the test of market demand and supply, and they may even maintain a "one prospers, all prosper; one suffers, all suffer" relationship with the international environment.

The capital market—the "big money client" that speaks louder than others—seems to be losing steam recently. Chinese stock investors, with their shares locked up in endless "bottoming," are no longer energetic in stock speculation and are displaying fatigue and indolence, resigning themselves to fate. The displayed boldness and extravagance as they charged valiantly into the market has now disappeared.

Land and housing prices look intimidating, but those with discerning eyes would laugh since these are actually bubbles. Whether it is for land or housing, even as prices have experienced multiple leaps from low levels, or high prices have jumped to abnormally high prices, the market purchasing power of these commodities is now muted. This is firstly due to the limited amounts that housing prices can drop, and secondly to excessively high prices. Its previous great appetite for "sucking" money no longer exists.

Although the "black hole effect" has lessened, the excess issuing of money has not ceased. The money flowing steadily into the Chinese economy will, now and then, gather at one place, creating a bulge. After it is put down by government policies, another bulge will appear, just like the Chinese saying "hardly has one gourd been pushed under water when another bobs up."

THE UNSTOPPABLE GROSS MONEY SUPPLY

China's gross money supply has always experienced explosive growth, and by 2010, the year-end balance of broad money supply (M2) reached ¥72.6 trillion, which is 1.8 times GDP.[13]

There are two reasons for the excessive issuing of money: the first is the relatively loose monetary policy implemented by the government, and the second is trade surplus.

There are three vehicles driving China's economic growth: investment, consumption, and exports. Domestic consumption has been relatively weak, and even though the call to stimulate domestic demand has been going on for years, the prospect of a prosperous nation and prosperous citizenry has yet to be realized; and the people are unwilling, and also unable, to freely spend their money. Investments and exports, on the contrary, have contributed greatly to China's economic growth.

When the economic crisis occurred, governments were even more inclined toward implementing loose monetary policies. The United States and European countries activated their printing presses and happily printed additional currency. Do not underestimate China's speed in issuing money as well. After the outbreak of the financial crisis, the Chinese government turned its monetary tightening policy into a monetary loosening policy. In 2009, China's newly increased credit hit a historic high and China's M2 growth rate far exceeded

China's GDP growth rate, even surpassing the M2 growth rate of the United States and other major economies.

China's large-scale release of credit was a masterstroke that had a leveraging significance in restoring confidence and reversing economic deterioration. However, this would only be a monetary "pseudo-honeymoon": once this "honeymoon" ended, problems would arise, resulting in risks of inflation expectations, asset bubbles, and deteriorating asset quality.

In addition to stimulating domestic demand, the central bank also needs to increase the money supply for the exchange of foreign currencies. For many years, China has been a country with a huge trade surplus. From the large amount of exports to foreign countries, Chinese enterprises acquired a large quantity of foreign currencies, with which they would complete the settlements with commercial banks. The commercial banks would then sell most of the foreign currencies to the central bank, and this was how foreign currencies flowed into the pool of foreign exchange reserves. Domestic enterprises needed to convert foreign currencies to renminbi. In order to stabilize the exchange rate (especially taking into account the stability of the exchange rate between the renminbi and the U.S. dollar), the central bank continued to expand the monetary base and to purchase foreign currencies in accordance with the policy of basing purchases on market demand and supply, adjusting by consulting the basket of currencies, and managing the floating exchange rate." The quantity of foreign currencies that needed to be purchased was not completely decided by the central bank, but rather by the amount of foreign currencies earned by Chinese enterprises, which thus formed the source of the need for large quantities of renminbi to purchase foreign currencies.

To prevent the renminbi from overflowing the market, the central bank issued a variety of short-term bills to buy up the excess base money. However, the central bank bills were unable to completely recover the excess base money. Yi Gang, the vice governor of the People's Bank of China and director of the State Administration of Foreign Exchange, said that by the end of 2010, the accumulated Chinese foreign exchange reserves stood at $2.85 trillion, and although the Chinese central bank used nearly ¥20 trillion to hedge it, only about 80 percent of the excess renminbi were hedged and 20 percent were still circulating in the market. Why not hedge it 100 percent to clean up all the excess money? Central bank decisions affect everyone, so recovering all the base money would not just harm the economy, it would also impact people's livelihood. With all kinds of intertwined and conflicting interests, the central bank simply could not issue bills as it saw fit.

THE BUSY "CAPITALISTS"

With the Chinese economy all fired up, idle capital, both within and outside of China, is watching enviously, and eagerly trying to be employed in grabbing a portion or two from the growth of the Chinese economy.

A large influx of international "hot" money has been making its way into China through various channels, thanks to the fact that the Chinese exchange rate is relatively stable, in addition to the combined presence of all kinds of preferential open-door policies and the popular expectation of the renminbi's appreciating. This idle capital has been similarly converted into renminbi through Chinese commercial banks.

Moreover, wealth accumulation by the people is no longer constrained to "silently depositing money into banks." China's banking interest rates have always been less than the inflation rate, and the people are becoming more willing to overconsume as they think that "instead of continually earning interest, why not use the money for investment or spend it?" The view on savings-type consumption is waning and this has increased the circulation rate of money.

The United States, unlike China, can issue paper money wantonly and export inflation to the whole world, thus conducting a covert plunder of the wealth of other countries. In contrast, when China issues money too quickly, it results in a significant contraction of the wealth of the Chinese people. A huge influx of funds will flow into the housing market and the stock market, and prices of assets will fluctuate greatly. The ghost of inflation will once again knock on China's doors.

With the combination of countries such as the United States exporting inflation to China like so much "hot" money rushing in ferociously, and China's implementation of a loose monetary policy, it is highly likely that inflation will be observed in China's commodity prices. So the bittersweet poison of inflation arrives, bringing damage to the people and the country. This is a severe test for the Chinese government's macroeconomic controls and regulations.

John Maynard Keynes knew full well the evils of a "disobedient currency." In his view, "there is no subtler, no surer means of overturning the existing basis of society than to debauch the currency. The process engages all the hidden forces of economic law on the side of destruction, and does it in a manner which not one man in a million can diagnose."[14]

Most of us hold insufficiently founded and dualistic views with regard to inflation. On one side, we love inflation as there will be a rise in the price of the goods we sell, which may be products we are producing or services we are providing; on the other hand, we hate inflation as we do not like to see a price increase in the goods we purchase; only a drop in those prices delights us.

However, we are not God. The things we often hope for tend not to materialize. But what truly disappoints us is that the reality is a world away from our beautiful dream. The price increases in the commodity we hope to increase do not happen as anticipated; rather, the price keeps falling, and the commodity we hope to see a price reduction in keeps climbing up. When we only slightly drop our guard, inflation pokes us in the eyes.

Is Money Honey or Poison in China?

The excess influx of money into the economy and market will not bring about an increase of commodities, though it will certainly increase the overall level of commodity prices. To give an example, a helicopter in midair threw out a large amount of cash to a closed micronation. The cash held by everyone in this "lucky nation" has now doubled. What will happen next? Will everyone there have twice the amount of commodities, or will the commodity prices in that nation double? . . . If you chose the latter, then congratulations, Friedman, the master of monetarism, will judge that you have answered correctly.

—Economist ZHOU QIREN[15]

OVERISSUE OF MONEY: "WATER DISGUISED AS HONEY"

An overissue of money seems beautiful in the beginning. With the increase of paper notes, companies see more profit, and those that guard their wealth get new clothes; a sudden increase of capital injection enters the stock markets and stock prices climb upward, bringing profits to investors; all these are really tangible benefits. With more cash in hand, bosses also raise the wages of workers, and payroll will appear fatter than before. With the increase of money, benefits are seen all around, everyone is supportive of the expansion, and the government also becomes well regarded. Economic news headlines read "Economy Grows Rapidly, Companies Perform Well, People See Increase in Salaries, and Live a Good Life."

In actual fact, this is merely superficial, and the overissue of money is "water disguised as honey." When money is first issued, it is viscous like slow-flowing honey, and bulges appear in places where it flows over. Some of these bulges attract investment and stimulate economic growth. However, with excess money circulating, these bulges even out over time; at the same time, given the stagnation in product supply, commodity prices increase. The good life of the people ends, and they are hit head-on by inflation.

Similar to the overissue of money, inflation does not sweep in like "the autumn leaves" in the beginning—inflation sneaks up silently at first. It also employs tactics and strategies in order to go unnoticed, like a man on a drinking binge: slightly tipsy in the beginning and feeling fabulous in the lightness this brings, but once he gets drunk, payback comes and knocks him out, causing havoc in his guts. The process of becoming sober again is a difficult one.

ALL THINGS UNDER INFLATION

The plight of different interest groups differs under inflation. American economist Murray Rothbard's classic view on inflation holds that inflation is a sacrifice of interests by one group of people in order to enable another group to benefit. Those who are nearer benefit first, and those who are in close proximity to the treasury will get loans faster, even though they may have spent all of their money before inflation began. There are many ways to spend money, whether through consumption or investment. They rush to spend the money before the currency depreciates, and with whatever time is left, they can simply relax, and quietly wait for the currency to depreciate. This type of investment reminds us of the unspoken rules in the world of art collection. When a certain calligrapher or painter gets old, collectors will rush to buy his works, not because there is a great improvement in the quality of his artwork; rather, these collectors are waiting for the artist's demise, so that the prices of his works will soar.

In China, real estate developers, local governments, and state-owned monopolies are the vested interest groups once inflation occurs. State-owned enterprises, with their natural advantage in the system, and advantages in policies and resource monopolization, will be the first to obtain bank loans and purchase large quantities of inexpensive resources. Moreover, they are at the forefront of the industry chain and possess relatively large bargaining power. Whether or not inflation does occur, they will also be able to raise prices, and the market will have no choice but to acquiesce.

People or groups that are the closest to the treasury have more channels through which to protect their wealth, and may even strike it rich with an "inflation fortune." Those who are at the lowest end of the money circulation chain will not be as lucky. They have less access to information and do not have adequate opportunity and capability to monopolize monetary resources, and thus can only watch inflation seep gradually into enterprise costs, daily necessities, and their savings.

China's manufacturing sector is low on the industrial food chain and does not enjoy vast pricing rights over raw materials. They have no choice but to swallow the bitter pill of price increases of raw materials. Moreover, as business is extremely competitive, it is hard for manufacturers to pass on the costs to consumers. Hence, their profits become even thinner and their survival becomes very much more difficult.

Ordinary folk are a similar target of inflation's plunder. On one hand, the imperfections of the household registration system, enterprise employment system, and social security system result in a large amount of resources being taken over by elite groups. Hence, the middle classes have few channels of investment and they tend to engage in savings-type investing. Also, flaws in medical treatment, pensions, and education greatly increase the living costs of the people, and to prepare for rainy days, these people prefer to put their money into banks. Once inflation strikes, their money that is in the banks will depreciate rapidly, resulting in the shrinking of their wealth.

So the overissue of money, which appears to satisfy everyone, ends up becoming a poison that delivers the opposite results as it gobbles up the entire economic gains of the country. This causes the Matthew effect of "the rich get richer, and the poor get poorer." If one day, commodity prices spiral out of control, everyone will lose. Even those who once benefited from price increases or decreases will be caught up by the pace of inflation and lose whatever they possess.

Where Is Chinese Monetary Policy Headed?

Markets are a great way to organize economic activity, but they need adult supervision.
—*Wall Street Journal* columnist DAVID WESSEL[16]

THE TWO CONSTRAINTS OF CREDIT

Ex-premier Zhu Rongji's bold method of directly restraining loans to curb inflation will no doubt produce instant results. However, times have changed. The situation that we faced in 1993 was monetary flooding caused by power borrowing, but today, market-oriented reforms have entered deep waters, and it is harder to enforce restraint. In addition, the government will also find it difficult to select the sector, department, or enterprise to which to apply its monetary policies. Once "credit constraints" are launched, everyone, whether they be "good guys" or "bad guys," will be knocked off.

For many enterprises, especially small and medium-size enterprises, 2011 was a year of difficulties which even surpassed the challenges faced in the so-called once-in-a-century financial crisis.

Statistics from the All-China Federation of Industry and Commerce revealed that 90 percent of small-scale enterprises were unable to obtain any loans from banks.[17] Well-publicized small loan companies were a shadow of their former self, providing only minuscule financing support compared to the large-scale financing needed to satisfy the demands of private enterprises. As the doors to legal financing closed shut, these small-scale enterprises were forced to borrow from private lenders, and often at startling interest rates. Using Wenzhou as an example, the interest rates charged by Wenzhou private lenders were on average four times higher than the benchmark interest rate. The interest rates for long-term private lending were between 3 and 4 percent per month. For short-term borrowing of less than one month, the interest rate could reach 8 percent, 10 percent, and even as high as 15 percent. Small and medium-size enterprises operating on thin margins were unable to work with such high interest rates.

With a sudden stop in money circulation, the abundance of money that used to flow swiftly turned from "a big river to a small stream; and from a small stream to a dry riverbed." Chinese enterprises, organizations, and individuals had to fight for the limited loan resources. This also became the breeding ground for crony capitalism and we were brought back to the era where power and relationships control everything, where those with the right family background and connections could devour everything and key state-owned enterprises could only beg for some crumbs. Small and medium-size enterprises, no matter how tough they were, could only look on, hungry.

THE AFTEREFFECTS OF PRICE CONTROLS
Price controls are also not advisable.

There are two main types of price control practiced by the government: first is the temporary type, where the government controls the commodity prices for a short period of time. Following the outbreak of the financial crisis, China's CPI index was relatively high, and in order to curb inflation, the Chinese government implemented a temporary price intervention policy. For instance, it injected national reserves into the market, and controlled speculation and profiteering from hoarding by dumping China's stores of rice and cotton onto the market. It also reduced the costs of agricultural products such as grains, vegetables, and pork by opening ETC channels and strengthening the links between supermarkets and farms.

The other type of price control is the long-term type, which is usually manifested as price controls of resources such as oil, electricity, and grain, as well as bulk commodities tied to national security. Be they temporary or long-term price controls, the primary consideration is balance of the macroeconomy.

The two-tier system launched in the 1980s was a prominent manifestation of price control by the government. In a two-tier system, there are two prices for one commodity, especially commodities such as production materials. One of them is the price within the plan that is controlled by the state and the other is the market-based price external to the plan. Of these two types of prices, commodities at out-of-the-plan prices are limited in quantity and more expensive. Some people with government background and control over resources were able to go anywhere and everywhere to get these commodities, resulting in the growth of a large number of profiteers who could handle the high-voltage cables of policy. Purchase contracts were speculated over and over again (just like during the times of the Dutch Tulip Bubble), and hence price controls actually drove the prices of products higher. Even Nobel Laureate in Economics Milton Friedman gently reminded us during his visit to China that we should not mix price liberalization with inflation. If the price is liberalized, only some commodities will see an increase in price. Although in the short term, people may feel pain, they will quickly realize that prices will not all rise one after another.

Temporary price controls can certainly ease inflationary pressures, but in the long term, these are not advisable as they only treat the symptoms and do not seek to get to the root of the problem.

As the commodity economy thrives, there will be a variety of commodities, and only the market can freely regulate the prices of each commodity. It is fundamentally difficult for the government to tangibly provide an optimal allocation of resources, so instead, misallocation may even occur, causing a distortion in the normal prices of various elements of production. Price controls of some commodities before the overissue of money may have temporarily curbed the prices of these commodities, but the monetary accumulation has not changed, and the extra money will flow into commodities not subjected to price controls. As in the balloon analogy given by Friedman: if you squeeze one end of the balloon, the air will rush to the other end, which will bulge. This is just like the saying "hardly has one gourd been pushed underwater when another bobs up." The government retains the right to conduct price interventions, which will once again increase its power to allocate resources, thus providing an opportunity for the breeding of corruption. Moreover, there is a cost involved in administrative intervention—be it the opening of a green channel, arranging for talks with the responsible persons of enterprises, or releasing the grain stored by the country—

these actions require manpower, material resources, and financial resources. Of course, such insanely difficult efforts may not be appreciated. In January 2008, the State Development and Reform Commission demanded that "price increase declarations and/or price adjustment records must be carried out for the six important commodities of refined grain and grain products; edible vegetable oil; pork, beef, mutton, and their products; milk; eggs; and liquefied petroleum gas." But in the eleven months since the implementation of price-fixing, there were six months where the CPI was higher than 7 percent, and the situation eased only after the deepening of the financial crisis.

OVERISSUE OF MONEY IS "THE HEART OF THE PROBLEM"

Preventing inflation also requires taking action at the root—i.e., the overissue of money. The root of inflation is the circulation of excess currency, and only by controlling the monetary quantity can inflation be effectively controlled. In the short term, the government needs to recover excess money, and in the long term it needs to control the amount of money issued. Once the monetary quantity in circulation is controlled, we would then be hitting at the "heart of the problem" behind the increase in commodity prices.

First, there is a need to reform the mode of economic growth that is driven by investments. Economic growth driven by investments will continue to expand the ratio of investment in the GDP, thus linking growth with investment. At the same time, the growth rate is also closely tied with the government's macroeconomic policies. The government encourages investment and releases a huge quantity of money, which attracts a joyful onslaught of investment, spurring rapid economic growth. The economic rebound triggered by the circulation of excess money will cause overheating, resulting in inflation and asset bubbles.

To effectively prevent the overheated economy from triggering even more asset bubbles, the government will implement numerous measures such as raising interest rates and bank reserve requirements in order to pour cold water onto the overheated economy. If too many policies to cool the economy are implemented at once, or if they are implemented too forcefully, the economy will suffer. The government will therefore stop at the appropriate time, and again implement policies to drive the economy, thus continuing this cycle of alternating economic driving and cooling measures.

An economy that is overly reliant on investment is inflexible, and a cycle will easily occur in which the economy is first tightened enough to stifle; and then, once stifled, it is loosened; and once loosened, it becomes "hot." In addition, the reliance on investment will trigger new risks, such as the increase of foreign exchange reserves and a flood of monetary liquidity, setting the scene for inflation.

Economist Wu Jinglian prescribed a remedy for us:

> To truly realize economic transformation, the fundamental momentum still lies in reforms, as pointed out by the Twelfth Five-Year Plan! Reforms were once driving the important engine of the fast-moving Chinese economic train for thirty years, and this fuel is still the most efficient one for China today. We must bear the labor pains of reforms with greater determination and courage, and better prepare the superstructure for the changes in the mode of economic development, so as to allow reforms to set a firm foundation for transformation.[18]

The calls for exchange rate reforms in China are getting louder and louder. China's relatively stable exchange rate, and the expectation of stability, has not only led the central bank to issue large quantities of base money in exchange for foreign currencies, but it has also provided a convenient channel for other countries (especially the United States) to export inflation to China. For example, when U.S. dollar–denominated oil has an extraordinary price increase, then the value of the dollar declines. However, as the dollar-to-renminbi exchange rate does not change, China will still import oil at a higher price, and inflation will then creep into China.

If China adopts a somewhat independent monetary policy, where on one hand, it uses a relatively flexible exchange rate mechanism, and on the other hand, it provides a definite anchor for the renminbi that allows it to remain steadfastly stable no matter what foul tempest of blood or madness happens in other countries, then this will ease the international inflation imbalance. Economists, however, are divided on what this anchor should be.

Zhang Wuchang (Steven N.S. Cheung), an economist who was inspired by the financial policies implemented by Zhu Rongji, repeatedly suggested that the anchor should be based on "a basket of commodities":

> Commodities by themselves are not money. The aggregate price (index) of the basket of fixed commodities is only a benchmark and anyone can trade in the market based on this index and without the involvement of the central bank. There is no price control as the relative prices of different commodities in the basket float freely. The central bank only takes charge of the benchmark index for market transactions, which is also known

as the price level. Based on the price theory, the non-control of relative
commodity prices is no control of prices.[19]

When economic logic meets politics, it will not always be that convincing
and forceful. Sometimes, there will be compromise, blockage or even backlash.
The anchor based on "a basket of commodities" sounds more like the utopia of
the monetary world. After all, the direction of China's monetary policy is not
only based on the opinions of economists, it is also based on politics, and of
course, on the people's livelihood.

CHAPTER FOUR

Why Does the Chinese Stock Market Run Contrary to the Chinese Economy?

China's Deviation from the Dog-Walking Model

The relationship between the economy and the stock market is like a man taking a walk with his dog. The man walks at a steady pace; the dog runs back and forth.

—German investor ANDRÉ KOSTOLANY[1]

CANINES WILL NOT walk in step behind their masters. On the contrary, they will be distracted, or even run in the opposite direction. Most of the time, however, stock markets will follow the economic curve, and move in tandem with the economy's rise and fall rather closely.

The Eastern canine that is the Chinese stock market often clashes with economic growth. It is a bit mysterious, perverse, and dares to break all heavenly rules and incur everybody's wrath. It dares to love and hate, and is uninhibited in its display of great joy and great sadness. It may therefore not be prudent for stock investors to invest purely in accordance with economic growth as a one-size-fits-all type of approach.

The Chinese stock market has experienced seven bulls and seven bears (referring to the Shanghai Stock Exchange): it has been very bullish or very bearish, and at the same time totally oblivious to the awe that steady GDP growth brings.

THE FIRST BULL AND BEAR MARKET

BULL MARKET: December 19, 1990, to May 26, 1992. After the commencement of operations of the Shanghai Stock Exchange, stock indices rose for two and a half years, and soared even higher after the lifting of trading limits. On April

13, 1992, Wei Wenyuan, the general manager of the Shanghai Stock Exchange (who was said to be so excited at the launch ceremony of the Shanghai Stock Exchange that he fainted), relaxed the trading limits for Zhejiang Phoenix and SVA Electron, and the Shanghai Stock Exchange sprang to life again. On May 20, the Shanghai Composite Index stood at 616 points and it was 1,265 points on May 21. By May 25, it had reached its highest level at 1,420 points. The fervor stirred up by rapidly rising stock prices blinded stock investors, and for a while, the "stock fever" was to be seen everywhere.

BEAR MARKET: May 26, 1992, to November 17, 1992. After the Shanghai stock market reached a fevered pitch, the government started to quietly cool it by issuing new stocks. However, the market continued to absorb the new stocks and the government could not do anything. Instead, it was the disorderliness of stock investors at Culture Square—the stock trading venue that can hold tens of thousands of people moving around, as if they were "swarming to the fair to sell cabbages"—that caused a spontaneous panic among investors. They began to dump stocks en masse and share prices nose-dived. Later, the stock market was affected by the August 10 stock market unrest, which led to bearish sentiment.[2] Within half a year, the Shanghai Stock Exchange fell from 1,429 points to 386 points.

Although they are both stock markets, for a long time, the Shanghai Stock Exchange and Shenzhen Stock Exchange did not share the same paths.

Compared to the continuously bullish market of the Shanghai Stock Exchange, the Shenzhen Stock Exchange was battered. In the early 1990s, the Shenzhen stock market became red-hot all of a sudden and stocks rose rapidly, doubling, and in some cases, even tripling or more within half a year. One of the top risers, Shenzhen Development, grew by more than 900 percent. The government became deeply concerned by the craze surrounding the Shenzhen stock market, and began to implement rectification measures such as narrowing the trading limit to 1 percent, making stock investors pay a 6 percent stamp duty, and collecting individual income adjustment taxes. With this series of unfavorable measures being implemented, the Shenzhen stock market started to weaken from December 8 onwards, and thus began its long decline. It was in such a desolate state that it even saw zero transactions on April 22, 1991. Beginning on September 7, and only after numerous meetings held by the Shenzhen government on revitalizing the market and financing, the Shenzhen stock market began to see a glimpse of its former self. The August 10 stock market unrest of 1992 solidified the notoriety of the Shenzhen stock market. It did not recover until 1996.

THE SECOND BULL AND BEAR MARKET

BULL MARKET: November 17, 1992, to February 16, 1993. After Deng Xiaoping made his Southern Tour speeches in 1992, economic development became the buzzword all over China. The credit and money supply skyrocketed, with the M2 growth rate exceeding 40 percent. This economic heat wave brought about prosperity in the stock market, which grew from 386 points on November 17, 1992, to 1,558 points on February 16, 1993. Within three months, the stock market rose by 303 percent.

BEAR MARKET: February 16, 1993, to July 29, 1994. The increase of money and credit resulted in soaring commodity prices and inflation. In June 1993, then Vice Premier Zhu Rongji imposed macroeconomic controls by tightening credit and money supply, and prohibiting actions that would disrupt financial order such as illegal capital financing. The stock market was affected and declined.

THE THIRD BULL AND BEAR MARKET

BULL MARKET: July 29, 1994, to September 13, 1994. With the stock market in the doldrums, the government, fearing social instability, issued three key favorable policies. These were: suspending the issuance of new stocks and listings for the year; strictly controlling the scale of share allocation of listed companies; and adopting measures to expand the scope of capital flowing into the market. This good news galvanized the stock market, and it kept rising to a peak of 1,052 points.

BEAR MARKET: September 13, 1994, to May 17, 1995. Stock prices were driven up by policies, and the market began to correct the rise. In addition, rumors of good and bad news filled the information network surrounding the stock market, resulting in volatility and jittery investors.

THE FOURTH BULL AND BEAR MARKET

BULL MARKET: May 18, 1995, to May 22, 1995. On February 23, 1995, the "327" Treasury Bond Futures Incident—a major scandal in the Chinese securities industry—occurred, and on May 17, the China Securities Regulatory Commission held a news conference to announce the closing of treasury bond futures trading.[3] Some people reacted with sadness, while others rejoiced. The death sentence of treasury bonds was celebrated by the stock market, and within three days the stock market rose from 582 points to 926 points.

BEAR MARKET: May 22, 1995, to January 19, 1996. On May 22, 1995, the State Council Securities Committee held its fifth meeting and announced that it would reveal the scale of stock issuance for the second quarter of that year.

The stock market was shocked and dived, and there were no notable results for the next half year.

THE FIFTH BULL AND BEAR MARKET

BULL MARKET: January 19, 1996, to May 12, 1997. In 1996, the Shenzhen stock market recovered and raced neck-and-neck with the Shanghai stock market, with both markets showcasing their best stocks and introducing blue chips. Some securities companies were even named as having been asked to manipulate the rise in stock prices. In addition, the good news of the lowering of interest rates on two occasions by the central bank also spurred the stock market. In short, the leaders were happy, stock investors were joyfully speculating, and the stock index returned to 1,510 points.

BEAR MARKET: May 12, 1997, to May 18, 1999. The stock market became conceited from its success and even asked for more, despite the policies and without regard for cooling measures applied from on high. However, overinvestment inevitably made this bull appear outwardly strong, while actually being inwardly weak, and the law of the market that dictates that a fall must follow a of rise began causing trouble. Management could not fulfill the market's insane demand for even more every time some was given, and they launched a round of cooling measures. The stock market began to lose its shine, and it remained bearish for two years.

THE SIXTH BULL AND BEAR MARKET

BULL MARKET: May 19, 1999, to June 14, 2001. With the stock market in the doldrums, people were disquieted. And more importantly, the government began to appreciate the stock market's financing function, or it saw the stock market as a key engine to help state-owned enterprises out of the mire of poverty. So, the government planned to support the market in order to change the sluggish situation, give play to the financing function of the stock market, and support the listing of state-owned enterprises. Breaking free of the doldrums would require a little bit of fresh fuel, and since Internet concept stocks were such a darling in foreign countries, the government decided to make use of them. With a strong boost from Internet concept stocks, the Shanghai Composite Index shot to its highest point.

BEAR MARKET: June 14, 2001, to June 6, 2005. The Shanghai Composite Index fell from 2,245 points to 998 points, and the bad news of the split-share structure was commonly seen as the cause of the long-term bearishness of the market. The trial implementation of reducing the holdings of state-owned shares, the great discussion over economist Wu Jinglian's claims that the stock market is one huge casino, and the frustration of the Chinese returnees from abroad over the failure of the ideals of marketization all resulted in wave after wave of panic in the market, so stock investors chose to exit.

THE SEVENTH BULL AND BEAR MARKET

BULL MARKET: June 6, 2005, to October 16, 2007. After the reforms of the split-share structure, foreign investments flowed in, and the scale of funds became larger. Private capital poured in to support the "four great pillars." From 2005 onward, China's lukewarm stock market ended its five-year bear run and began to soar. In 2007, the bulls hit the sky with the Shanghai Composite Index rising 96.66 percent for the entire year. During this period, the Shanghai Composite Index saw a peak of 6124.04 points. The combined value of the Shenzhen and Shanghai stock markets increased from ¥8 trillion at the end of 2006, to ¥32 trillion by the end of 2007, becoming the fourth largest market by value in the world. In December 2007, the combined total number of accounts of the Shenzhen and Shanghai stock markets reached 136 million.

BEAR MARKET: October 17, 2007, to the end of October 2008. Markets have their cycles, and tens of thousands of stock investors will keep an eye on the market with hopes for a bull run. However, a bear market can occur for the slightest reason. A statement made on October 17, 2007, by Tu Guangshao, then vice chairman of the China Securities Regulatory Commission, that "Hong Kong has proposed share calls of listing companies" had the unexpected effect of bringing panic to the stock market; both the Shenzhen and Shanghai stock markets plummeted. The financial tsunami at the other side of the Pacific Ocean finally triggered a butterfly effect and the stock market nose-dived, bringing the stock market to below 1,700 points. In the first half of 2008, the decline of the A Share Index was the fastest in the world. The situation only picked up in the second half of the year, with the Shanghai Composite Index declining 65.39 percent for the whole year, ranking at number thirteen, the worst-performing stock market in the world.

There are endless surprises, troubles and joys in the Chinese stock market, and the ups and downs have always maintained close yet distant links with the general trend of China's economic growth. It will be futile, no matter how sharp a person is, to uncover the endogenous relationship between the stock market curve and GDP growth. In 2010, there was a small commotion regarding the man-and-dog theory, to the extent that even the normally composed *People's Daily* also spoke out:

Even though the domestic economy registered strong growth in 2010, the A Share Index did not benefit much from it, and on the contrary, became one of the worst-performing stock markets in the world in 2010. As of the closing on December 25, China's A Share market fell 11.75 percent for the whole year and is ranked second to last globally.

The strong rebound of the A Share market in 2009 filled everyone with the expectation that the market would do well in 2010, too. But, reality struck investors hard. Stock markets are the barometers of the economy. In 2010, China's economic performance was much better than that of any other country, with a year-on-year GDP growth of 10.6 percent during the first three quarters. In addition, China had also surpassed Japan for two consecutive quarters to become the second largest economy in the world. So why does the performance of the Chinese stock market deviate so much from that of the real economy?[4]

Lifting the Veil of the Policy-Driven Market

The work of the China Securities Regulatory Commission is the most sensitive, akin to sitting on the mouth of the volcano, and everyone has to be mentally prepared. When share prices sky-rocket, the powers above will object, fearing something will go wrong; when share prices plummet, those below will object and the people will give up; and when share prices are neither rising nor falling, everyone will object, because you are no longer taking charge of the market.

—LIU HONGRU[5]

REVOLVING AROUND THE "POLICY-DRIVEN MARKET"

On March 31, 1995, when sixty-five-year-old Liu Hongru retired from the chairmanship of the China Securities Regulatory Commission, he delivered the emotional statement above based on personal realizations.

The Chinese stock market, whether it is going up or down, must revolve around policies great or small. The stock market's concern and keenness over news conferences announcing new policies is far greater than over news conferences announcing GDP growth figures. Sometimes, a small rumor can even precipitate a drop or rise in the stock market.

In late May 1990, rumors that the state planned to reorganize the Shenzhen Stock Exchange resulted in a surge of share prices, and within one month, shares of Vanke Group rose 380 percent, Shenzhen Anda rose 380 percent, and Shenzhen Development rose 100 percent.

On May 30, 2007, with the stock market bubble growing steadily, the government suddenly revised stamp duties upward. The market fell sharply, and within five trading days it had retreated by 21 percent.

After seventeen years, the stock market is still good for nothing and will rise or fall every time it senses a hint of policy changes. It seems that no progress has been made.

The looming shadow of an "invisible hand" can be seen in the seven bulls and seven bears of the stock market, and the government's beautiful vision can also be divined by observing the market's uneven path: it is best that the stock market rise steadily without any sudden changes, as both rising too quickly and falling too fast are problematic. The government fears the formation of bubbles and inflation when the stock market rises, so it pours cold water to douse the passion for investment. The government also fears instability when the stock market falls, which will make people lose confidence in future economic growth, so it comes up with favorable policies to support the market.

At times, during certain key moments when the stock market is falling, large amounts of mysterious capital appear from nowhere, or a certain large-cap stock might get propped up by some "veiled" capital. This is not a case of some hitherto unknown wealthy benefactor's coming forward to help rescue the stock market, as stories involving actual money and finance are rarely as legendary and dramatic as those in soap operas. The public might not even applaud one who seeks recognition for good deeds such as these. Ensuring GDP growth and stabilizing enterprise are what's most important, so the overwhelming tendency is toward doing good anonymously. Knowing this, it becomes easier for us to understand the capers of the "Eastern dog" that is the Chinese stock market.

From 2001 to 2005, China endured a prolonged bear market. Stock markets all over the world were announcing good news, and only the Chinese stock market was lukewarm. The dog's master—the Chinese economy—was also doing spectacularly well, with steady economic growth and subdued inflation. It was a moment for the "Chinese miracle" to shine, but the "Eastern dog" was acting abnormal and lethargic and thus had to be left far behind by its master. Stock investors waited anxiously and hoped that the government would provide a strong boost, but the government, in a departure from its usual self, only quietly adopted a wait-and-see attitude. The government knew full well that the macroeconomy was doing well, enterprises were not worried about the lack of funding, and the people were confident regarding economic growth, so they did not feel the need to act.

After the outbreak of the 2008 financial crisis, China's stock market plummeted because of all sorts of negative news—international stock markets fell, and small and medium-size enterprises were closing down en masse—as well as from the fatal wounds of the previous bubble buildup. However, after a short slump, the Chinese stock market did not hit rock bottom but hovered at around 2,000 points. This was not bad, given that stock markets all over the world were nose-diving. At that time, who was the hidden person trying to break the fall? Numerous enterprises, organizations, and individuals rushed to enter the market when it was at 5,000 or 6,000 points, and they were all crying and lamenting about their high entry point: "I am locked in a bad position by the stocks" and "I am suffering tremendous losses." They were unable to do much to support the market, so the mysterious funds to buttress it must have come from someone important. The ¥4 trillion infrastructure investment plan and huge investments by local governments were all positive signs for the capital market, which fueled the rise of the Shanghai Composite Index for three consecutive months in the first quarter of 2009, with a quarterly rise of more than 30.34 percent.

Countries were suffering hard times, small and medium-size enterprises in China were complaining of their struggles, and even the untouchable real estate prices began falling as the economy wandered in the dark, not knowing when it would see the light at the end of the tunnel. At this critical moment, what was needed was for the people to trust the stock market and regain confidence. When the economy is doing well, no one takes notice of the barometer that is the stock market. But when the economy is in recession, grasping at every straw one can reach is the thing to do. With just one ray of sunlight on the stock market, confidence would be restored.

THE DEPENDENCE ON POLICY

As its name suggests, the main hero of the capital market is the market itself. On October 20, 1995, when Gao Xiqing stepped down as vice chairman of the China Securities Regulatory Commission, he wrote a letter to Lou Jiwei, director-general of the Macroeconomic Control Department of the State Commission for Restructuring of the Economy, in which he said:

The only reason for the existence of the China Securities Regulatory Commission is to make sure that the information on the securities market is adequate, prompt, and transmitted accurately, so as to ensure that investors can compete in this market that is "outwardly fair." From the perspective of the whole society, the stock market is the only place where investors can invest in independently . . .[6]

However, the capital market is not as independent and free as it should be. It suffers from being greatly policy dependent and, as such, does not respond readily to market laws. Sometimes, a slim financial internal reference report from the central government brings more sparkle to the eyes of investors than a thick book on the essentials of investment by Warren Buffett.

The investors' and the market's obsession and dependence on authority and policies are based on a judgment made from past experiences. The sudden rise and fall of the Chinese market and the sudden changes in big cap stocks are more or less linked to policy. Therefore, a person will make huge losses if he ignores the policies.

The government's previous interventions were based on the fear of risks in the stock market, and that the people would be overjoyed and lose control when it rose—losing their humanity. Or that if the stock market fell, the people would be depressed and jump to their deaths—losing their lives. In the early 1990s, the "invisible hand" could be seen everywhere, even more so in the capital market where there were risks that threatened stability.

Moreover, the government's attitude toward the stock market was to "try and see." If the stock market were to "make trouble" by bringing about additional cases like the Shenzhen "August 10th" stock market unrest that was described as being "extremely despicable in means and plot," the stock market could easily be viewed as an evil contraption, and shutting it down would be just an administrative matter. Hence, the people pay more attention to the policies than to their understanding of the laws of the market since a positive or negative policy will directly determine the future of the capital market.

Also, the capital market was messy in the early stages of the stock market, like the chaotic revelry brought about by dancing demons. Sometimes the stock market rose rapidly like the "Chinese rocket Shenzhou-6," and sometimes, it fell sharply like a "scorned wife jumping off the cliff to her death." There were all types of black box operations and shady deals, and some investors would just dip into their pocketbooks without even knowing what stocks were: the market environment was chaotic and the laws of investment were a complete mess. Investors were confused and disoriented, and besides policy, there was no better reference point for investments.

Economist Xu Xiaonian deemed that the policy cycles also affected the people's tendency to "think that policies can save the market":

> When the market is bearish, the government will think of ways to revive it by issuing editorials, taking about the vision, injecting capital, issuing funds, and reducing stamp duty. When the market is bullish, the government will think of ways to warn about the risks by raising stamp duty, conducting large financing, regulating fund positions, and viciously punishing violations. These cycles have been basically the same over the past ten years or so, with the only differences being in time and point.
>
> A businessman I met in Shenzhen who speculates in stocks once told me he never reads company reports. This is not because he does not understand the content of the reports, but that there is no use in reading the reports. Every night he watches the television news and in the morning he reads the newspapers in detail so as to comprehend the spirit behind the speeches of the leaders, and ponder over the policy direction before deciding on what to buy in the stock market.
>
> We have treated saving the market as a norm. Not only has this become a convention, it has nearly become an institution, and the expectations of stock investors are likewise being solidified. When the market falls, all eyes are on the government. After propping up the market, it rises rapidly and the government has to come in again to intervene, causing it to then slump. The stock market has once again gotten stuck in a policy-driven cycle. And ordinary investors are perpetually those who are hurt.[7]

With further market-oriented developments in the capital market, the positive roles of the market, including financing, regulatory controls and enriching the people, have become more prominent, and there is no longer the possibility of shutting down the capital market. However, with the government continuing in its regulation and control of the capital market with the intention of spurring economic growth and stabilizing the enterprises, and with the people getting used to the idea of administrative power, the concept that policies indeed influence market trends will become a reality.

China's Stock Market Goes Crazy over Gambling, Becoming a Misappropriation-of-Money City

On one hand, this classic zero-sum game created numerous wealthy people that we may or may not know; and on the other hand, it left a black hole of bad assets worth trillions of yuan in the Chinese financial system. Most of the time, the rich people and the bad assets are just two sides of a coin. The rich people have emerged slowly out from the black box, but the bad assets have not. Finance is only one aspect of this black box.

—Independent observer YUAN JIAN[8]

THE PHANTOM OF SPECULATION

The Chinese stock market suffers a serious problem of speculation.

When the market hit 6,000 points, myths of moneymaking and a quick path to wealth filled the entire atmosphere and everyone looked forward to the stock market hitting another new high, but instead the stock market fell. The past prophecies of the so-called stock gurus failed to come to pass, stocks rumored to definitely climb higher actually dropped lower, and even the stocks of giants such as Vanke and Mengniu also fell. The spectacular upward trend ended in dismay, and the gains made were easily lost with the downward trend.

Be it bear market or bull market, it is beyond doubt that the overall trend of the Chinese stock market is bright. The general state of Chinese economic prosperity dictates that the stock market will have an upward trend. From 2005 to 2007, the stock market rose as often as five times, making the world sit up at take notice. The steady growth of the Chinese economic environment is tangible, but China's GDP has not grown by five times, and profits of Chinese enterprises have also not soared by five times. China's stock market growth is induced by large influxes of "hot" money, especially of boundless private capital. The grand sight of "everyone playing stocks" has appeared, and no matter how little money each person plays, it merges into a gushing torrent. As can be seen from the annual stock turnover rate of nearly 1,200 percent in the Chinese stock market, the value of the Chinese stock market has not reached the stratosphere, and both investors and supervisory agencies are not yet mature. Be they listed companies, investors, or shareholders, their inclination to gamble is too strong, and this increases the speculative nature of the Chinese stock market.

AN ALIENATED MONEY CITY

Before the stock reforms of 2005, the split-share structure was known as the original sin of market speculation.[9] The split-share structure prohibited the trading of nontradable shares in the market, which meant that two-thirds of a listed company's shares would not be floated on the market. It was difficult to reflect the value of a listed company based on one-third of its shares and big investors could easily exploit this to create a capital storm and cause the stock price to fluctuate widely. The situation was so bad that some people cried out that

> The Chinese stock market has become chaotic and disorderly, with no independent supply-and-demand relationship, no basis for price-setting, and no inherent space for making choices. The basis of credibility of the Chinese stock market has been lost, and the series of innovations of the basic system attempted by the China Securities Regulatory Commission were hard to understand and bear, making people worried and hesitant![10]

Even Shang Fulin, chairman of the China Securities Regulatory Commission, pointed out that numerous flaws existed in the split-share structure:

> Under the split-share structure setup, pricing of stock includes not only the basic fundamentals of the company, but also the anticipation of the two-thirds of shares that have yet to be floated on the market. Objectively, this results in a smaller scale of floated shares of a listed company, increases the speculative nature of the stock market, higher fluctuation of the stock prices, and a distortion of the pricing mechanism.[11]

In China, the stock market has to a large degree been alienated as a money market, and financing has become an important function. The Chinese stock market system has also been largely designed with the intention of allowing the maximization of financing. Waves of money have gushed in, enlarging the financing plate, thanks to a large quantity of new stocks being issued on the boards of small and medium-size enterprises and growth enterprises, as well as rounds of financing conducted by large cap stocks. From 1990 to November 2010, the total financing in the A Share market was ¥3.642946 trillion, a financing rate that can be compared to bursting blood vessels. From 1990 to June 2010, the cash dividend in the A Share market was ¥1.604937 trillion. The total financing was 2.27 times that of total dividends.[12]

Under the cover of "marketization," numerous companies, regardless of performance or quality, all rushed to get listed, competing at "sucking blood."

Although the best days of the stock market are yet to come, the "four highs" are very common: issuing shares at high prices, issuing of additional shares at high prices, issuing of convertible bonds in high quantities, and shares allocation at high prices.

The price-earnings ratio and the issue prices of new stocks are getting higher and higher. Among the first batch of startup companies that was listed in 2009, the price-earnings ratio has increased forty times, with Ultrapower being the highest at ¥58, and Lummy Pharmaceutical the lowest at ¥16.50. Once, the average dynamic price-earnings ratio on the growth enterprise board was more than one hundred times, implying that share prices had deviated drastically from the intrinsic values of the enterprises, and that the growth prospects of these enterprises were far from being as bright as described when they were listed. The most direct proof of this are the successive resignation letters tendered by senior management.

Between the beginning of 2011 and November 16 of the same year, there were a total of 424 resignation announcements from listed companies on the small and medium-size enterprise board and the growth enterprise board. Reasons for the resignations varied, including too long a separation from their families, poor physical health, and the like. For instance, on July 29, 2011, Cong Langbo, director-cum–deputy general manager of SJ Environmental Protection, and Zhang Jie, director of the company, separately tendered their resignations. Before departing, they cashed out their shares for a combined amount as high as ¥2.4 million.[13] In short, with these people reducing their holdings and cashing out, it is clear that they would not be accompanying investors in planning for the long term.

Discerning stock investors will realize that getting listed is like a bottomless pit. Many listed companies have outstanding performance during the initial public offering, but once listed, they deliver poor financial statements within a year or even six months.

High premium prices cannot be used as a comparison to a high growth rate of small and medium-size enterprises since the capital market has lost its ability to select strong growth and high-value enterprises. A small and medium-size enterprise can become a new elite business overnight by using the capital market as a jumping board. However, at the same time, enterprises that are tagged "high-growth" and "high-tech" may also disintegrate quickly and become just flashes in the pan.

With No House Rules in the "Casino," What Can the "Gamblers" Do?

From the beginning, China's stock market has not followed any standards. If it continues on this path, it will not become a good investment ground for investors. Stock prices are abnormally high, and therefore, a considerable portion of the shares have no investment value. Also, from a deeper perspective, because of the violations and illegal activities that are common in the stock market, investors are not seeing returns, and the stock market has become a haven for speculation. This is like the foreigners' saying, "China's stock market is like a casino, and furthermore, one without rules." There are house rules in a casino; for instance, you are not to peep at the cards of others. But in our stock market, some people do peep at the cards of others, and they cheat, and swindle. They have perfected the skills of being big investors, speculators, and manipulators of stock prices.

—Economist WU JINGLIAN[14]

STOCK MARKET BUBBLES

Julius Fučík reminds us, "Be on guard!"[15] In the capital market, we often need such reminders to be cautious. We charge into the stock market eagerly and without hesitation, but the results tend to be far from the beautiful picture we initially dreamed. We encounter multiple dilemmas of whether to sell or not, whether to buy or not, but still, we are unable to escape from the fate of the majority of retail investors—i.e., repeated losses.

More than one person has sternly warned us that the Chinese stock market is like a large casino. We harbor such detestation for actual casinos because they can make a person indulge and lose his fortune overnight. However, when it comes to gambling in the capital market, we seem to enjoy it; and with the capital market becoming more and more bustling, there are more and more people taking part in the gamble.

The "gambling" nature of the Chinese stock market is reflected in its excessively speculative nature. As the most important approach to capitalization, the stock market securitizes the assets and future income of listed companies. The securitization of capital greatly increases the capital supply of a country, while also increasing the cash flow of the listed company. The risks of asset securitization of the listed company itself are relatively small, but the securitization of future expectations is filled with numerous risks.

The Gospel according to Matthew in the New Testament sternly reminds us to "Enter through the narrow gate. For wide is the gate and broad is the road that leads to destruction, and many enter through it. But small is the gate and narrow the road that leads to life, and only a few find it."[16] The strength of the enterprise results from playing the intense commercial game of competition. The more an enterprise does not enter the glorious land, the smaller the door will become, and the so-called "luck" and "dreams" will not stay forever, and will abandon the enterprise. "Only one in a thousand can maintain the lead in an industry for ten years, and only one in ten thousand can stay in the lead of an industry for twenty years." Chinese enterprises similarly cannot escape from a fate where "for every sailing ship, there are tens of millions of sunken vessels." Many enterprises do not possess the natural endowment of being "one in ten thousand," and although they may be red-hot in China, or even all over the world, within a few years, they may not be able to easily reach the level of being everlasting.

Nevertheless, the price-earnings ratio of the Chinese stock market is ridiculously high, and can reach as high as sixty times, far ahead of the twenty to 25 percent price/earnings-ratios of Western countries. There are a lot of factors determining whether an enterprise's prospects are wide or narrow. The financial contractual nature of the future growth of enterprises results in two different worlds of shares and listed companies, and such a differentiation may present two different extremes. Stock prices may deviate from company performance and rise freely or fall sharply without stopping. There are also a number of stocks that fluctuate widely as the result of manipulation by big investors. Even though there are stern measures to crack down on such big investors, and these measures are getting harsher, cases of big investors manipulating stocks still occur. This is analogous to playing card games where the big investors can see the cards of others, cheat, and speculate, while the majority of retail investors can only imitate the cards played by others.

Two professors from Chicago conducted a quantitative analysis of the speculative nature of stock markets and found out that the speculative factor in the United States stock market was between 15 and 20 percent, while the speculative factor of the Chinese stock market had already exceeded 60 percent. Hence, a person should not underestimate the bubble of speculation that exists in China. Economist Wu Jinglian, once said that, "In 2001, there were some people who said that they wanted to fly away from the Earth although they were held back by their hair, and this gave rise to many criticisms. But now, who can say that there is no bubble in the stock market?"[17]

SETTING THE STAGE

The bubble will burst one day. China's stock market is one big bubble, and some stocks have also formed their own smaller bubbles. With public talk building, and bets being placed by big investors, the bubble will become larger and larger.

Dubious tales emerge again and again that are along the lines of what the Chinese express as "three tiger sightings make a tiger real" and "popular opinion becomes hot enough to melt iron." If you initially had some reservations over the future of a particular enterprise, the so-called experts would solemnly inform you that the enterprise's high growth has been strictly and scientifically validated, and the enterprise would also promptly display its excellent financial statements to entice you and suggest that the enterprise has a very bright future. Would not your heart's reservations just disappear?

Noise and false information keeps emerging in the capital market. The stronger these are, the more influential they are on investors' anticipation of the listed company's future, easily causing stock prices to deviate from their original value.

The capital market is a zero-sum game, where one man's gain will be another man's loss. In order to make more money, investors will attempt ways and means to get others to lose money.

An investor once made this analogy on the horrors of a stock market bubble: whenever the "bloodsucking bat" goes on its journey, it will always leave behind a path of destruction in its wake, with the path getting bigger and more deadly. In order to create a bubble fueled by ill intentions, large organizations will do their best to create a scenario, and the smaller organizations will tag along with the arrangement. Only unknowing retail investors have to diligently watch to see what happens. Usually, just a few can clearly see what is going on behind closed doors. The continual rise in stock prices only succeeds in allowing small investors to enjoy some benefits, or giving them the illusion that the mirage is becoming reality. When these small investors arrive in huge numbers, the bubble bursts, leaving behind nothing but their remains.

A large number of the investors are disadvantaged by the lack of market information. Their conclusions on the anticipated future of stocks are mainly based on the financial statements released by the companies in question, current trends, and the references provided by professionals, such as analysts. The company financial statements, the current trend of the stocks, or the views of analysts all provide a selection basis for stock investors. However, we cannot deny that these can be susceptible to manipulation—e.g., the listed company may amend its financial statement to make it look much better than it is in reality. Therefore, a huge rise in stocks may be due to manipulation by the organizations. In addition, analysts are not prophets and may just be the hired experts of some big investors. The information in the capital market is vague, and investors have to be prudent—"listening and watching everywhere"—when making a move in the capital market. Nevertheless, share investors are not completely rational. Incorrect information and the accompanying ill-suited or erroneous mentality have prepackaged the outcome so that most of them will not win in the stock market.

RETAIL INVESTORS LED BY THEIR NOSES

Daniel Kahneman, a psychologist and winner of the Nobel Prize in Economics, proposed the Prospect Theory.[18] There are three basic principles to this theory: most people will turn risk-averse when receiving gains; most people will seek risks when facing potential losses; and people are more sensitive to losses than gains Kahneman suggested two experimental games that are still persuasive today.

In the first game, you have two choices: Option A is to receive ¥1,000. Option B is to have a 50 percent chance of receiving ¥2,000, with a 50 percent chance of receiving nothing.

Which would you choose? Experimentation showed that most people chose Option A, which reveals that when an assured gain is within their grasp, people tend to be risk-averse.

In the second game, you also have two choices: Option A is to definitely lose ¥1,000. Option B is to have a 50 percent chance of losing ¥2,000, with a 50 percent chance of losing nothing.

In this situation, which would you choose? Experimentation showed that most people chose Option B, which reveals that when faced with a certain loss, people will take more risks.

Someone once conducted a review of the 1995 transaction records of 334 traders at the Chicago Board Options Exchange and discovered that, when faced with more and more gains, the investor invested less and less; and the more risk-averse she or he was, the shorter the time she or he held on to profitable trades, meaning that the turnover rate is higher and selling of shares is likely when there is a small gain. At the same time, in the midst of continual losses, there will be a tendency in the investor to gamble and hope for recovery via a "lucky strike." Only a few will sell their stocks, while most will continue to hold them and fight to the death with the stock market.

Also, although retail investors cannot essentially decide the movement of the stock market, they can influence the direction of stock prices through excessively sensitive sentiments. Compared with the joy derived from gains, the pain caused by losses leaves a deeper heartache for retail investors. Their excessive inflexibility regarding losses will drag them into the whirlpool of irrationality. When stock prices rise, they will carry broad smiles. But when stock prices fall, they become depressed immediately, and with investors exiting the market, prices cannot be supported, so will continue to fall.

Furthermore, retail investors display a herd mentality. Incorrect information causes these investors to lose confidence. Their decision may easily be influenced by the so-called expert-supported "insider news," and they get very passionate about "recommended stock commentaries." When people rush in when the price is rising, they want to rush in too; and when people exit when the price is low, they want to exit, too. In the end, they will discover that they have lost more than they have gained.

Many people will find the following story familiar:

You invest in a listed company with stock on the growth enterprise board, a recognizable name, and satisfactory performance. When the stock rises from ¥20 to ¥21, you sell it and earn ¥1. You feel good about yourself. However, the market index is still rising, and you regret selling early, since the stock you sold previously has gone up to ¥25. Given such a good market, you feel you should buy in again. Hence, you choose a stock valued at ¥25 and exit when it hits ¥28, earning ¥3 for each share. By doing this repeatedly, you earn a few thousand yuan. You start to think differently about yourself: you can actually speculate in stocks, and you can create a legend of "no losses" around yourself. In your opinion, those investors who lost a lot in stock speculation are not skillful after all.

The market index continues to climb. You wander outside the market, considering for the umpteenth time about whether you should go in. With the market on an upward trend and stock prices rising one after another, you wonder if a bubble has formed. However, when you listen to the opinions around you, you hear many analysts saying with certainty that this is a bull market, and you can even earn money by closing your eyes and speculating. You keep receiving information that some stocks will see a huge rise in their price. You decide to buy more at ¥40 per share, thinking to sell it when it reaches ¥41. But the market seems to read your mind, and as soon as you enter into the market, it falls. This golden stock plummets and now you have no choice but to hold on to the stock. Sometime later, the market recovers somewhat. With this recovery, you smile and enter the market again. The next day, the market slumps and the stocks you buy fall. You think to yourself, this may be the bottom and you enter into the market again. On the third day, the market falls further, and your pocket-book feels the pain. You are not resigned to your fate, and decide to engage in a prolonged battle with the market. Nevertheless, the market continues to fall, and the level you thought was the bottom is actually the peak. You had actually gone in at the peak.

Independent commentator Yuan Jian made this perceptive remark:

> The cold fact is that there remain only two kinds of enterprises since China's reform of the ownership system: the power enterprise and the non-power enterprise. In the China of today, such a classification may in practice be even more suitable than the traditional classification of the state-owned enterprise and private enterprise. Some local authorities use the stock market to shift the crisis in local state-owned enterprises to the whole of society; those who monopolize capital use the stock market to rob the wealth of society; and the objective market participation of small and medium-size enterprises served as a cover for the two abovementioned functions, which have also become the flower vase that enhances the legitimacy of the stock market.[19]

In this sense, when the stock market went "crazy" over gambling, it became a "place of decadent indulgence" for big investors who were disguised in order to prevent the public from differentiating between good and evil, robbing the public of its wealth, and causing fear among the people.

Where Has the "Night Watchman" of the Capital Market Gone?

If we say that the thirty years before reform and opening up was an era in which the central and local governments were uncovering productivity, switching social development modes, and promoting the capitalization of social wealth, then the thirty years after that should be the era in which governments avoid impeding of profits, maintain a distance from the market, and polish their inspection and management skills. At that time, we will smile when we recall today's talk of "encouraging listing and issuing shares" or "management city."

　　—WANG AN[20]

THE MARKET NEEDS A "NIGHT WATCHMAN"

The capital market is both a beauty and a beast. Once it gets out of control, the capital market will descend into chaos, with different groups emerging and using all kinds of skills to complicate the bottom line of morality, laws, and regulations, causing the situation to get out of hand. Therefore, only by finding a "night watchman" that is independent, objective, discreet, and does not engage in wrongdoing, will the stock market in China become reliable.

On July 2, 1997, the State Council announced that the Shanghai Stock Exchange and Shenzhen Stock Exchange would be under the direct management of the China Securities Regulatory Commission, and this implied that the China Securities Regulatory Commission would now be the "night watchman."

Chen Zhiwu, professor of finance at the Yale School of Management, hit the nail on the head when he spelled out the function of the "night watchman":

> What kind of regulatory model does China need? The China Securities Regulatory Commission and other administrative departments are not subject to the supervision of the NPC Standing Committee nor under the independent review of the judiciary. Hence, we can limit the functions and powers of the China Securities Regulatory Commission to that of a supervisory role and specify that it may only get involved or intervene in the market when the market is dysfunctional. However, if a reliable supervisory punishment and control mechanism to which the market is held accountable is not established at the same time, then there is no reason for the China Securities Regulatory Commission not to increase and expand its own powers. The purpose of setting up the China Securities Regulatory Commission is to make it a judge over the securities market, not to make it the administrative manager of all the listed companies, securities companies, and the securities market, nor to make it the agency that executes macroeconomic policies. But in reality, the China Securities Regulatory Commission still resembles an administrative manager.[21]

The stock reforms pushed forward by the China Securities Regulatory Commission in 2005 were referred to as a master stroke of the capital market. Shang Fulin, the chairman of the China Securities Regulatory Commission (who seems easygoing, amiable, and soft-spoken while issuing stern warnings and mildly reminding investors to "talk big picture, talk politics"), actually has a firm character, courage, and determination with the tenacity of "an arrow that does not return when shot." He ignored opposition from state-owned enterprises, local governments, and even foreign funds, and supported the stock reforms.

On April 29, 2005, the China Securities Regulatory Commission promulgated the *Circular on Issues Relating to the Pilot Reform of Split-Share Structure of Listed Companies* and proposed the reform idea of combining considerations. Hence, the reform of the split-share structure which characterized the Chinese stock market officially began. The reform's purpose was to change abnormal equity allocation, permit nontradable shares to enter the market directly, and ensure the balance of interests of small and medium-size investors among the holders of nontradable shares—i.e., the structural investors and later buyers of tradable shares—so as to strengthen the capitalization of the Chinese stock market.

Consideration is crucial in stock reform. As the holders of nontradable shares do not purchase the shares in the market using cash, but instead receive the shares and controlling stakes at a capital valuation that is lower than the market price, the interests of holders of tradable shares will be harmed if nontradable shares are allowed to be traded on the market at the same price as tradable shares. Thus, the China Securities Regulatory Commission proposed the adoption of the method of consideration compensation. How much price compensation would be considered reasonable? In a clever move, the China Securities Regulatory Commission threw this ball back to the market and allowed the listed companies to decide. To prevent the holders of nontradable shares from "bullying," the China Securities Regulatory Commission also set a restriction on this stock reform, stipulating that the reform plan must receive the consent of two-thirds of the holders of tradable shares and two-thirds of all shareholders. This stipulation ensured the smooth implementation of this stock reform.

To the ordinary investor, this stock reform was a celebration of democracy in the capital market, but to the holders of nontradable shares, it was a day of loss. They put up a stiff opposition, trying various ways and means to thwart the change, and mobilized opinions from all sides to protest, putting up a stiff opposition. Among them, Sany Heavy Industry Director Liang Wengen's attitude and extreme "large pig bringing down food to small piglets" rhetoric represented how they felt: "A large pig leads a group of small piglets and sees a bucket of pig feed. If the large pig does not bring down the pig feed, the small piglets will have nothing to eat. Now, the large pig has brought down the pig feed, but the small piglets are beginning to complain and want more. How can this be?"[22] However, the outcome was a foregone conclusion, and all the objections and disgruntlement were wasted efforts.

From April 29, 2005—when Sany Heavy Industry, Qinghua Tongfang, Zijiang Enterprise, and Jinniu Energy were selected as the first-batch companies in the stock reform—until December 31, 2006, when 1,303 companies completed or were entering into the stock reform procedures, the market value grew to

¥6050.447 billion. In addition, the Chinese stock market shook off the slump of the past five years, with the Shanghai Composite Index rising by 130 percent in the whole of 2006. The A Share market became the third largest IPO market in the world, the combined market value of both the Shanghai and Shenzhen stock market was ¥9059.9 billion, and listed companies issued ¥8.5 billion in dividend payments.[23] Also, the ratio of the stock market to GDP rose from 17.7 percent before stock reform to 44 percent. After a chase, the stock market finally moved closer in alignment with its master, the Chinese economy.

THERE IS NO MARKET WITH CONCLUSIVE REMEDIES

There is no market with conclusive remedies. The collapse of the split-share structure did not mean that all the elements that had gone against market-oriented principles were eliminated. The stock reform of 2005 only removed the chronic disease left behind by the misplaced investment mechanism. A large number of challenges still remained.

In 1992, the steadily progressing securities market was met with controversy and its future was uncertain. During his Southern Tour, Deng Xiaoping encouraged the people to "make a move":

Are securities and the stock market good or bad? Do they entail any dangers? Are they peculiar to capitalism? Can socialism make use of them? We allow people to reserve their judgment, but we must try these things out. If, after one or two years of experimentation, they prove feasible, we can expand them. Otherwise, we can put a stop to them and be done with it. We can stop them all at once or gradually, totally or partially. What is there to be afraid of? So long as we keep this attitude, everything will be all right, and we shall not make any major mistakes.[24]

Now, the boat that is the stock market has steered into the heart of the river, and it would be wishful thinking to just "close it." The management can, from an index complex, cancel everything as well, as shares are not votes. As the saying goes "if it is destined, then you will have it ultimately, if it is not destined, then there is no point insisting on it"; if the capital market is provided with a transparent disclosure of information, fair investment opportunities, transparent and sound polices, and a deepened market-oriented operation, the stock market will naturally move along with the overall economic trend. Finally, matters in the stock market will still be decided by the stock market.

CHAPTER FIVE

Why Is the Nation of China Prosperous, While Her Citizens Are Not?

The Rise of China Is as Fast as a Hare, While the Rise of Citizens' Wages Is as Slow as a Tortoise

Wherever there is great property, there is great inequality. For one very rich man, there must be at least five hundred poor, and the affluence of the few supposes the indigence of the many.

—ADAM SMITH[1]

"SMALL RICHES" IN THE CONTEXT OF THE NATION'S WEALTH

On a summer day in 2011, there was a quiet screening of a small budget film entitled *The Piano in a Factory*.

Thanks to factory reforms, Chen Guilin, a casting plant worker in his forties, who worked in a large state-owned enterprise in the northeast, was laid off along with his wife. As he was able to play the harmonium, he and some other workers who were also laid off hastily set up a theatrical troupe to perform at events such as weddings and funerals in order to make ends meet. Life got worse when his materialistic wife got involved with a businessman selling counterfeit drugs, and he had to compete with her over custody of his daughter. His daughter issued a challenge, saying she would follow whichever parent was able to give her a piano. So Chen Guilin and his equally destitute friends worked together in a run-down, abandoned workshop to build a steel piano for his daughter.

During the divorce scene, the male lead has this classic dialogue:

"Chen Guilin, will the child be happy with you?"
"Don't threaten me with happiness. Xiao Yuan is very happy."

In a single instant, all of life's frustrations that lurk behind the face's wrinkles were revealed for all to see.

Today, against the colorful backdrop of the country's rising prosperity, commoners like us all live in varying degrees within the shroud of the sad story of

The Piano in a Factory. Cloudy dreams, the pride of "who says I don't care," and a motley of lights and shadows, are interwoven into a materialistic lifestyle; and within that weave, an appearance of happiness is quietly portrayed. If one or the other is lacking, happiness would simply seem incomplete. At times, a tinge of sadness may arise, and at other times, there is neither grief nor sorrow.

Our country is moving farther and farther down the road of great wealth. As a country with nearly a 10 percent growth rate, China has seen rapid expansion and distribution of wealth within a short span of time. We are collectively moving from being moderately prosperous to having overall prosperity. "Overall prosperity" is, indeed, a tempting notion.

From the macro point of view, the country is moving toward great wealth, yet we must not neglect the "small wealth" of the individual. Are you wealthy?

Given the large definitely rich" chassis of China, we, the commoners in China, should also enjoy receiving the benefits of being "definitely rich."

In 1978, the mean annual disposable income per household for China's urban residents was only ¥343.40. By 2007, it had risen forty times to ¥13,785.80. The per capita net income of rural residents also increased from ¥133.60 in 1978 to ¥4,140.40.[2] We have prospered. Your wages have increased, your buying power has grown, and the ways to acquire wealth have also diversified.

WHICH LEVEL OF THE WEALTH PYRAMID DO YOU BELONG TO?

Without a doubt, the entire wealth pyramid is growing. However, you will discover that the pride in watching your nation rise to great power does not bring the same amount of joy to your life. Regardless of whether your income increases rapidly or slowly, it will not be able to keep up with the increase in corporate and government revenue. You are amazed at corporate and government revenue growth figures, but the incremental increases on your paycheck happen slowly. It is like the race between the hare and the tortoise: the national wealth grows at the speed of the hare, while your salary grows at the speed of the tortoise.

Figures cited by the Jiu San Society in 2010, revealed that there was a gradual decline in the proportion of residents' income relative to gross national income. The ratio of workers' remuneration to GDP dropped from 68.6 percent in 1992 to 52.3 percent in 2007. In 2008, figures in the National Economic and Social Development Statistics Bulletin showed that China's per capita income that year was ¥9,800, while per capita GDP was ¥23,800. The ratio of per capita income to per capita GDP was 41.2 percent.

From 1995 to 2007, national fiscal levies increased overall by 5.7 times and the average annual growth rate was 16 percent, while average disposable income of urban residents increased by 8 percent annually, and net income in rural areas only rose by 6.2 percent.[3]

You may be glad that you have an easier and more prosperous life than the previous generation, but when you compare yourself with your peers who may be at the top or upper-middle levels of the wealth pyramid, you may feel less equal, relatively poorer, and depressed. Compared with the rapid growth of the country as a whole, the rise of the nation is a topic that is irrelevant to your personal level of affluence.

There is a huge wealth gap between those at the top and those at the bottom of the pyramid.

The Gini coefficient is the conventional measure used by people for income analysis, and an important indicator of the differences in residents' internal revenue allocation. It is a number between zero and one: the higher the Gini coefficient, the greater the gap in wealth distribution. According to the standard, a Gini coefficient that is less than 0.2 indicates absolute income equality; a value between 0.2 and 0.3 indicates relative equality; a value below 0.3 indicates stability; a value between 0.3 and 0.4 indicates relatively reasonable income equality (0.4 is the warning threshold); a value between 0.4 and 0.5 indicates a relatively great income gap (0.5 is the critical line); and a value higher than 0.6 (0.6 is the unrest line) indicates severe income disparity. In 2008, China's Gini coefficient was 0.469, which was already past the critical threshold and nearing the crisis point. Some people describe the wealth disparity in China as such: "In this income pyramid, the highest level is formed by the top 10 percent high-income earners of the total population, whose savings account for almost half of the total national private wealth. At the base of the pyramid is the poorest 10 percent of the total population, and the majority of these people are accumulating debts."

Li Shi, director of the Income Distribution and Poverty Research Center at Beijing Normal University, determined from his research that the income disparity between the top and bottom 10 percent of the population had increased from 7.3 times in 1998 to twenty-three times in 2007. Also among these statistics was the fact that, at the end of 2008, the pension for civil servants was 2.1 times that of enterprises, and the monthly pension of public institutions was 1.8 times that of enterprises.[4]

BEHIND "DEFINITELY RICH" LIE THE SORROW AND MISERY OF THE COMMON MAN

Today follows yesterday and tomorrow leaves the past behind. This cycle repeats itself, and all that is left as evidence that time has gone by is the comparison of a bunch of abstract and boring figures. As time passes, the people's emotional experiences also change.

As a supporter of the "Beijing Consensus" and the "China model," Professor Yao Yang of Peking University, believes that a neutral government, fiscal decentralization, the new road to democratization, and the pragmatic attitude of the Communist Party of China are all factors that led to the miraculous rise of China. However, Yao Yang is not as optimistic as he was before. He is beginning to worry that the aura of the nation's wealth is losing its charm:

> Household income, which forms part of the national income, is declining. Thus, although there is economic expansion, citizens do not feel that their income is progressing in the same manner. Furthermore, besides economic development, people begin to hope for improvement in well-being. The government's old method of using economic development to appease social discontent is starting to fail.
>
> More importantly, the government's continual efforts to grow GDP have often been done at the cost of people's economic and political rights. But the people will not always remain silent in the face of such violations, and their dissatisfaction will eventually turn into recurrent protests.[5]

Our country is moving so rapidly that she does not even have a chance to stop and look at the people who are stumbling and falling behind, or see the kind of life and emotional ups and downs that they are experiencing. Changes to the map of wealth happen suddenly and the hidden stories of hurt and losses that affect families, friendships, and love, much like that in *The Piano in a Factory*, are all related in some way to the huge rich-poor divide and the fact that the country is prospering but its citizens are not. Perhaps even they themselves are unsure how to keep up with the bustling times, whom they should blame, or who should be lending them a helping hand.

What is irrefutable is that the widening income gap has deepened their sense of frustration and deprivation. Their antagonism toward the rich and powerful is growing stronger, and the incidence of mass unrest is rising. The "China Model" has cast countless shadows, one of which is social anomie, which is growing and increasingly causing the "China Model" to lose its original luster.

A poem by Gerard Manley Hopkins celebrates "All things counter, original, spare, strange; / Whatever is fickle, freckled (who knows how?) / With swift, slow; sweet, sour; adazzle, dim; . . ."[6] As we slowly savor this enormous feast called "the wealth of our nation," besides enjoying some morsels of national pride, we will also get lumps of mortal sorrow and misery stuck in our throats.

The New "Zhou Bapi" Also Knows to Imitate a Cock's Crow in the Middle of the Night

[The] nagging and pervasive tradeoff . . . between equality and efficiency . . . is, in my view, our biggest socioeconomic tradeoff, and it plagues us in dozens of dimensions of social policy. We can't have our cake of market efficiency and share it equally.

—ARTHUR OKUN[7]

THE AFTERMATH OF THE STORY OF CAPITAL INCLINE

There is no direct relationship between the wealth of a nation and the wealth of her citizens. The connection is complicated and confusing. As the mighty GDP begins to flow toward the people, cracks, sand dunes, lakes, and swamps appear from time to time and continually divert the GDP flow. By the time GDP really reaches the individual, it has become a mere trickle.

The heavy reliance on capital and the dependence on labor costs of China's gradual reforms determine the capital incline in various policies and lead to the formation of an income distribution model that uses capital rather than labor as the allocation reference. At the initial stage of reform and opening up, there was an extreme shortage of capital and an abundant, almost inexhaustible supply of labor. In order to stimulate economic growth, all policies inevitably tilted toward and even fawned on capital; and the capital-decides-income trend was thus formed. The tolerance and magnanimity of policies toward capital led to even more brazen capital greed, and labor wages were driven down without restriction.

As the reforms progressed, capital accumulated rapidly, and there was a relative shortage of labor supply. However, an employer-led profit distribution pattern had already taken shape, and the inertia of capital incline policies continued. There was still a lot of room for capital to flex its muscles, while the voice of the labor force "carried little weight." It is no wonder that a book entitled *Why Are the Chinese Industrious and Yet Not Rich?* deeply resonated with the people.[8] "Loss will continue if we go on" in this manner. People suddenly realized that they have been living in a morally confusing era where "perspiration is worthless," where even the old maxim "diligence leads to wealth" sounds gloomy and hopeless in this bizarre and ever changing world.

The initial distribution pattern is a decisive factor in determining the prosperity of the country and personal income. In China, the proportion of wages is on average less than 10 percent of the costs of business operations, whereas it accounts for about 50 percent in developed countries. The bankruptcy of

General Motors is an obvious example. In a once-in-a-century economic crisis, the century-old GM brand came to an end. A large part of the reason for GM's bankruptcy was the fact that the market was shrinking, yet GM's costs—of which labor costs were the most outstanding—were not reduced accordingly. The United States car industry had always had the tradition of offering high wages. In comparison with Honda, Toyota, and other foreign car manufacturers in the United States who pay workers about $25 per hour, GM and other American car giants paid an average of $70 per hour. In addition, GM had to bear other costs that came with the century-old brand, such as the pensions and medical expenses of a large number of retired workers, etc.

China's labor force is the biggest and, relatively, also the cheapest. This became the human capital advantage that aided China's economic takeoff. For the same amount of labor, Chinese laborers receive lower wages than their Western counterparts. Whichever way you turn, we will come back to the circle of the demographic dividend. In 2007, the Academy of Social Sciences published the *Annual Report on China's Enterprises Competitiveness: Blue Book of China's Enterprises,* which proposed that behind the thriving and prosperous scene of corporate profits lay the dark truth about low wages, the huge focus on corporate income statements, and the unseen payroll where benefits are absolutely repressed. From 1990 to 2005, the proportion of workers' wages in the GDP fell from 53.4 percent to 41.4 percent, while the proportion of business profits in the GDP increased from 21.9 percent to 29.6 percent. In 1998, the total wage bill of state-owned and above-scale industrial enterprises was still 2.4 times corporate profits; but by 2005, that had dropped to 0.43. In the same time period, the proportion of industrial enterprise profits from industry rose from 4.3 percent to 21.36 percent.

Professor Zheng Gongcheng of Renmin University deconstructed it this way:

After wealth is created, a portion goes to state tax, and this amount is increasing. There is no drop in investment income of enterprises, so labor income decreases. Thus, if the proportion of labor income increases, the country's wealth gap will effectively be controlled. Generally in developed countries, the proportion of labor income in the initial distribution is at least 55 percent or above; ours is currently less than 40 percent. As such, imagine with me, for example, ten percentage points of the 2008 GDP of thirty trillion is three trillion; if wages were to increase by three trillion, we could expect that the living conditions of ordinary workers would be greatly improved.[9]

Once the gate to the market is opened, a trickle of freedom will become a tidal wave and the nation's protection of workers' income level will be pushed aside. Large profit-driven enterprises carry out their own valuation of labor. In addition, there is an excess supply of labor. Thus, whether intentionally or unintentionally, they become the new "Zhou Bapi,"[10] who knows to imitate a cock's crow in the middle of the night—i.e., they will know well how to use all ways and means to further their own interests, for example, cutting labor costs by refusing to provide employees with social insurance, housing funds, etc.

THE DISADVANTAGED LABOR FORCE

Compared to the strong and assertive employer representatives who hold down wages, the labor force is greatly disadvantaged.

When the author Liang Xiaosheng visited a silk factory that had nearly one hundred female workers and discovered that their wages were extremely low, he asked, "Sir, these female workers are all your fellow townsfolk; isn't the salary that you are paying them too low?"

The potbellied, black-haired boss laughed,

No, no, I think it's not low at all. Precisely because they are from my hometown, I gave them the priority in recruitment! The younger women will soon get married in a few years, and then they will have their house and dowry. This is something which their parents would like to give them but can't. So, I think of it this way: apart from their biological parents, I am probably considered the second greatest benefactor in their lives!

He turned and asked the ladies, who were laboring hard at work, "Do you want a raise?"

"No . . ."

Although the response was generally a muted one, a smile still flashed across the boss's face.[11]

If business operators consider themselves "messiahs," it would be unrealistic to hope that they will one day "have compassion." What is comforting for workers is that as labor surpluses disappear, the "powerful voice" of the employers will also gradually become a thing of the past, and wages can finally get out of the pit and make a gentle, upward climb. However, to completely reverse the unjust labor distribution pattern and improve workers' remuneration, we would still need to constantly strengthen the workers' right to speak before the employers and continue to improve codetermination wage mechanisms and support measures. This is a long-drawn-out and laborious process that requires constant mediation between the workers and employers, as well as strong institutional and legal support and protection from the government.

The Nation's Wealth Pie Is Being Divided into Smaller and Smaller Slices

The outstanding faults of the economic society in which we live
are its failure to provide for full employment and its arbitrary and
inequitable distribution of wealth and incomes.
— JOHN MAYNARD KEYNES[12]

GOVERNMENT FINANCES PLAY A BIG ROLE

The country's wealth pie looks big, but as different parties each take a slice, the wealth is suddenly diminished. By the time it reaches the people, there are only crumbs left.

Governmental finance takes the biggest chunk of the GDP pie. From 2007 to 2009, China's fiscal revenue accounted for 19.9 percent, 19.5 percent, and 20.4 percent of the GDP respectively. If government funds, state capital budget, and social insurance funds are included, the proportion of GDP accounted for increases to 27.6 percent, 27.9 percent, and 30 percent respectively.[13] Comparing to other countries, this proportion of government revenue relative to GDP is not particularly outstanding. However, when compared vertically in terms of resident income, there is some unfairness. In 2009, for example, fiscal revenue in the government budget was 6.85 trillion, equivalent to the disposable income of nearly 400 million urban residents in a year. In 2008, government revenue was also equivalent to the income of 390 million urban residents in that same year, or the net income of 1.29 billion farmers.

Huge administrative costs are also highly controversial government fiscal expenditures.

During two conferences in March 2009, the government work report by Premier Wen Jiabao showed that there were some problems in the government itself. For example, public consumption was not standardized; there was extravagant waste; and an excess of new construction and expansions of office buildings of administrative entities, constructions of luxury office buildings and hotels, etc. During the two conferences in 2010, Premier Wen Jiabao again stressed in his government report:

We must insist on frugal administration, oppose extravagance and waste, and constantly reduce administrative costs. There is a need to strictly control government building construction, to prohibit high-end office décor, to carry out system reforms for more efficient public services, bus services etc., and enforce stricter controls on public funds leaving the country.[14]

Ye Qing, the deputy director of the Hubei Provincial Bureau of Statistics, listed several sets of relevant statistics indicating that in the twenty-five years between 1978 and 2003, China's fiscal revenue grew about twenty-eight times from ¥113.2 billion to ¥3 trillion; administrative costs in the same period of time increased eighty-seven times, from less than ¥5 billion to ¥700 billion. The proportion of administrative costs to total expenditure had risen to 19.03 percent by 2003. This was very much higher than the 2.38 percent in Japan, 4.19 percent in the United Kingdom, 5.06 percent in South Korea, 6.5 percent in France, 7.1 percent in Canada, and 9.9 percent in the United States.

In 2006, National People's Congress representative Liu Mancang and Chinese People's Political Consultative Conference member Liu Guangfu highlighted the fact that "Every year, the expenses covering government cars used for private purposes by government officials at all levels exceeds ¥200 billion. That is almost as high as the defense expenditure in 2006."[15]

China's administrative expenses remain high. In the ¥8.5 trillion national budget of 2010, the general public services expenditure was nearly ¥860 billion, or 10.18 percent of the total budget.

Besides administrative costs, rent-seeking is another huge channel through which national wealth is lost. Hu Angang of Tsinghua University, an expert on national conditions, estimated that in the second half of the 1990s, China's corruption-based economic loss was, on average, between ¥987.5 billion and ¥1.257 trillion annually, equivalent to 13.2 to 16.8 percent of the GDP.

A LARGE FIGURE ON A VOIDED CHECK

Furthermore, we do not get a single cent of the state-owned assets that should be ours.

In the list of the world's top five hundred companies published by the British *Financial Times* on May 29, 2009, forty-seven of the enterprises were from China. Their total market value was greater than those from Japan and the United Kingdom. Among them, PetroChina, Industrial and Commercial Bank of China, and China Mobile ranked second, fourth, and fifth respectively. In 2009, the total value of state-owned land and assets amounted to about ¥79 trillion, which, when divided by an average of 1.3 billion, resulted in each person possessing as much as ¥60,000 worth of state-owned assets in 2009.

However, state-owned assets are owned by the state, after all. Although ¥60,000 is "credited" to you, when family income is actually calculated, this amount is clearly not included at all. It is a voided check. This voided check for ¥60,000 will not buy you bread, eggs, or pork, and it will most definitely not get you a house. It cannot be used for investments, nor does it bring dividends.

Most of us are unable to get hold of the ¥60,000 that supposedly belongs to us, but some people— those who work in the system of state-owned enterprises —are able to obtain these funds. As the money they spend is not their own, there are no limits on how they spend it. Sometimes, greed enters their hearts and they pocket all the money for themselves. The common folk may still be in the dark about such covert and dishonest activities.

Everyone should get an average of ¥60,000, which is not a small amount. People have continually suggested that this money cannot remain on a voided check, and reasonable changes must be made to the current method of distribution of state-owned assets so that the people can directly enjoy tangible benefits. Some have advocated combining the equity of state-owned assets and enterprises and establishing a state-owned assets fund. Managers can then allocate this fund to the 1.3 billion Chinese people in the form of shares. In this way, the people can truly become state-owned assets holders and practically get their share. The profits from state-owned enterprises can then directly belong to the ordinary folk, and people can truly enjoy the benefits that economic growth brings.

The population of China is as high as 1.3 billion people. National conditions are complex and "sharing property among the people" may not be realistic. However, even though we can change the initial and subsequent distribution patterns, it is also possible to change the current "wealthy nation, poor citizens" structure of benefits. Raising wages; increasing investment in areas such as education, health care, employment, and pension; and strengthening the protection of the people's property rights are all able to directly or indirectly increase citizens' wealth.

Elderly Issues: The Sad Twilight Years

Based on their intuition, most people think that ¥30,000 is obviously not enough, while ¥10 million is a bit excessive. My apologies, but I beg to differ—if there is continual and unrestrained issuing of currency, a pension of ¥10 million may not be enough to

last through old age. With regard to this issue, we must rationally
analyze the past twenty years.

—ZHONG WEI, Center for Financial Research,
Beijing Normal University[16]

SHORTFALL IN PENSION INSURANCE

We cannot resist the changes that the natural law of aging brings to our evanescent youth. The only difference is its duration. Elderly support is an issue in life that not only society but every family must face. Uncontrolled population growth ruthlessly eroded the foundations of society, and after a relatively long period of awakening, from the initial trial stages to now, China has been resolutely implementing family planning policies to slow down population growth. China's rapid train of life has finally slowed down after much struggling to tear it away from centuries-old childbearing values and desires. On the other hand, family planning has produced a large generation of 4-2-1 families. China now has more than 100 million single-child families. More and more family resources are put toward the raising of children. Parents and parents of parents, all compete to gather more resources to bring up their children.

However, a shift toward conservatism has always been quietly taking place. As the generation of single children grows up and settles down, and life expectancy increases, the burden of caring for parents and grandparents falls upon the third generation. The cycle of nurturing is no longer the life experience of two generations, but three.

The features that reflect societal trends are undergoing this quiet change. The 4-2-1 and 8-4-2-1 new, inverted family structures brought about by family planning are a test for the people who are situated in position "2." They face various pressures related to economic and emotional issues that come with supporting the elderly. When people are resolving their problems and asserting their independence and freedom as well, they will also find it hard not to look at society and wonder what kind of solutions society is providing for these situations they are personally experiencing.

A pension insurance system is society's first line of defense in managing elderly support.

In 1997, China began implementing the pension insurance system. The system's policies are such that an employee's pension insurance would consist of two parts. One part would be the individual account that businesses and individuals contribute to; the other part would be the basic pension fund, which is 20 percent of the average wage of workers in each region, and contributions are made by enterprises paying 5 percent of the individual's total wages.

The implementation of the pension insurance individual account system is helpful in alleviating the stresses of elderly support. However, because it was implemented rather late, there are issues of historical debts. Those who were already working or had already retired when the Social Security System was implemented were not able to accumulate the pension funds in their earlier years. This shortfall had to be borne by society, and later, by the contributors, thus increasing the hidden burden on the pension insurance system. In addition, some companies have not been contributing enough pension funds because of inefficiency, or they have been maliciously holding back contributions in order to cut costs. This has resulted in a deepening gap in the financing of pensions.

From 1998 onward, China implemented the pension insurance fund's special transfer payment system to settle historical debts, and subsidies have been consistently increasing. They have grown from ¥2.4 billion in 1998 to ¥87.3 billion in 2009. Within twelve years, there was a total of ¥448.3 billion worth of subsidies but this is still far from being sufficient. The shortfall is as much as ¥1 trillion.[17]

From his role as governor of the central bank, to that of a mayor managing the economy, to party chief of the National Council of Social Security Fund, Dai Xianglong's job has always involved money. However, he took up office when there was already a huge ¥2 trillion pension gap, and every day he has had to work anxiously to bridge this gap. "According to the standards of the United Nations, our country became an aging population in 1997; but after we became an aging population, a shortfall appeared in the pension fund's income and expenditure."[18]

CAN YOU AFFORD TO TAKE CARE OF YOUR PARENTS?
Regarding the independent financial capacity of the elderly in China, by the time they enter their golden years, the savings of a majority of them will have been depleted. They spend too much money and effort in raising their children. Even when their children are grown up, they are still willing to prolong their mission in order to help their children purchase houses and take care of the next generation. They even use their pension and pension insurance premiums, which are their main source of income, to help their children build up their careers and families. Parents no longer have savings of their own, and the burden of taking care of and protecting them in their golden years naturally falls on their children.

If you are not born in a rich family, if your parents are not high-ranking officials or wealthy, or if they are not even considered minor officials and they have not saved up enough money for retirement—or perhaps, they were not doing well in their previous post, or have already gone bankrupt and are unable to even obtain a bit of a pension—then the responsibility for your parents' happiness will fall solely on you. The brutal truth is that you are still too poor to even help yourself and are trying to climb the "survival" ladder alone. Everybody, whether they be outsiders or yourself, finds that their income is just always average and never enough, and it is always quickly consumed by a thick wad of monthly bills. Everything requires money—your children's education, high housing costs, social activities, food, accommodation, transport, etc. . . .

After several rounds of paying bills, there is not much money left. You are barely able to take care of yourself—how will you be able to ensure that your parents enjoy their golden years comfortably?

The main expenditure in supporting the elderly comes when their health deteriorates. When parents fall sick, heavy expenses follow: medical bills, nursing care, nutritional fees, and other such costs "plunder" a family's already impoverished financial resources. The stress of supporting parents is not just financial: there are also psychological pressures and opportunity costs. In a situation where support must be given to "the old above, and the young below," many people feel obliged to spend more time and effort on their family and this affects their career development. On the other hand, in order to ease economic stress, children are forced to work harder or take on more jobs, and thus increasingly neglect caring for the spiritual and emotional needs of the elderly. This is especially so when "empty nests" start to form and the elderly person's dream of a happy family becomes less and less obtainable.

In addition, you have to plan for your own future. Some say that ¥10 million is needed for retirement in the future, and there are old people who have ¥3 million in savings, yet still that is not enough to buy box lunches. In short, future retirement has become a daunting prospect.

"EVERYONE HAS A SHARE" IS WISHFUL THINKING

As the practice of raising children to provide for your old age declines, indisputably, the social security system has to step forward. However, the social security system is only able to guarantee the basic necessities of life. It is still far from being able to meet the comfort levels most people look for. Also, many have eagerly waited for the much-talked-about welfare state for such a long time that they have become disillusioned. The overwhelming momentum of economic growth and strong idealistic thinking has given birth to a welfare-state utopia. People believe that modernization can result in the creation of a high-welfare state by a progressive government. Indeed, many countries have boldly led their people into enjoying the benefits of the welfare state. Whether rich or poor, citizens can receive nondiscriminatory access to national welfare and care. This includes education, medicine, transportation, housing, and pensions.

In China, an "everyone gets a share" distribution method is not really feasible.

The basic idea that China is a "developing country" determines that its national income is insufficient. Although GDP growth figures are more and more dazzling with each year, the economic foundation is weak, so it is not easy to become prosperous rapidly. The Chinese government is thus unable to fork out enough money to "give everyone a share." The late start of the social security system, coupled with other historical legacies, resulted in a gaping shortfall in the pension system. This has become a concern in China's elderly care.

Judging from the soft power of national sustainable development, if China prematurely implements a blanket high-welfare system when the culture, moral values, and character of the people are not yet at the level to be able to enjoy welfare and are instead still at the level of being continuously innovated, then a system that supports laziness is likely be formed. Such a system lacks vitality and activity, and is not conducive for the development of the country as a whole.

When the children's real economic strength is put to the test, the custom of raising children to provide for one's old age, which is supported solely by filial piety, will inevitably die out. Although the pension insurance system is committed to the welfare of the people, it is merely able to assure survival, and the Engel coefficient will be particularly large. Finally, you are your own keeper. To avoid the embarrassment of economic distress in old age, one must learn to plan ahead and to prepare early for retirement.

But for a significantly large group of people, their concern is not about having enough to save because they earn little and are already unable to cut expenditures. With such great pressure from both sides, their household budget becomes like "a mouse in a bellows."

THE WEALTH PARADOX—"INDUSTRIOUS AND YET NOT RICH"

No matter how much we try, we are still unable to grasp the wealth paradox of "industrious and yet not rich." On the whole, China's family unit is becoming better off, yet because of factors such as system costs, opportunity costs, rent-seeking, and personal hardworking habits, the income curve of the people has not risen smoothly.

Housing plays a major role in a family's expenditure. Once a house is bought, a drastic situation of surrendering, deploying all resources, and emptying all savings may come into play. When you purchase a house, you have to make mortgage payments, and at the same time, support the elderly and send children to school. Sum up all these bills, and your annual income gets depleted. There is absolutely nothing left to save for future retirement. To quote a contemporary proverb, retirement savings are like a road from Mars to Earth, where a shadow of the destination cannot even be seen.

Even if you have some savings, the ultimate beneficiary might not be you. In 2007, HSBC conducted an annual survey entitled "The Future of Retirement" in fifteen countries and regions around the world. The findings from Mainland China revealed that only 9 percent of those surveyed believed they had prepared sufficiently for retirement, 32 percent of the respondents said they did not have retirement plans, and up to 41 percent saved for their children; only 14 percent saved for retirement.

Even if you work extremely hard and save a large sum of money, the purchasing power of renminbi falls because of inflation, and the value of the money you save in the bank shrinks dramatically. You may have made a long list of retirement plans for that sum of money, such as traveling, learning calligraphy, or even philanthropy. Yet in the end, you are terrified to find out that the money is only enough to buy your box lunches.

The cruel realities of old age are perhaps even more disturbing than those of youth. The years have eroded not only your energy, but also your financial resources, material resources, and time.

Hospitals Happily Earning Money

Whom do we turn to when we are sick? In my opinion, medical financial security needs to be established and even more so, a medical service system has to be established. China is not a developed country but a large amount of high-quality medical service capabilities have already been mobilized and accumulated long ago. Thus the areas in need of "health care reform" are mainly in financial security—whether payment is made personally by commercial insurance, or by the government. But China's problem is twofold: there is the question of who pays for medical bills, and also the question of how to mobilize more resources for the health care sector. If we believe that what we have is just a medical financial security issue, and that, by settling payment difficulties, there will automatically be a guaranteed provision of medical services, then we are very mistaken. This is a noteworthy point for future "health care reform."

—Economist ZHOU QIREN[19]

"EXPENSIVE MEDICAL SERVICES"

Health care reform is surging forward with great momentum but the worry that "you can have anything, but don't fall sick" has not abated. The feeling that seeing a doctor is expensive and difficult still exists and prevents people from having a positive health care experience.

The occasional cough and headache are small issues. Although you are no doctor, you can still go to the pharmacy to get drugs for minor ailments. By relying on common sense or following the advice of books, you may be able to somehow cure the problem. But if more serious symptoms occur, such as sharp pains in the head, sudden fever, or dizziness, or you are unable to determine which part of the body is malfunctioning, you should not take matters lightly or blindly follow a prescription, in case to do so is merely to delay obtaining the correct treatment. So you arrive at the hospital full of apprehension, and the doctor starts with a long diagnostic checklist and sends you on a visit to every single department. Medical tests are expensive, and the more high-tech a procedure is, the more sophisticated and recently imported from overseas the equipment, the higher the fees are. When the test results come back and it turns out you have just a minor illness, you are, of course, glad. Although you may have spent a lot of money unnecessarily, at least you bought peace of mind.

If what you have is not a minor illness, then you must prepare yourself for a large investment. The doctor patiently suggests and encourages you to accept treatment using the most advanced and painless technology. For the sake of your health, you have no choice but to take the kind doctor's advice. Your wallet grows thinner and thinner, and you might even throw in a few years' savings.

You are not the only one complaining that medical services are costly. This is a general feeling among people. Statistics from the Department of Health show that in 2008, average outpatient expenses were ¥146.50 per person per visit, and average inpatient expenses were ¥5,463.80 per person per visit. There is an upward trend in the proportion of personal payments. The proportion of personal payments of total health expenditures rose from 20.4 percent in 1978 to 45.2 percent in 2007. The third National Health Services Survey in 2005 revealed that 45.8 percent of people in China did not seek treatment when sick, and 29.6 percent should have been hospitalized but were not.

THE STENCH OF MONEY ON "WHITE-CLOTHED ANGELS"

Lifesaving hospitals can no longer nobly claim that their purpose is "public welfare." Other than borrowing the brand name "public welfare," nothing has changed in the way doctors greet us with a cold shoulder and an expressionless face, tarnishing the real meaning of "public welfare." Instead, the steady stream of patients that come and go are detecting the smell of money from these doctors.

The statistics from the Department of Health website also show that the total national health expenditure (referring to the total funds spent by the entire nation on health care services that year) rose from ¥11.021 billion in 1978 to ¥1,128.95 billion in 2007: an increase of 102 times. In addition, individual health expenditure rose from ¥2.252 billion in 1978 to ¥509.866 billion in 2007, which is an increase of about 226 times. That is far higher than the growth of GDP and per capita income of urban and rural households over the same period.

Members of the National Committee of the Chinese People's Political Consultative Conference and Secretary-General Wu Mingjiang of the Chinese Medical Association revealed a set of data to the media showing that public hospitals in China are not really public. Only 10 percent of funds are invested by the state, while the hospital has to self-finance the remaining 90 percent. As per the saying, "there is no wool without sheep," 90 percent of hospital funds come from patients.

MARKETIZED, YET STILL INCOMPETENT

"Marketization" has always been a buzzword in health care reform; and when health care becomes marketized, a medical market that is highly efficient, fair, and competitive can be created. This was once the beautiful blueprint for health care reform. Now that more than 90 percent of funding comes from patients, hospitals no longer blindly follow in the footsteps of government finances. Is this not the medical field becoming marketized?

Actually, China's medical field has not really become marketized. Marketization was once welcomed with great fanfare but that was mostly a gimmick. It pretended to make its rounds in the medical field and then quietly slipped out of the window, leaving patients to support the hospital with money from their own pockets. In more precise terms, the Chinese medical field is suffering from marketization paraplegia.

China's health care industry has never been fully marketized. On the contrary, thanks to the singular voice claiming that the medical field is special because it concerns life and health, the government has never completely withdrawn from the Chinese medical market. Quoting statistics from the Department of Health again, in 2005, 82.8 percent of hospitals across the country, 95.1 percent of all hospital beds, and 90.4 percent of health care workers belonged to state-owned and collective organizations, while 52.8 percent of all hospitals, 80.1 percent of hospital beds, and 77 percent of health personnel worked directly with government-run medical institutions. The power of appointment of the vast majority of hospital directors lies in the hands of the government, and the personnel boards of hospitals are also directly or indirectly subject to government influence. Although hospitals work by the appointment system, it is still the responsibility of health administration departments to determine if doctors are legally qualified for practice. When public hospitals look at increasing the number of doctors and nurses, they have to check to determine if they have achieved the bottom line of the establishment.

There is an endless stream of patients seeking treatment and the danger is that hospitals become overcrowded. Even if hospitals want to expand, they are unable to make that decision on their own. Is opening a hospital like opening a small store where all you need is a bright red stamp from the Ministry of Industry and Commerce? The medical field is related to life, and approval from the health administrative authorities is required. The relevant departments even have to approve new departments and staff expansions.

With regard to the management system, hospitals do not have complete autonomy or voice: they only operate within the government's framework. Financially, the government does not play a blanket role. It only carries a small part of the financial burden, leaving the bulk to the hospitals themselves.

The lack of financial support from the government is a clear reason why hospitals are lamenting, "There is not enough money." There is also an unspoken rule that hospitals still have to cope with a large group of people who do not have enough coverage, so require extremely cheap public health and medical treatment. This group of people takes away another portion of the income pie that should belong to the hospitals.

In 2006, the former state deputy minister of health Yin Dakui provided some surprising data: "80 percent of the government's investment in medical expenses goes toward servicing groups that mainly comprise 8.5 million party and government cadres (Chinese Academy of Sciences survey report). In addition, according to the Ministry of Supervision and Ministry of Personnel, two million cadres at all levels from the national party and government departments are on long-term medical leave, out of which, 400,000 cadres occupy cadre hospital wards, guest houses, and resorts on a long-term basis. The yearly expenditure is about ¥50 billion." In 2007, the government health expenditure was also just under ¥229.71 billion.[20]

The government only manages the hospital but does not provide fiduciary support. So the hospitals have to provide for themselves by "putting their hands to work." Be it quickly or slowly, in order to catch up with the profit trend of marketization, hospitals still have to strive to earn money. Whether supporting doctors by providing drugs or supporting doctors with technology, the money comes from the pockets of consumers. Under the weight of economic burden, the humanitarian ideal of "saving the dying and injured" has been corrupted, and it is no longer surprising that hospitals work to get rich from patients. In July 2007, the Fourth Hospital of Fuzhou even reported a strange case when a patient made nineteen appointments to see the doctor for his illness and the doctor handed him nineteen prescriptions!

COMPLAINTS FROM PUBLIC HOSPITALS

Consumers may complain that it is difficult and expensive to see a doctor but public hospitals also have their share of grievances. Wu Mingjiang, a former hospital director, raised a complaint that is worth our consideration:

> Despite the high cost of medical care, honestly, once you deduct the hospital's day-to-day operating expenses, it would be considered remarkable for the hospital to see an 8 percent profit each year. In fact, it is the system that causes high medical expenses. Patients always claim that doctors earn too much, and I admit that there are some specialists whose income is very high because of their expertise, and it is also true that there is a minority of unethical doctors with dishonest medical practices. Within the hospital, however, there are quite a number of young residents who earn only about ¥2,000 a month total. They have to maintain a simple lifestyle and dare not even think about buying an apartment. Why do we lose so many young doctors? Their income is too low![21]

Public hospitals are nonprofit organizations that are rarely questioned and generally acknowledged as truthful by people. Since government funding is weak, they have to be self-reliant and at the same time fight the collaborative war over "free medical care" with the government. Moreover, their competitors are weak private hospitals and foreign hospitals. Because of favorable climatic, geographical, and human conditions, public hospitals are therefore able to boldly set their prices high, as though they were selling abalone or shark's fin. Only doctors know the truth about whether money is being truthfully spent to get quality abalone and shark's fin, as there is insufficient information, and ordinary people can make nothing of it.

The Era of Monopoly: Power Connections Trump Hard Work

Traditionally, the liberals have always stressed the relationship
between the plight of disadvantaged groups and broader social
issues such as discrimination and social class boundaries. In contrast, the conservatives emphasize the important role that differences in values among the various groups and competitiveness
play in explaining the experiences of the disadvantaged sectors.

—Sociologist WILLIAM WILSON (in translation)[22]

THE ERA OF "CONNECTIONS"

Nowadays, phrases such as "connections" and "dishonesty" are more popular
than "hard work."

In 2010, the arrested perpetrator who injured two girls in a car accident in
the new Hebei University district arrogantly challenged, "Report me if you dare!
My dad is Li Gang." "Connections" are especially in vogue: "My father is the
magistrate," "My dad is a wealthy businessman," "My father is a celebrity." In
short, all types of "fathers" are being flashed out by these "second-generation
officials," "second-generation wealthy," "second-generation celebrities," and
"second-generation soldiers," who enjoy showing off, are obsessed with vanity
and fame, or use their fathers as shields when they get into trouble.

The high-profile and attention-grabbing "connections" precisely exemplify
how wealth, capital, and reputation have become socially monopolized capital.
Whether you are rich or poor, powerful or not, famous or not, directly affects
how high the ceiling of opportunity you or your descendants may reach.

Wealth and social capital are becoming more and more overbearing, and
their arrogant insolence comes with an abundant tendency of "winner takes all."

Emerson brilliantly sums up opportunity in this manner:

> Actually, opportunities do not follow any norms. Not only do they belong
> to a small minority who are prepared and able to seize them, they also
> belong to some people who were predestined and fated to meet them.
> Usually, they fall into people's paths in an elusive and fortuitous manner.
> Denying this point means never being able to understand why someone
> can guard the roulette wheel his entire life and still remain a pauper while
> another may walk into the casino just once and instantaneously win a
> million dollars.[23]

The opportunities that the first-generation entrepreneurs were destined for
were found in the great environment of "reform and opening up." The initial

stage of reform and opening up was one that was chaotic, full of confusion and murk, but at the same time, there were countless dazzling opportunities in its wake. This chaotic situation led to people using various means, even unscrupulous ones, to seize every opportunity and procure wealth.

Today, these bizarre yet dazzling times have passed, leaving only a crystallized situation where social resources and benefits are held in the hands of a small minority. By leveraging their own capital or power, they have taken the best resources and the right to speak. Others who later wished to enter their ranks would have to wade through miles of water—e.g., the household registration system, the socially structured division of labor mechanism, wealth distribution system, etc.—which have become huge, glaring barriers between the two.

THE GRADUALLY FADING HALO OF EDUCATION

Education, a factor once reputed as to most fully embody equal opportunities and the principles of justice in the distribution of social wealth, is now becoming an increasingly gloomy facet of life.

In 2010, the *Education Expenses of Chinese Families* report released jointly by Sina Education Channel and other investigative bodies revealed that 61.9 percent of Internet users are not satisfied with their present situation, and are anxiously hoping to change the status quo through education.

Many parents hope and expect their "sons to become dragons and daughters to become phoenixes." This is also the most logical way for them to extend their personal ideals. They hope that through education, their entire family's social status can be improved, and they can break through the impenetrable strata and open the way for vertical mobility across all walks of life. "No matter how tough life is, the child must not suffer; no matter how poor we are, we must not be stingy toward education." This slogan has been increasingly raised, and the education of children has become an important catalyst leading to a rapid emptying of parents' wallets.

As China's economy grows, education costs also increase along with everything else. From 2004 to 2008, the national expenditure on education doubled, maintaining an annual growth rate of more than 16 percent. It grew from ¥724.26 billion in 2004 to ¥145,007.4 billion in 2008. Education accounts for up to 3.48 percent of the nation's gross domestic product.[24] Nevertheless, education costs still make up a large part of parents' expenditure.

If there is no worry about children's school fees, there would be other new items to worry about: school selection fees, books expenses, various types of school expenses as well as endless courses such as Mathematics Olympiad preparations, piano lessons, painting classes, etc. Among the numerous expenses, the one that has increased the most is the school selection fee. In 2011 in Beijing, the school selection fee from kindergarten to primary school was as high as ¥250,000. This ¥250,000 includes clearly marked amounts for the Board of Education, human relations fees, as well as agent fees. The expenses for junior high school and high school are not low either. Apart from school selection fees and tuition fees, there are also home-tutoring costs which can range from tens to hundreds of yuan, as well as additional training and crash courses which can go up to tens of thousands of yuan. From the first to third year of middle school, this adds up to a minimum of more than tens of thousands to as much as several hundreds of thousands. University costs are also high. The total expenditure for four years in university reaches at least ¥60,000.

In 2009, the Social Research Center of China Youth Daily conducted a survey on 2,157 people through Sina. Of those surveyed, 74.7 percent believed that education costs are the greatest burden for ordinary families in urban and rural areas; 36.2 percent of respondents said that education expenditure made up 10 to 30 percent of their annual family income; 29.5 percent said that their education expenditure was between 30 and 50 percent; 12.8 percent said their expenditure was between 50 and 80 percent; and 8.4 percent spent more than 80 percent of their annual income on education.

Despite its high costs, education is not necessarily the direct route to success. Various factors, such as the continuous expansion of universities, high education becoming irrelevant or out of touch with the market, the structural imbalance between education and the market, China's economic structural imbalances, etc., have all made it increasingly difficult for university graduates to find employment. In the face of cruel realities, their yearning to become a part of high society has become more and more like a wishful dream. This group of young people, once passionate and energetic, is now confused, sad, and lost. Some of them even become depressed, embittered, or harbor other more extreme emotions. As they are not well employed, they are labeled as "boomerang children or elderly parasites," "school failures," "ants," and other derogatory names; none of the labels are glamorous or honorable.

THE "LOVE AND HATE" OF PATRIMONY

Many people have publicly expressed their disgust for patrimony, yet many are unable to get out of the cycles of patrimony. Those who repeatedly blame patrimony could very well be the beneficiaries of such. The college entrance examination is a relatively fair system that promotes mobility up the social ladder. Unfortunately, after the entrance exam, patrimony comes into play at every opportunity. Once there is a graduate in the family, the entire family relationship chain becomes abnormally active. The contacts and resources accumulated over previous generations become more important than ever. Whether it is an intergenerational transfer of power or one of wealth, it will have an explosive effect on the employment food chain.

In 2007, the *2006 Graduate Employment Survey* published by the Committee of Communist Youth League, Central School Department, and Public Policy Research, Peking University, showed that 41.61 percent of the students think that going through the family and personal social relations, friends and relatives, etc., is the most effective way to obtain a job. Among the students from the major cities, this ratio was as high as 51.29 percent.

The children of the rich and powerful, or of celebrities, have much easier access than other children when it comes to employment or establishing a business. The parents of these scions of the rich have not only accumulated wealth but have also woven a network of relationships. These parents are well aware of the amazing benefits of this good relationship network, and they hope to bind both wealth and social capital together, and pass this magic bundle to their next generation. That way, the safety net that comes with the inheritance will be higher.

In September 2011, the son of famous singer Li Shuangjiang became the target of public criticism for unlawful driving and assault. A columnist at *West China City Daily* wrote about the incident,

> When an accident takes place, we should not demand that Li Shuangjiang and his son have higher moral standards than others. Moral values can only come from self-discipline and not from external discipline. In a law-governed society, the law should be the only criterion, and not who the father is—regardless of whether your father's last name is "power," "celebrity," or "wealth."[25]

The law should be able to overlook your father's last name, be it "power," "celebrity," or "wealth." However, when these fathers lead the way for such social stratification to become more deeply ingrained in society, the law will be even less able to impartially govern.

CHAPTER SIX

Why Are Centralized Enterprises Sluggish, While Private Enterprises Are Lively?

The "Eldest Son" Superiority of Centralized Enterprises

Whether it is determined from resource aggregation, the requirements of heavy and chemical industries, or the strength that is
desperately needed in the era of global competition, the manifes-
tations of nationalism at this present stage are closely intertwined
with financial and industrial oligarchs. China is not alone in this:
all countries that have huge sovereign wealth funds have similar
factors—from Norway and Kuwait to Singapore, to name a few.
Centralized enterprise is the typical style of nationalism.
  —Financial commentator YE TAN[1]

THE "ELDEST SON'S" PURSE

For a considerable time, China's economic superiority was described in this way:
the state-owned economy is thriving like one branch of a tree that overshadows
the others, there are no other offshoots, and likewise the success or failure and
ups or downs of the economy hinge solely on state-owned enterprises.

But even the palm and back of a hand have differences between them, not to
mention particular phases of the transition of a traditional planned economy to
a market economy. Preferences will inevitably appear in the country's policies.

China's reform and opening up produced three major interest groups: state-
owned enterprises, foreign investment, and private enterprises. Among these,
state-owned enterprises obtained the most preferential policies because of
their natural institutional advantages. From capital, personnel, and technology, to resources—almost all of the preferential policies toward state-owned
enterprises opened wide the doors to these advantages. Even those state-owned
enterprises that were inefficient received "poverty alleviation" because of their
noble descent.

Private enterprises could not hold a candle to the powerful financial advantages of state-owned enterprises.

The financial advantages of state-owned enterprises were first manifested in easier access to bank loans. State-owned enterprises were likelier to gain large loans to launch a large project, carry out particular reforms, or conduct mergers and acquisitions and investments. In March 2007, Sinopec, Fujian Province, Saudi Aramco, and ExxonMobil established a joint venture, the Fujian Refining and Petrochemical Co., Ltd. Sinopec raised a total of ¥33.3 billion in syndicated financing for its refining and marketing projects in Fujian; and the loans were entirely provided by domestic banks.[2]

In September 2009, China National Petroleum Corporation (CNPC) announced that it had signed a long-term strategic cooperation agreement with the China Development Bank (CDB), and that within the next five years CDB would use a preferential interest rate to provide a $30 billion line of credit to CNPC. The many private enterprises that fight for bank loans until they are bruised and bloody form a stark contrast to the state-owned enterprises that find financing as easily as turning over the palm of one's hand. Moreover, as soon as there is macroeconomic or industrial depression, state-owned enterprises also have the easiest access to government subsidies. In 2010 alone, CNPC received ¥1.599 billion in government subsidies, and Yangtze Power received as much as ¥1.847 billion.

Capital markets have also become the geomantic treasure for the funding of state-owned enterprise. In the late 1990s, the decision makers did everything possible to finance low efficiency state-owned enterprises. They found that the stock market is a good thing, and hence they allocated large quantities of listing indicators to state-owned enterprises.[3] Regardless of the level of efficiency, all could be assigned a share of the stock market. During the most frenzied time, even the All-China Women's Federation was assigned a listing indicator. The electronic military enterprise BOE Technology Group Co., Ltd., had been called the wonder of the stock market. Thanks to poor management, BOE was headed for a total loss: in just seven years, from 2002 to 2009, the company's net profit losses amounted to more than ¥3.77 billion, and in 2005, liabilities reached ¥17.3 billion.

But the company's huge losses did not stop it, in the slightest, from riding on the crest of its success in the capital markets. Accompanying its entry into the domain of LCD panels in 2002, BOE's financing became smoother, the scale of its capital increased from ¥2.2 billion to ¥18 billion. Dividends were ¥66 million in that period, and shareholders' equity investment losses were ¥2 billion. BOE had repeated losses, and not only did it not go bankrupt, it became bolder in the financing markets, and the China Securities Regulatory Commission (CSRC) still approved their development plans. The bottom line is that the government can pay off the remainder of the debt. Backed by this dowry of government credit, even when facing the worst, BOE could even be married off in glory in the capital markets. As the saying goes, "The emperor's daughter does not worry about getting married."

NATURAL MONOPOLY IN A SPECIAL CONTEXT

The "special treatment" that state-owned enterprises enjoyed was also reflected in permitting and maintaining the existence of state-owned enterprises' monopolistic advantages. The monopolistic advantages of state-owned enterprises were displayed in their dominance in some special domains: private enterprises lacked reasonable and legitimate entry channels, price controls existed in the market and interfered with the normal competition between private enterprises and state-owned enterprises, and so on.

In 2006, the State-owned Assets Supervision and Administration Commission (SASAC) director made clear that the seven major industries—defense, power generation and distribution, petroleum and petrochemicals, telecommunications, coal, civil aviation, and shipping—were absolutely controlled by state-owned enterprises. In the eighty industries of the society, seventy-two kinds allow state-owned capital to enter, sixty-two kinds allow foreign capital to enter, and only forty-one kinds allow private capital to enter.[4]

After the 2008 financial crisis, a new term appeared: *renationalization*. Renationalization refers to implementing certain market-oriented reforms in iron and steel, coal, and other industries, and also permitting a large amount of private capital to enter the above mentioned domains, thereby obtaining certain rights to current operations and development. However, under the policy's guidance or coercion, private capital was once again excluded and marginalized by state-owned capital. In response to the 2008 financial crisis, the government's ¥4 trillion investment plan (the plan to revitalize the top ten industries), and the orientation of the financial environment, all intentionally or unintentionally caused the phenomenon of renationalization to appear in some domains such as steel, iron, and coal.

For example, the "ten industrial restructuring and revitalization plan"— including automobile, steel, textile, equipment manufacturing, shipbuilding, telecommunications, light industry, petrochemicals, nonferrous metals, and logistics—exhibits the government's shady support for state-owned enterprises. Some state-owned enterprises directly and proudly ascended onto the nation's special protection list, as in the identification of China State Shipbuilding Corporation (CSSC) and China Shipbuilding Industry Corporation (CSIC) as the two leading companies focused on the development of the

shipbuilding industry. Also, there were revitalization plans as well as empha-
sizing support of automotive industry bases: the bases of the big three car
manufacturers—FAW Group Corporation, Dongfeng Motor Corporation and
SAIC Motor Corporation, Ltd.—along with the three small-scale car manufacturers—Beijing Jeep, Tianjin Xiali, and Guangzhou Peugeot Automobile
Company (GPAC). In addition, the planning of the steel industry also made
clear "the promotion of transregional regrouping for Anben Steel Group Company, the Pangang Group, Dongbei Special Steel Group, Baosteel Group and
Baogang Steel Group, and Ningbo Steel, etc., and the advancement of regional
restructuring for Tianjin Pipe and Tiantie, Tianjin Steel, Tianjin Metallurgical
Company, TISCO and iron and steel enterprises in the province, etc."[5]

Price controls are also a tall glass door, weakening the competitiveness of
private enterprises through administrative measures, and providing state-
owned enterprises low-priced resources and policy protection. Take the "dual
pricing system" launched in the 1980s as an example. This particular pricing
mechanism caused private enterprises to be sidelined, and township enterprises also were not able to participate. Zhou Yaoting of the Wuxi Hongdou
Group of Jiangsu township enterprises recalls it in this way:

Red beans developed, and the country had never given away one kilogram of diesel or one kilogram of cotton yarn, and had never had any raw
materials that were part of any plan. In 1985 and around 1986, the textile
industries had extreme shortages of raw materials, many factories were
forced to stop, our enterprises had no cotton yarn to do foreign trade, and
I wanted to go to the Wuxi City department to fight for something. Of
course, the answer would be no, because you are township enterprises,
so it would be impossible to be given one kilogram of cotton yarn. I said,
"state-owned enterprises are the Big Brother, we township enterprises are
the Little Brother, and Little Brother is learning from Big Brother. Could
you make the textile companies give us a little bit of cotton yarn?" The
department cadre replied to me: "You township enterprises are Little
Brother? You cannot be called that."[6]

From a market perspective, state-owned enterprises and private enterprises
have no intrinsic differences. State-owned enterprises similarly survive for
profit and provide products to customers. They don't need to assume public
responsibility and should stand on the same competitive platform as private
enterprises. But the policy will inevitably turn to the "origin of heroes," and
with the magic wand of the state-owned system, state-owned enterprises can

easily obtain financing and cheap resources, and attract talent. The positions of nobility and grassroots are vastly and materially different.

Private Enterprises Survive in the Cracks

Regarding China's transition from a planned economy to a market economy, if China is compared to Russia, the secret of China's success in the past twenty years is that in addition to the original state-owned enterprises, many new companies were also set up. This is a very important factor.

—MASAHIKO AOKI, president and chief research officer of the Research Institute of Economy, Trade and Industry, Tokyo, Japan[7]

THE STRONG TEST SUBJECTS OF SYSTEM REFORM

Many private enterprises that emerged from the heaviness of history, once the cruel reality of the hardship and shame of the old days had been swept away, have become the masters of fate, their names proudly listed on various fortune lists, and have become the wealth creation idols that many people prostrate themselves to worship.

However, people see the scenery in front of them. And if they turn around suddenly, they will be able to hear a slight sigh. The sadness and hardship of those living in the cracks has been exposed.

The variability of policy is what most causes private enterprises to flounder, toss, and turn. The experimental nature of China's system reform has caused many open market policies to be fickle, continuously walking, looking, stopping, worried that disaster will strike. Thus, from time to time, the arm of regulation is extended. However, because of lack of experience, this regulatory arm has an inevitable tendency or habit of adopting simple and crude methods. The policies are continually changed back and forth and thus produce policy risk. Things that have previously been characterized as good could be considered outrageous if the policy changes. Moreover, taking into consideration the authoritative and exemplary nature of policies, almost all policies that are introduced—especially those policies aimed at bringing order out of chaos—are often accompanied by punishment to one party as a "warning to others." State-owned enterprises are the eldest son and have a responsibility to avoid large moves that disrupt the economy.

If they make the wrong move and shake the economic base, how can it not lead to disaster? Foreign investment is a foreign wealth monk: it can not only recite scriptures but also provide capital. But to avoid leaving behind stereotypes, it cannot offend too many people. Only the private enterprises have a grassroots background, are not concerned about economic pedigree, and lack much financial backing. They are also too aggressive and active, often playing the system, and walking a fine line regarding policies and laws. So it would be most appropriate to place the blame on the private economy as a warning to others.

After several periods of macroeconomic regulation and control, many private enterprises have experienced displacement injuries. To this day, some retain lingering bruises. To this day, those who experienced or witnessed the "Eight Kings" incident of 1982 will break out in cold sweat in reaction to mere memories.

On January 11 and April 13, 1982, the State Council twice issued stern regulatory documents:

> Regarding serious crimes that damage the economy, regardless of the person that commits them, that person's professional association, or whether he holds a high or a low post, all must receive just and stern enforcement of the law, without the slightest exception, partiality, intercession, or cover up. If there are any violations, all parties will be investigated and held responsible.[8]

The famous Eight Kings of Wenzhou were "planted" in the midst of mutations of these policies.

The Eight Kings of Wenzhou are "Motor King" Hu Jinlin, "Coil King" Zheng Xiangqing, "Catalog King" Ye Jianhua, "Screw King" Liu Dayuan, "Miner's Lamp King" Cheng Buqing, "Contract King" Li Fangping, "Electric Appliances King" Zheng Yuanzhong, and "Flea Market King" Wang Maiqian. At the time, the Eight Kings were at the center of the limelight, so naturally, they were classified as priority targets within the scope of fighting "criminal activity" in the economic arena. In the blink of an eye, the Eight Kings plummeted from the pinnacle of life to rock bottom—for example, the ill-fated Cheng Buqing, whose hands were tied behind his back as he was taken into custody and denounced and reviled on a public stage. Liu Dayuan became the only "king" who did not go to jail. Even though he avoided that fate, he fell into despair and lost his passion for business, so it was hard for him to regain yesterday's glory.

The issue of property rights is also a headache for many, especially early-stage private enterprises. For various historical reasons, the property rights of many private enterprises are not precise. Imprecise property rights are a taboo of business. When these are undetermined, those involved in the business will most likely end up "making someone else's wedding dress." An entrepreneur spends a lot of energy, finances, and wisdom in order to prove that the business he established is his own. But once the concerned parties meet behind closed doors to discuss enterprise ownership, there will inevitably be a divergence of interests, and there may be a conflict that destroys the enterprise. This is another scar that remains on the body of private enterprises.

THE LONELINESS OF GRASSROOTS

China's private capital is ill fated. This is also reflected in its rise from the grassroots with only meager support. If the growth of state-owned enterprises is further weakened, they will still have the powerful financial backing of the government. Regarding banks, I'm afraid that there are no mortgage bargaining chips that are better than government credit. Thus, large state-owned enterprises and listed companies have stable cash flow, wide financing channels, and a standardized financial system, and they can be high-quality banking customers. Alternately, banks adopt a "suspect the poor, favor the rich" attitude in their treatment of private enterprises. Private enterprises have inherent issues, including poor financing capacity and inadequate power to impose norms and regulations of the financial system. Furthermore, they often lack decent assets that are highly insurable and easily realized, such as land and real estate. Thus, private enterprises incessantly complain that they get the cold shoulder from banks more easily, especially where a tightening of credit is concerned.

In terms of industry's space to expand, private enterprises still face many glass doors. With the introduction of "A Few Suggestions from the State Council on Encouraging, Supporting, and Guiding Individual and Private Operations, and Other Non-public Systems of Economic Development" and "A Few Suggestions from the State Council on Encouraging and Guiding the Healthy Development of Private Investment," etc., the private economy's industrial space was further expanded at the legal and policy level. However, this was far from adequate.

Feng Lun, chairman of the Vantone Group and one of the representatives of private entrepreneurs, wrote an article titled "Crossing the River of History" in which he states,

> Private capital has always been ancillary or supplemental to state-owned capital. Therefore, the best way to protect itself is either to leave the monopolized field of state-owned capital and be content with dominating in just a small corner—do a little small-scale trading, actively engage in charities, repair roads and bridges, or enter into a partnership or joint venture with state-owned capital to create a mixed economy pattern. It is to use one's own professional competence with strict management to increase the value of state-owned capital, and at the same time, allow

private capital to gain the recognition of society's mainstream values, and create a relatively safe development environment. In the future, with the establishment and development of a harmonious society, private capital will be plentiful, small scale, with widespread employment that involves a large number of the population. And its space of existence will be limited to areas that are either not in conflict with state-owned capital or which state-owned capital has relinquished. Faced with state-owned capital, private capital has always adhered only to a position of cooperation rather than competition, supplementation rather than replacement, and connection without transgression. All in order to advance and retreat with ease, and maintain sustainable development.[9]

Public opinion also holds private entrepreneurs as highly controversial. Perhaps the ancient view that "no business is free from evil" is too deeply rooted. When our nation was defeated, the merchants and prostitutes did not worry about national hatred or the enemy of their families, and continued to do business even with the enemy side. These sorts of stories have been told often and have been widely heard. Thus, private entrepreneurs have yet to cast off the hat of blame for being "rich and merciless." The Rich List is just one example. Every year, wealthy people fall off the Rich List because of past crimes or current crimes that cascade one after another. The Rich List has thus become an ominous thing. People have characterized it as the "Sacked List," "Deception List," and even "Butchers' List." The chairman and CEO of the Giant Interactive social network, Shi Yuzhu, has a stomach full of bitter grievances to spill.

Society's expectations of me are higher than they are for Chen Tianqiao and Dinglei because I used to be a loser. The winner-takes-all mentality is in the bones of the Chinese people.... I could not make any statements after finishing work on the Hope Primary School. If I said anything, the media would scold me, stating that the investment in Huaxia Bank to see a return was also my fault. When they could not find any other problems with me, they said I was involved in speculation."[10]

They are like grassroots mayflies that develop quietly and continue to rise toward the light. The ups and downs of their fortunes are precisely concentrated in the drastic changes throughout the history of this era. Trendy heroes are also great criminals. Regardless of how far the rivers and lakes flow, or how high the temples rise, they have struggled to rise from the rubble and grow from the gravel.

The Greater the Era, the More Natural Selection Is Involved

In terms of common sense, the development of the private economy represents vast ideological progress. I think it is important to
allow it to exist without too many imposed issues.
— HARRY M. MARKOWITZ, Nobel Laureate in Economics[11]

UNEXPECTED GROWTH

Despite policy support, financing, the opening of space within industry, and additional aspects, private enterprises suffered discrimination, and many advantageous resources were forcibly assigned to state-owned enterprises. However, it is undeniable that it is precisely under the guidance of mainstream reform that these people (who were scattered in every corner as peddlers and menial servants, owners of small workshops and mom-and-pop stores) would have the opportunity to create wealth, smoothly meet the standards of mainstream economic performance, and exhibit full economic vitality.

In 2003, the State Council set up a nonpublic economic development research group. Li Yining, who was over seventy years old, was entrusted with the great responsibility of leading more than twenty officials dispatched to the two provinces of Guangdong and Liaoning in order to thoroughly interact with the population, interview, and investigate (them). The research group wrote a seventeen-page report, "Recommendations on the Promotion of Non-public Economic Development"—the first prototype of "Thirty-six Articles About the Nonpublic Economy." The survey shows that every day in China, there are more than 1,500 newly formed private enterprises. In 2003 alone, private enterprise capital funds increased to ¥1 trillion. In the last ten years, these companies provided nearly 7 percent of jobs, and successfully absorbed 70 percent of the rural labor force, making a significant contribution to social and economic development.

To be fully compared with the growth pattern of the private economy, many with a monopoly position in industry, and state-owned enterprises with a mentality of "if you want money, you get money, if you want resources, you get resources," exhibited weaknesses that caused people to be disappointed.

The 1980s were a glorious era for state-owned enterprises. There was even the happy scene of "coming alive quickly," which inspired people. But with the continued deepening of reform, state-owned enterprises increasingly revealed a trend of being tough and thick-skinned. They behaved in very perfunctory ways regarding various reform measures, whether it was akin to taking strong medicine or performing serious surgery.

The government has implemented many reforms of state-owned enterprises, such as the substitution of tax payment for profit delivery, the contract system, the separation of government function from enterprise management, and structural optimization. Among these reforms, in July 1992 alone, the State Council issued the State-Owned Industrial Enterprises to Change Their Operational Mechanism Ordinance, which gave state-owned enterprises fourteen items of autonomy. This meant that the hands and feet of state-owned enterprises were gradually set free, and they could independently feed off the market. However, the state-owned enterprises, whose reins had been loosened, seemed to be used to captivity. With a hasty entrance to the marketplace, there were actually some who did not know what to do because they were far removed from grassroots private enterprises and that kind of ferociousness. State-owned enterprises behaved in a lukewarm way toward a number of reform measures, causing paradoxes to emerge—the more the state-owned enterprises were reformed, the greater the losses. Some once-prosperous state-owned enterprises also continuously declined.

In September 1995, the *People's Daily* published an article titled "A Report from the 'Eighth Five-Year Plan (1991–95),'" which analyzed three major dilemmas faced by state-owned enterprises: high losses (the losses to state-owned enterprise were increasing at a rate of 14.2 percent annually, and the average annual loss exceeded ¥50 billion); inefficient use of enterprise funds and increases in product inventory by 30 percent annually; and the 5.4 percent decrease in the comprehensive economic efficiency index of state-owned industries compared to the "Seventh Five-Year Plan" period (1986–90). By 1996, the net sales profit rate in the budgets of state-owned enterprises slumped with total losses 28.6 times greater than that of 1985. This year, the number of state-owned enterprises nationwide that have gone bankrupt is 6,232.

COMMON ASPIRATION OF THE PEOPLE: THE CATFISH EFFECT

The economic vitality of the state-owned enterprises is not as good as that of private enterprises. This is not only because of the consensus, of which people are already well aware, but also because those in power have likewise realized that the private economy has been introduced, and that this could trigger a greater "catfish effect,"[12] from which they could stimulate the vitality of the entire economic system.

In September of 1997, the 15th National Congress of the Communist Party of China (CPC) proposed that the basic economic system of the initial stage of socialism in our country was one in which public ownership was the dominant body, and more diverse forms of ownership developed together. The report also suggested that the state-owned economy should implement a strategic shift, with advance and retreat, to "grasp the large (state-owned enterprises) and let go of the small (state-owned enterprises)" and do something but not everything. The strategy of privatization was placed on the agenda: state-owned enterprises would maintain their monopolistic advantage in upstream energy industries (iron and steel, energy, automotive, aviation, telecommunications, electricity, banking, insurance, media, large-scale machines, and the military); and at the same time, state-owned enterprises would substantially exit from areas that were fully competitive. As a result, the curtain was officially opened to privatization, joint-stock reform emerged, and the whole field was set ablaze.

Under the burgeoning trend of privatization, the reform of state-owned enterprises continued to advance, but the outcome of the reform remained unsatisfactory. According to Kong Shanguang's statistics, from 1998 to 2005, the earnings of state-owned enterprises were nearly ¥5 trillion, with losses of nearly ¥2 trillion, and profits of about ¥3 trillion. Over the same period of time, up to ¥1 trillion of state funds were used to increase corporate liquidity for state-owned enterprises, and for innovation funds, for three items of cost, to reimburse enterprises, and to subsidize losses. The market allocation efficiency that was triggered by state-owned enterprises taking advantage of cheap funds caused the country to lose nearly ¥1.6 trillion; and at the same time, the Ministry of Finance wrote off ¥750 billion in losses in 2003 and 2004.[13]

No one would willingly recognize that their role was insignificant or candidly admit defeat. However, these brutal figures are, one by one, helping people gain insight into the "ways of the world" of various economic sectors. The private economy is unhesitatingly gushing out, but state-owned enterprises are becoming a little lost on the road of pampered luxury. It is without question that the more constant interaction there is in a great era, the more room there is for natural selection to function.

"Spending Their Own Money Would Cause Their Hearts to Ache"

Every individual necessarily labors to render the annual revenue of the society as great as he can. He generally, indeed, neither intends to promote the public interest, nor knows how much he is promoting it. By preferring the support of domestic to that of foreign industry, he intends only his own security; and by directing that industry in such a manner as its produce may be of the greatest

value, he intends only his own gain, and he is in this, as in many
other cases, led by an invisible hand to promote an end which was
no part of his intention.

—ADAM SMITH[14]

THE DIFFERENCES BETWEEN "PUBLIC" AND "PRIVATE"

The government pampers state-owned enterprises—providing maximum con-
cessions in policies, financing, and industry space—and has essentially provided
them with the best Chinese medicine doctors and the best Western medicine
doctors in order to fundamentally cure their ills. They have tasted the physical
fitness of Chinese medicine, and have undergone bone- and tendon-rending
surgery. However, the reforms are still unsatisfactory. The imagined vitality has
yet to appear in state-owned enterprises. On the contrary, private enterprises
had not been "cradled in the palm of the (government's) hands for fear that
they would melt," and neither had they assumed the powerful presence and
professional authority of a "Tiger Mom." They still had the posture of people
who have been cast out to fend for themselves. But they have broken through
numerous barriers, growing lush with admirable vitality and vigor.

After repeated transformation and rescuing, many state-owned enterprises
still remain immersed in the morass of loss. It is just as a perplexed Ling Zhijun
stated, "In the last several years, we have written numerous prescriptions for
state-owned enterprises, and after every dose, everyone proclaims, 'he's alive.'
I don't know how many times he's been 'alive' now. If I settle down and take
another look, I discover that he's still 'not alive.' Could these drugs be effective
in the future if they are taken once more?"[15] Perhaps we can no longer give
state-owned enterprises too many feelings of monopolistic superiority.

I have taken great pains to try to find the root of human nature. These
admonitions have been around since ancient times: "Objects are other peoples'
goodness, children are their own goodness," and "Spending other people's
money is like running water, but spending one's own money causes heartache."

For the most vivid example, there is none better than the "iron rice bowls"
of the people's communes, and the responsibility of the household contract
and accountability system.

The People's communes focused on one word: "public." In the original agricultural cooperatives, farmers' private property was confiscated, such as private
plots, livestock, and fruit trees, production tools, and even their household
tables and chairs. Banks could forcefully take deposits from farmers in the form
of large quantities of steel and water, and euphemistically call it an "investment."
Thirty years later, Bo Yibo's interpretation of this confiscation of assets became

this verse: "see the money and want it, see the goods and transfer them, see the house and demolish it, see the grain and pick it."

Even if there are so many of them that they are a formidable force, farmers are still persuaded to contribute their own property by a variety of public opinions and slogans. Regardless of how beautiful the blueprint for the future may be, they still will not be confounded by the leaders' enthusiasm until they cannot distinguish between public and private. But they are silent even while choking with fury, and can only privately grumble. Not only have their finances been confiscated, their people have also been dragged to become collective labor and can only eat in public canteens. Among those that have been organized into collectives, there is the thinking that they no longer need to waste their brain cells to think about anything because the government has already given them their future, and their work and even basic living needs have all been planned. Most farmers go along with political policies in a muddleheaded way and continue to be dizzied by the beautified, fuzzy blueprint. Policymakers, on the other hand, use their blind optimism to carry out their solid and irrefutable demonstration, sure in their moral assumptions that farmers are highly conscious that their passion for work will be thoroughly motivated by "distribution according to one's needs."

However, the people's communes did not push China further toward socialism. Instead, they caused many mistakes. Even if these errors were contrary to common sense, people were totally unaware: grandiose reports such as "the average yield per *mu* is 500,000 kilograms of sweet potato; 300,000 kilograms of sugar cane; and 25,000 *jin* of rice" were believed by leaders, who repeatedly lamented, "How will this much food be consumed?" When the grain was harvested, the people were busy making "iron and steel," and the grains rotted and molded on the ground. Famine unexpectedly engulfed the populace. There were food shortages, and increasing numbers of people died as a result of the famine. The so-called inspiration of "each according to his needs" caused cascading declines in farmers' production initiative, and when hunger arrived, people neither had the strength nor the enthusiasm to "embrace" the people's commune. The history of the people's communes went from brilliant to tragic, and the beautiful blueprint of "communism" also became increasingly decadent in the midst of hunger.

An opposite scenario occurred after the implementation of the household contract responsibility system. All of the villages were experiencing days of happiness: men were working from morning until night, their skin tanned until black, and they were still having a great time. They did not delay their efforts even in order to eat lunch, so they hastily ate a few mouthfuls of the food that their wives brought to the field. From the establishment of people's communes, women who had not gone to work in the fields had to take advantage of the light from the moon and stars to pull weeds after working busily all day. Regardless of whether the land was arable or not, they would select and sow the seeds to the best of their efforts.

After the Party attempted to use coercive force to politically achieve the unified leadership of the farmers, they used the collective labor method to achieve the communist blueprint. However, the communist ideals were too distant, and the choices of the collective-style system did not generate more enthusiasm for labor among the farmers. Those moral constraints that were piled up by slogans and denouncements clearly could not fill in the deficiencies in the system.

The fundamental, qualitative differences between the people's communes and the household contract responsibility system clearly cannot be fully equated with the differences between state-owned enterprises and private enterprises. However, a look at incentives and how "spending one's own money causes heartache" show that the two have areas of convergence.

THE CONFUSION OF SUPERCOMPANIES

Today's state-owned enterprises now appear more like supercompanies. They are the companies of the nation's populace, and all of the people are shareholders of these state-owned enterprises, so there are more than 1.3 billion shareholders. If the assets grew even larger, then they would have to be divided among 1.3 billion people, becoming so thin that we could see through them. At the same time, the people are not directly involved in the management and decision making of these enterprises, and also will not get bonuses. Therefore, very few people take their own innate assets that they own as a right of their natal nationality (i.e., state-owned assets) very seriously. It is not within their supervisory control and area of concern to know the spending and earning potential of these companies and to consider the negative aspects of such things—e.g., how much money the company has wasted and how much has been lost to the corruption of associated managers.

Moreover, from a practical point of view, the dissipation is as powerful as the number of shareholders is great. It is not realistic to allow 1.3 billion people with "seven mouths and eight tongues (all talking at once, with a clash of many opinions)" to manage a company, so as a result agents have emerged. However, agents are just stewards in their principal identity, with only the right to manage and very little ownership, so it is also extremely difficult for them to generate accord with the owners. Instead, it is as if they are "working for others and spending others' money." Therefore, when they spend money, it is also reckless, and their hearts will not be distressed to the point of bloodshed when losing a few hundred thousand, millions, or even tens of millions. They can cold-heartedly assure themselves that what was lost was not theirs, it belonged to the country. If they screw up, it will not be labeled with such sensitive words as greed and corruption, but only as an investment mistake. Moreover, the courts will not force them out of their family property or foreclose the business in order to pay their debts. More than one billion shareholders are utterly helpless, not to mention that their voting rights are useless.

Thus, it is difficult to motivate enthusiasm and diligence for reform in leaders of state-owned enterprises when relying on moral constraints alone. The only way is to strengthen the structure of the institution is by managing the board of directors, shareholders' meetings, audits, and other aspects more closely, placing rigid constraints upon the leaders of state-owned enterprises, and enhancing the leaders' enthusiasm through good incentives to facilitate the feeling that "spending other people's money also causes heartache."

"LET THE TOILING MASSES GET THEIR HANDS DIRTY TO SUPPORT THEMSELVES"

The distance between the ownership and management of state-owned enterprises and that of private enterprises is relative to the distance between the ends of the earth. Ownership and management within individual companies in the private economy is often uniform, from the small startups and family-run shops, to the large multinational private enterprises. The husband and wife who own a grocery store and give tens of dollars in extra change when selling a carton of cigarettes would have aching hearts for half a day. If they again lose more money, it is their own money, and losing it is equal to cutting their own flesh. It means that in their daily lives they will have several kilograms less meat, one fewer toy to buy for their children, one less item of clothing that the wife may buy . . . in summary, this tangible loss would cause them to personally perceive a genuinely painful experience.

Once there is a philosophy of "letting the toiling masses get their hands dirty to support themselves," there is no need for rigid moral and institutional constraints. The people will not fear difficulty or painstaking efforts. When given rain, they will soar, and when given sunshine, they will be magnificent. There is a world of difference between this and state-owned enterprises, which still remain tepid, despite countless people pushing them and driving them along. No wonder economist Friedrich Hayek resolutely defended economic freedom.

He believed that "only when incentives of private liberal institutions exist, will it be possible for the information that is dispersed among millions of economic people to be effectively collected and utilized. If there is no 'carrot' of profit gain and no big 'stick' of bankruptcy, then no system of innovation will appear."[16]

In China, state-owned enterprises, which were the first to occupy a strong position in the market, did not obtain it through the early development of the market, but based on political considerations and provisions from authority figures. If there were no market, no competition mechanism would be introduced, and they alone would dominate, occupying the entire pasture, and catching all of the sheep. Every businessman in the world wants to monopolize the market. Once they monopolize the market, these monopolies can make exorbitant demands, while consumers are constrained by their despotic power, and can only swallow their cries. Administrative monopolies are especially like this. Through legal or administrative means, the government forcibly transforms a monopoly on the market into the right to monopolize power. This power has already ceased to be the rights signified by a market monopoly. Once administrative monopolies have been formed, enterprises that are outside of the range allowed by the government—even if they try every means possible—will still have difficulty entering the already monopolized fields. Even if they rashly enter these fields, they may also need to hastily exit because of conflicts with the law and the official policy's bottom line.

State-owned enterprises were almost living day to day by "extending their hands to receive clothing and opening their mouths to be fed": if they had no money, they extended their hands to the government for help, or they reached out to the community, disguising it as enhancing their financing capacity. Using the guise of a market-oriented storefront, they gained cheap resources and reduced production costs. They were the dominant party in any industry, were solipsistic regarding prices, and fixed the numbers according to their wants. At any rate, the consumers did not use their feet or even their spittle to cast their vote until they had the ambition to boycott the company's products.

Regardless of whether it is a business or an individual, one is often somewhat ungrateful in one's view toward their affluent environment. The more one has sufficient materials, the more disdain one feels for these supplies. The more "chic" one pretends to be, the less significance they see in this easily obtained "great wealth." It is only when truly suffering from cold and hunger, that we know the preciousness of a coat or a morsel of food.

Entrepreneur Liu Chuanzhi's saying has resonated with more than one person:

You young people belong to the group of people who have never starved.
So when you eat roast pork, you don't feel the same as when I—who has
experienced starvation—eat roast pork.[17]

State-owned enterprises that have been pampered for a long time grow con-
taminated with inertia and are compromised in terms of growth and innovation.
Just as in the curse "wealth never survives three generations," when everything
comes too easily, one inevitably becomes smug, sighing that life is good, while
squandering one's wealth with impunity and failing to think ahead, until all at
once, the family property is decimated or even destroyed.

Private enterprises, which are caught in the cracks between state-owned
capital and foreign investments, are far worse off when compared to the good
life of state-owned enterprises. A considerable portion of China's private entrepreneurs did not start out as "big spenders," nor did they have earth-shattering
moves. On the contrary, they are the ones who were consistently hard-pressed
for money. When publishing a book or biography during a time when they are
personally flourishing, many private entrepreneurs often begin with "I was a
bitter child," taking care of cattle, setting up stalls, serving as an apprentice,
posting small advertisements ... he lacked the elegant demeanor and the "Midas
touch" of people who had returned from studying overseas and the elite; and it
is only in recent years that he became a legend.

Using Wenzhou as an example, Wenzhou does not, in the slightest, deserve
to be called a vast territory with abundant natural resources. It is only a palm-
size track of land that backs up to a mountain, but does not overshadow it, and
it is near the sea, but does not swallow it. It abuts a waterway, but this is a dead
end. Wenzhou business people often lack "legendary" backgrounds, have not
been highly educated, and moreover, are not returnees from overseas. They
have not followed a planned trajectory over the years with an outlook on the
next few years—or ten years or even several decades—ahead of them. They
identify as merely farmers and small-business owners. They have no chance
at the protective umbrella of policy. On the contrary, when policy stepped on
its powerful brakes, these people got thrown against the windshield, and when
pressure came from all sides like dark clouds gathering overhead, they became
targets, chastised in speech and in writing, typical examples of "a warning
to others." It is exactly in these poor dregs of Wenzhou, so naturally devoid
of natural resources that even grass cannot grow there, that there are large
groups of disadvantaged people who are in the situation of being at the end of
their rope. Yet they continually blossom, erupting with the unlimited energy

and vitality of the private economy, becoming another paradox in economic propositions.

Most private entrepreneurs have ambitions to build their careers. In order to achieve professional success, they rack their brains to draw on all of their social resources, and they have a very powerful subjectivity and initiative for wealth creation. The opening of the market economy, then, has provided the objective conditions for them to reasonably and legally gain gradual freedoms to mobilize resources, and survive and even thrive in a variety of cracks.

This is the era of the rise of the startup. It is also a time of continuous delivery and the emergence of new eras—eras of pushing out the old and bringing in the new. The increasing triviality inadvertently reveals indescribable magnificence, and perhaps, this has never been accidental.

CHAPTER SEVEN

Why Can't Mighty Reforms Produce Mighty Enterprises?

The Primary Reason Is That the Commercial DNA Is Broken

If a man is fortunate he will, before he dies, gather up as much as
he can of his civilized heritage and transmit it to his children. And
to his final breath he will be grateful for this inexhaustible legacy,
knowing that it is our nourishing mother and our lasting life.

—WILL DURANT[1]

THE FRACTURING OF THE BUSINESS GENE

Over more than thirty years, there have been historical changes. With the
opening and closing of significant doors, the private economy is developing
like a raging fire, bringing sweeping changes to our time from the economic
fringes that have gradually become rooted in the center of the economic stage.

However, the domain of fortune that has been formed after many years of
metamorphosis and long-term sharpening invariably has carelessly exposed a
regrettable gap—fresh, mighty, and admirable enterprises. The heavyweight
standard measure of corporate development and brand quality—the Fortune
500—includes only a handful of our private enterprises; although many companies have already made it big and have even gone out of the country to build
networks overseas and reap those benefits. But much like soldiers on the bat-
tlefield in autumn, it seems that they haven't yet given much business wealth
to the community. What we see more are abstract figures, which, one by one,
represent wealth accumulation. Faith, convictions, and rules do not stir the soul
of business. Many enterprises have not yet disembarked from the cycle of fate
that dictates, "there will always be someone who emerges in each generation,
but their influence will be felt for only a few years." There is a variety of reasons
for the fall of an enterprise. Some have sunk during large shifts in economic
trends, and some have died in the gutter.

THE FRUIT OF CHINA'S ACTIONS IS ROOTED IN
CHINA'S PARTICULAR BACKGROUND

The pace of change in China is far faster than the circumstances that we have imagined. After accumulating vast knowledge and catching up, China's smooth integration into the market economy took only thirty years; it took the Western world two hundred years. The world changes rapidly, and now that China is in the midst of major enterprises, its late start is a rare advantage, but also a tough trial. Once it cannot keep up with the beat and rhythm of change, it will face extinction.

The fractured commercial DNA that is from a deficient business gene has brought about the primary reason for what is lacking in mighty enterprises.

China's business culture penetrates all the way down. It is always stumbling, with not enough to fill the gaps. Throughout Chinese history, business people have always been biased in favor of supporting the first name that appears. In the long river of history, they are annihilated in various political games, but they tenaciously form a number of economic fragments, continuing to maintain secrecy and using a low-profile method, dedicated to silently changing China's development gene.

The older generation of business people—no matter how beautiful and brilliant they were, no matter how much ambition and hope were mingled in them—would come to an end like fireworks. The profound knowledge that had been painted over with the gold powder of the "creation of wealth" also vanished, leaving behind just the memory of ostentatiousness. We are anxiously awaiting the stories of murky worldliness that are hobbling over to us from the foggy depths of history. They are mostly witticisms based on business epiphanies, and are mixed with cosmetic cover-ups, and the uncommon brilliance of corporate wealth and wisdom. China's commercial DNA is fractured across the board, and it is difficult to carry the DNA forward from beginning to end in a single breath.

John King Fairbank has asserted that, "In the development of China's long drama of history, the Chinese merchant class has not occupied a prominent position. It has only been the supporting actor—perhaps having a few lines—ordered about by emperors, bureaucrats, diplomats, generals, propagandists, and party bosses."[2] Before the liberation, business people did not evolve within the feudal system. Under feudalism, the state system had the intense color of personal leadership. The establishment of a national bureaucracy was at the center of institutional strengthening, and the country's political goals were for a strong nation, which ignored domestic wealth and the enrichment of the people, thus marginalizing business people. In a society of official ideology that had an exceedingly thick political flavor, business people had to wear many layers of political clothes in order to survive. And they had to spend a lot of time currying political favor, carefully surviving in the cracks. The overemphasis on political flattery caused merchant groups to inordinately chase profit through patronage while ignoring the establishment of their own system of thought, which caused the inherited fractures of business wealth.

In *The Metabolism of Modern Chinese Society*, social historian Chen Xulu states that

> ancient China was static, with solidly congealed social strata. Modern China is dynamic, with a rapid social metabolism. This is also different from the West, where social change has been achieved via self-renewal mechanisms since the Middle Ages and into modern times. Modern China's social metabolism has been, to a large degree, due to a rapid succession of external shocks, and an internalization of nonnative elements through unique social mechanisms. This has promoted ethnic conflict and class antagonism, expressed as waves of change one after another, and zigzag innovation.[3]

Modern society experienced powerful external shocks, and business people finally had the opportunity to escape the official ideology and restrictions of the powerful feudal shell. However, it was regrettable that the business people, who had broken away from a variety of feudal shackles, did not thoroughly remake themselves. The nation remained poor and weak, and wavered with the ups and downs of the country's fortunes; not to mention that the storms of the era and its accidents were all an unbearable burden for them.

These gloomy changes were too severe and rapid, and the traditional inheritance patterns that were inherited from generation to generation were hanging by a thread, ready to break at any time. Whether it is a family business or a traditional business group, none have found a better model for doing business, and have finally reverted to obscurity—fallen silent.

THE HARM OF HATING THE WEALTHY

The most complete rupture of the business gene was still to come. When the Political Bureau meeting convened in September 1948, Mao Zedong, Liu Shaoqi, and others made it clear that "after the national government came into our possession, China's main internal contradiction was the dichotomy between the proletariat and the bourgeoisie." In the winter of 1951, the CPC Central Committee launched the large-scale "three evils" campaign against corruption, waste, and bureaucracy, with a movement to suppress the widespread occurrence of corruption. This ostentatious anticorruption movement quickly expanded to become the "five evils" campaign against bribery, tax evasion, the theft of state property, cutting corners, and the theft of economic intelligence. When the prosperity of the political movement increased, more and more national capitalists were included within the range of what was being opposed, labeled undesirable elements within national capital, and exposed to the collective hatred and exclusion of the people. This highlights the infamy of entrepreneurs during that time. People still hated the wealthy, looked down upon engaging in business, and hated business people, trade, money, and wealth. Once people gained an opportunity to crusade against them, they became frenzied and greedy, and stopped at nothing to condemn the "contemptible behavior" of amassing wealth.

The collective chord of wealth abhorrence determined the entrepreneurs' precarious position in those extraordinary times. Any of their movements can send them into the mouth of the storm, and they rarely received special asylum. After several political movements and social transformations, the wealth of many national capitalists was looted, and some even lost their lives. People who never tire of immersing themselves in political movements may be completely unaware that they have squandered an amount of rare wealth. National entrepreneurs who have survived in the cracks of bureaucratic capital and foreign capital are the result of an ebbing tide. They have mastered Chinese and Western methods of operation, created enormous social wealth, excellent products, and benchmarks for those who came later to the industry to learn from them. But many national capitalists have lost their wealth and even their lives in several political movements and social transformations. When the people never tire of movements that condemn capitalists, and they do not think about how they have strangled a generation of national entrepreneurs, they cause fractures in Chinese entrepreneurship that become irretrievable losses to China's economy.

HERITAGE THAT IS NOT SOLID

Today, the gates to the market are open, with a variety of resources gushing forth, and the business gene that was once suppressed has shed its poverty and been resurrected. Take the once flourishing Ming and Qing dynasty merchants of Shanxi, for example; while they also copied their predecessors to create amazing wealth, their road to fortune held many occasions of scheming. They rely on natural resources, and walk the paths of both black and white. They are intimate with influential connections, have incisive interpretations based on their knowledge of "down" and "sell," and are often dubbed the "nouveau riche" in public opinion. They have made amazing marks on business, but they have not formed a system of business philosophy, and are lacking in regard to business ethics. After long years of erosion, there is no trace of the statecraft inherited from the Ming and Qing dynasty Shanxi merchants.

After reform and opening up, China's entrepreneurs, who had disappeared, were invited back. After three decades, these entrepreneurs, who were ready to move rapidly into their positions just as a rider whips his horses into a full gallop, eventually had to face the fact that they were aging. As the famous general Lian Po said in the idiom, "I am now old. Can I still be of use?"

The next generation of entrepreneurs will eventually take the elder generation's scepter of wealth. To this day, the family business model remains the main model of private enterprise. Vice Chairman Zhuang Congsheng of the China Federation of Industry and Commerce said that according to estimates, family-run enterprises account for more than 95 percent of all private enterprise. Moreover, with the exception of a few entrepreneurs—such as Liu Chuanzhi, the chairman of the board of Lenovo Group, who explicitly expressed a desire to "build a family business without kinship," and He Xiangjian, who resigned as chairman of the board of the electrical appliance company The Midea Group, which he founded—most private entrepreneurs still want to assure that they pass the baton of wealth on to the next generation.

Regarding the current macroeconomic environment that has gone from disorder to an excessively ordered market environment, there are many remaining variables. Inevitably, and regardless of the past, present or future, regardless of whether they are first or second generation, or have glamorous backgrounds, business people are dragged down by lingering bitterness and apprehension. Second generation entrepreneurs likewise need to make an arduous journey and struggle in China's rugged business territory. The so-called "winner takes all" path to success is nothing more than persisting to the end to become the last survivor.

Although second-generation entrepreneurs have experienced staff employment—creating industries and various other professional domains—they are defective because they have been less susceptible to the suffering of aspiration. Their suffering is not that of the "frustration of spirit and will, exhaustion of muscles and bones, exposure to starvation and poverty, and harassment from troubles and setbacks." Second-generation entrepreneurs who lack the education of frustration may have apparent weakness regarding toughness, bravery, the bearing of hardship, endurance for hard work, and other entrepreneurial qualities. Furthermore, second-generation entrepreneurs, especially the second-generation wealthy, continue to struggle with a veritable vortex of ill repute. Some of them flaunt their wealth, gamble, abuse drugs, and even commit crimes, and the people are nervous about letting the wealthy second-generation entrepreneurs take care of the country's financial territory and future.

Perhaps it is difficult to handle wealth. The disorderly, chaotic, and romantic era of blurred business is long gone. Countless people have attempted to modify this new world with gorgeous rhetoric, but it has stripped off its external layers, and only the ancient rules of the jungle remain, stubbornly persisting from the depths of history to the present. Which methods will the young or relatively young people use to master wealth? This is the great unknown to which no conclusive answer can be given.

There are many things that can change overnight, such as fate, the future, a pessimistic outlook, and even systems. But elements such as entrepreneurship, market awareness, and business beliefs, on the other hand, require experience and study. The second-generation entrepreneurs lack that refinement which develops time; hence the brand-new entrepreneurial spirit that has gradually accumulated via reform and opening up has less promise of immortality and endurance.

Having a Desire to Be Big but Lacking Strength

Somehow over the years, folks have gotten the impression that Wal-Mart was something I dreamed up out of the blue as a middle-aged man, and that it was just this great idea that turned into an overnight success. It's true that I was forty-four when we opened our first Wal-Mart in 1962, but the store was totally an outgrowth of everything we'd been doing since Newport—another case of me being unable to leave well enough alone, another experiment. And like most other overnight successes, it was about twenty years in the making.

—SAM WALTON[4]

THE DREAM OF THE FORTUNE 500

"In China, no enterprises have failed because of excessively slow development. There are only enterprises that have collapsed from developing too quickly." This is a foreign management expert's evaluation of Chinese enterprises, and we cannot avoid being a little ashamed in hearing this.

Every entrepreneur has the dream of becoming bigger and stronger. However, these unrealizable dreams of a golden age cannot bear the slightest bit of reality and are broken with a gentle poke. There are many Chinese entrepreneurs obsessed with being area chiefs, industry chiefs, and even world chiefs, but their dreams have been washed away by reality beyond recognition. Many Chinese entrepreneurs have all had similar mantras and aspirations: to advance to the Fortune 500 within five years. But time cannot conform to the wishful thinking of these smug business heroes, drawing them an ideal curve.

The chairman of the Dongsheng Group, Guo Jiaxue, has always dreamt of the Fortune 500: "With calculations of Dongsheng's ¥17 billion of operating income this year, if I maintain a 17 percent growth rate annually, we can reach sales revenue of ¥100 billion after fifteen years, approximately $12 billion. The Fortune 500 companies have their ups and downs, and it is certain that through our own efforts and performance, we can create a Fortune Global 500 enterprise in the market economy." Because of shareholder accounts, tensions in the capital chain, and other troubles caused by a multitude of negative factors, Dongsheng's Guo Jiaxue frankly had to give up his Fortune 500 mantra. "This ideal has been shattered. I will no longer strive for the ideal of building a Fortune 500 company. This ideal will never again exist."[5]

The ten-year plan of Prince Milk China's famous dairy enterprise has also caused its industry peers to stay as quiet as cicadas in winter. "From January 1, 2007 (before and after being listed on the market), the three-year production and sales doubled to ¥6 billion, and then reached ¥40 billion after three years. Total output is projected to rise steadily up to 2016, when it will reach ¥100 billion, with an annual profit of ¥15 billion, and tax revenue of ¥8 billion or more." This kind of pronouncement and aspiration did not remain realistic for very long, and with a lack of commodities, insufficient funds to cover payroll, production arrestment, debt payments, and other fatal injuries looming, Prince Milk's capital chain was deeply fractured and the organization lost its former high spirits.

THE "SPEED WINS" COMPLEX

Many private entrepreneurs in China are obsessed with winning via speed and enterprise size. They are keen to have the speed and efficiency to conquer the world. This speed and scale complex is related to the following factors: entrepreneurs are blindly optimistic. An entrepreneur's optimism index and the enterprise's operating conditions are positively correlated: when an enterprise has operational difficulties, the entrepreneur is self-aware and recognizes that too much optimism and seriousness is extremely foolish because it hurts the vitality of the business and can even cause its demise. But as companies continue to expand, praise accumulates from within the enterprise and from the external spotlight. The aura around the entrepreneurs' bodies transforms them from venture mortals into venture gods who think that their luck, charm, and leadership abilities are sufficient to ensure that their brilliance will continue to exist, and that they may easily escape the fate of going "from prosperity to ruin." But in fact, enterprise operations are like the wind and waves of the sea. When enterprises expand, they can enhance their ability to withstand storms. But the wind—i.e., operational risks—is continually increasing, and when that happens, enterprises need to sail much more carefully.

Facing multifold temptations as the gates to the market opened, various kinds of opportunities surged out, and a large volume of foreign investment flowed into China in search of a lush habitat for financial resources. Chinese enterprises were faced with plentiful resources, numerous funds, a large market, and other attractive opportunities. Compared to small and medium-size enterprises, enterprises that had developed to a certain scale had a better chance of coming into contact with different forms of opportunities. They also had a particular vigor to transform the potential of these temptations into corporate firepower. However, some entrepreneurs started to lose ground when they were unable to withstand the waving hand of temptation.

During an investigation of China, Japanese management scholar Kenichi Ohmae had this to say:

> There are too many opportunities in China, and that makes it difficult for China's entrepreneurs to focus on one area in order to produce excellent results in that particular arena. But focus is the only way to make money. Coca-Cola concentrated on making Coke, becoming the world's leader in the field of consumer goods. Toyota focused on making cars, becoming Japan's most profitable company. Enter an industry, specialize, and then globalize. This is the only way to make money . . . Wanting to read summaries of management books, wanting to use just five years to catch up to what took Japan fifty years to learn, this is exactly what China intends to do. However, management is a continuous feedback process. If you only learn in this "concentrated" way and then rush to take action or allow other people to transform the organization, this is simply like "artificially made children."[6]

THE GAP BETWEEN IDEALS AND STRENGTH
IN THE "PRISONER'S DILEMMA"

"Traveling thousands of miles for a dream," one does not need to conceal lofty goals, but many enterprises in China actually lack the strength to become bigger. Relying on labor bonuses, suddenly reduced system costs, the qualitative improvement of talent, and other late-developer advantages, the competitiveness of China's private economy has grown stronger and developed considerably. However, with the progression of the market economy and other various elements, bonuses gradually disappeared. At the same time, the congenital deficiencies of the private enterprises remained in the areas of technology, capital, and management. Technology remained weak, and China continued to imitate Western technology, following its every footstep. Private enterprise lacked competitive brands and value-adding products.

Moreover, the larger the enterprise, the higher the degree of diversification, and the greater level of demand on management, culture, and systems. Many enterprises are busy with "aspirations" to "spread the vendor's stall wide" (i.e., expand the business platform). It is difficult for them to establish and conduct a large-scale expansion of management, culture, corporate structure, and management performance within a short amount of time. When technological advancement lags far behind business expansion, this foreshadows a corporate crisis.

Many Chinese management experts have emerged, such as Liu Chuanzhi, Zhang Ruimin, and Niu Gensheng. But they are far from reaching the level of "established values, methodology, and achievement that produces companies with a far-reaching impact on business management methods around the world."[7] In 2007, Lenovo's acquisition of IBM's mergers and acquisitions business happened much smoother than expected, and the new company's business gradually got onto the right track. However, Liu Chuanzhi remained anxious, because he believed that China's enterprises lacked unique management ideas as well as business culture. In fact, more worries were still to come. The subsequent financial crisis proved Liu Chuanzhi's anxiety. The financial crisis caused Lenovo to fall into a quagmire of consecutive losses. Liu Chuanzhi had to make another vigorous effort to turn the tide. This seemed to tell people that if a company the size of Lenovo was left without a figure such as Liu Chuanzhi, it would continue to operate, but only while stumbling and limping. At Lenovo, the imprint of individual heroism is so deep that it is not a good thing.

Entrepreneurs often face the embarrassment of being like a fish in water with regard to business model innovation and market competitiveness, but repeatedly beached and bewildered regarding management. In particular, the larger the enterprise, the more that its management operates in confusion, making management issues therefore more prominent. For this reason, many Chinese companies have headaches that spur the proliferation of MBAs and EMBAs in China. This causes the airborne troops (i.e., the highly educated professionals flying in and out of the country) to frequently fall into the predicament of being misguided in dogmatically mimicking Western management and producing strange variations of theory—as when plants change depending on growing environment. In a survey, five out of ten of the top Chinese entrepreneurs said that their favorite books are *Built to Last* and *Good to Great,* and their favorite character is management expert Peter F. Drucker. This shows that Chinese entrepreneurs seek to learn from "management" authorities if they are thirsty.

In fact, "becoming bigger and stronger" is excusable, and those who do not acknowledge this ambition are supercilious. However, whether being bigger and stronger is the long-term or short-term goal of enterprise development, business leaders act in accordance with the strengths and needs of the enterprise. If people can see the good in wanting to become bigger and stronger, then this dream is not a scourge, but an effective incentive.

Moreover, we need to clearly understand that the truly mighty enterprises in the world are not mighty because of their monstrous size, but rather thanks to the spirit of competitiveness at their core. Such qualities are difficult to imitate, as are talented management teams, the ability to continuously innovate, reasonable and effective rules and regulations, and a higher level of brand recognition and reputation.

When enterprises become bigger and stronger, they must endure loneliness and withstand temptation. Among Fortune Global 500 companies, not one has escaped the necessary passage of time before seeing success. The successful ones crawl along in one industry for many years before they metamorphose into industry tycoons. Their annual growth rate may not be so brilliant, but they are able to maintain stability through decades and even centuries of sustained growth. They do not value the short-lived and are persistent in being a company for the ages. Similarly, Chinese enterprises also need to experience countless transitions and transformations, and to undergo the reincarnation of traveling the road from hell to heaven, ultimately to enter into the present day with the attitude of a mighty enterprise.

The Private Arena: The Hero Loves but Has No Path to Attainment—"Heroes" Love Finances but Obtain Them with Ill-Gotten Gains

As I look back on my life's work, I'm probably most proud of having helped to create a company that by virtue of its values, practices, and success has had a tremendous impact on the way companies are managed around the world. And I'm particularly proud that I'm leaving behind an ongoing organization that can live on as a role model long after I'm gone.

—Hewlett-Packard cofounder WILLIAM R. HEWLETT[8]

RULES OF THE JUNGLE ON THE INTERNET

In 2010, an evil war occurred on the Chinese Internet. The combatants were Tencent, the "public enemy," versus Qihoo 360, the "warrior of idealism." No matter on which side, they all felt extremely aggrieved, and both sides continually resorted to evil tricks that violated market principles. They even used tactics so lowly as to fall into the "three indiscriminate" occupations of "prostitute, actor, and beggar." In order to protect the interests of their users, they had to take the risk of praising virtue and punishing vice. During the Spring Festival of 2010, the battle began when Tencent suddenly launched the free security program QQ Doctor. This made Qihoo 360's CEO, Zhou Hongyi, anxious, and he hurried back to Beijing on the second day of the New Year in order to convene his staff to deal with this sudden emergency: "This technique is meant to make them invincible against competitors. . . . We cannot let them kill us with this one trick. I am definitely going to resist."[9]

In April 2010, Tencent launched QQ Computer Manager, which contained a cloud security system to kill Trojans, fix system bugs, and perform real-time protection and many other security functions that were no different than 360's Security Guard program. This increased the feeling of crisis at Qihoo 360.

On September 7, Qihoo 360 expanded a counterattack and released the personal privacy protection tool 360 Privacy Protection, of which QQ software was a major target. Tencent responded by publishing a piece on September 28 entitled "360 Browser Suspected of Pornographic Website Promotion and Undergoing Public Security Criminal Investigation." And on October 27, Kingsoft, Baidu, and others jointly issued a declaration "to oppose 360's unfair competition and strengthen industry self-regulation." Once again, Qihoo 360 counterattacked, and the moves grew still more ruthless: on October 29 they introduced a security tool called Koukou Bodyguard to help customers block QQ advertising.

More stand-in and hand-to-hand combat was to come. At 6:19 p.m. on the evening of November 3, 2010, Tencent posted "a letter to the majority of QQ users," stating that it had made the difficult decision to "disable QQ software on computers that have had Qihoo 360 software installed." Qihoo 360 then took on a tearjerking victim identity: the company had arrived at a critical life-

or-death moment and asked its users to show their support by boycotting QQ for three days.

In "Cracking China's Internet Jungle Funds," *Chinese Entrepreneur* asked a question regarding the war between Tencent and Qihoo 360 that exposed and thoroughly revealed the evil gene in the Chinese Internet business. This industry has no lack of "large companies," but who will be able to become a "mighty company"?

It was an evil war of "kill or be killed" that unceasingly hijacked users' interests and revealed the barbaric practices of the Internet. There has been market-oriented development until today, but large and small unofficial commercial arenas still persist. When business grudges cannot be solved through market-based means, more underhanded methods are used, and market rules may as well exist in name only.

THE TIMELINESS OF WILD GROWTH

In *Wild Growth*, private entrepreneur Feng Lun described the savage character:

> In the era of the private arena, private enterprises seem either like bandits or knights. Because we were restricted for a long time in the old system of the past, as soon as we left it behind, there was actually a special kind of happiness, one of ease and freedom. The arena can be regarded as made up of informal organizations, belonging to a marginal kind of structure that exists in between the courts and the common people. Those in private enterprises who are in these marginal structures are free. In that free state, people will choose their allies and enemies, and they will feel great happiness and mental pleasure, as if they were being knights errant.[10]

It cannot be denied that in the beginning of reform and opening up, or during the business startup period, barbaric growth did indeed have its space of existence. Writer Gao Mengling said that "this is a revolution in the economic field, and the first people to conduct revolutions are often a 'ruffian movement.' In Mao Zedong's words, they flash like lights in the sand that are washed over by big waves, because these people have the daring spirit to rush and break through."[11] At the beginning of reform and opening up, the market had just opened up a crack in its door and everything was in a state of chaos. If everything were in strict compliance with the market rules and things were done by the book according to market rules, then things would have probably died a "death by accident or violence" long ago.

During the period of enterprise start-ups, there were "congenital" weaknesses. Capital, talent, and the market were all relatively weak, and the interests-oriented barbaric growth was conducive toward enterprises setting up shop too quickly in order to dominate the market in the shortest amount of time, so as to ensure that those enterprises would occupy the highest ground quickly, and gain the right to survive among the fierce competition in the industry.

However, as the market economy continued to improve and enterprises grew bigger and stronger, barbaric growth became more and more useless; enterprises needed to act according to the rules of the market, adhere to fair competition, value the interests of consumers in the increasingly standardized market, and take off the coat of savage growth. If people still adhered to the arena approach and quickly picked allies and enemies in market competition, they would not only harm their competitors, they would damage the interests of consumers, as well as the entire industry chain.

The dairy earthquake of 2008 is one example. Worn out by the melamine crisis, the entire industry was devastated and people everywhere were railing against it. Even the top companies in the dairy industry, the Yili Group and Mengniu Dairy, had been poisoned. Consumers were almost at the point of flushing at the mere mention of milk. In the final analysis, it was determined that while the entire dairy industry was engaged in the one-sided pursuit of maximizing interests and speed, it relied too heavily on bulk milk resources, pushed down prices and safety standards of raw and unpasteurized milk, adopted a policy of "plugging leaks," and only superficially dealt with any issues. Product quality could not be guaranteed. Everything finally came to light in 2008, and the dairy enterprises that had tried to be so clever may as well have lifted up a huge stone and smashed it onto their own feet. The dairy industry was discredited and descended into a full-blown crisis.

Even more worrisome was that the rise of big business not only failed to purify the industry environment, but also brought sharks into the ecology. As the size of their enterprises continually increase, some large enterprises have taken on a self-inflated sense of being king of the hill, and their goals have become rooted in nakedly undisguised bloodlust; others absolutely cannot violate their territory, and the area outside of their territory must be barren so as not to give others an opportunity to survive. In the Internet industry, it is common practice for large companies to suppress small companies. If they see a small company with a bit of potential, they do everything possible and look for every opportunity to wipe them out through poaching, imitating their counterpart's products, and so on. Small companies already lack confidence. Tossed about a few times, their vitality is greatly injured, they develop only with great difficulty; they will finally reach a point at which they have run their course and perish without outside interference. There are rumors that because there are too many sharks in the Internet industry, entrepreneurs should first set up several major premises before starting their business: who is the number one company in this industry? Who is most likely to be able to exterminate me? How long can I sustain this for? It suggests a tragedy like going to war: "The wind rustles, the river water is cold, and the brave soldier is never to return."

As weights, weather vanes, and touchstones are tools to measure the quality of things, such as heaviness, wind direction, and mineral quality, the pursuit of interests tests the very core of capital, and that is not an unreasonable method of measurement. However, "gentlemen love fortune when obtained in a proper way." The outlaw era is a thing of the past, and if people tenaciously hang onto barbaric growth, it only produces more reshuffling in the industry, and wickedness will break out in the entire industry. Everyone is a victim, and the only, ancient iron law of growth is to "throw away one's butcher knife and immediately become a Buddha."

Chinese Business People Do Not Have a Sufficient Understanding of Politics

China's reform was not a complete victory. Economic reform came from strategies that ranged from easy to difficult and originated in the nonstate-owned sector. On the one hand, this reduced resistance toward, and increased facilitation of, reform. On the other hand, this allowed the propagation of a dual-track rent-seeking environment which disseminated trickery and Machiavellian acts of corruption. The two natures of reform's future were grimly placed before us. One path was the road of the market economy under the rule of law of a political civilization; and one path was the road of crony capitalism. In the battle between these two roads, the latter appeared to be more aggressive and compelling. We must clearly recognize the threat that this trend poses to our nation's prospects and future. In my opinion, the only way to overcome this danger is for the ruling and opposition parties, across the board, to make joint efforts to practically promote reform, to establish a market economy of justice and rule of law.... The delay in economic and political reform has resulted in two serious consequences: first, China's economy has continued to rely on capital and other resources in an input-driven, extensive growth mode, running madly all the way, which has triggered a series of social and economic problems. Second are the rent-setting and rent-seeking activities and the consequent corruption, a widening gap between rich and poor, and an intensifying breakdown of social standards, values, and norms. All of these have caused strong dissatisfaction in people from all walks of life.

—WU JINGLIAN[12]

THE MANIPULATION OF POLICY TOWARD HOT OR COLD

Private enterprise and politics have differences, which can mainly be grasped on the macro- and micro-level.

China's private entrepreneurs—i.e., the beneficiaries of reform—bear the pressure and impact of social transformation. The increasingly open system has provided them with the space to breathe and survive, and they have been able to put up their fists. At the same time, because of the exploratory and progressive nature of China's reform, many measures are being implemented on a trial basis. If the response is too heated, then they stop; if the response is cool, then they continue. In this way, authorities repeatedly test the general trend of insight and acumen of private enterprises with regard to macroeconomic policy. Although the general direction in which China will promote reform has already been set, once the reality shifts, hesitation and anxiety are inevitable. When the private economy sees the sun, it is brilliant. Characteristically herdlike behavior is exacerbated by authorities' fear that the private economy will "risk the world's great condemnation," causing the overheating of the economy, and interfering with the normal economic order. Private enterprises are innately inadequate, as they are in a disadvantaged position in which financing is difficult and barriers to industry entrance are frequent. Meanwhile, because China's reforms are gradual, private entrepreneurs are continuing to break through the layers of institutional barriers, inevitably hovering in the gray areas of the law. When the systems tighten up, the blame will be suddenly placed on them.

About every three to five years, the government conducts a macro-adjustment, and private enterprises bear the brunt of it, becoming the "frontline soldiers" of macro-control. If private enterprises do not know how to understand the times, and risk marching forward or breaking into some sensitive areas, they will have stepped on political power lines; and their political risk will have suddenly increased.

Iron is an obvious example. In 2003, there had been some hot investment spurts in the heavy industry field. The central government worried that the economy would become overheated, so it rapidly stepped on the brakes. On December 23, 2003, the State Council issued "The State Council Notice of Several Suggestions to the Development and Reform Commission and Other Departments for the Suppression of Blind Investment in the Iron and Steel, Electrolytic Aluminum, and Cement Industries," which demanded the containing of blind investment and low-level redundant construction. At the time, Dai Guofang of Tieben Iron and Steel Co., Ltd., in Changzhou City, Jiangsu Province, was high spirited, and worked hard in order to "catch up to Baosteel within three years," and reach the ambitious goal of "striving to the Global 500." He obtained ¥4.339 billion in credit from six financial institutions and received nearly 9400 acres of land. However, because his actions were inflated, he didn't know how to restrain himself. Tieben, Ltd. became the target of the investigation team's focused examination, and Dai Guofang went to jail. Li Su, chairman of the Hejun Vanguard Group, which had inspected Tieben on several occasions, told the media: "At the time, Tieben was arguably the 'best domestic steel mill' from the perspective of iron and steel technology, and its input-output was extremely reasonable. Even if other steel mills had issues, it could still make money." Unfortunately, macro-control has always been broad and sweeping, and the government obviously would not concern itself with regretful matters on a case-by-case basis. More than anyone else, Dai Guofang himself secretly sighed with the most intense regret, because he did not know how to mediate the political situation.

Even if some reforms try to provide an improved environment for the development of the private economy, reforms that give private enterprises more independence will also cause them to be pulled into the political whirlpool, and property rights for enterprises is a typical representation of that phenomenon. With the implementation of the "privatization" strategy in 1998, property rights reform also began. Many enterprises that relied on the prestige of state-owned capital, or depended on the private capital of state-owned capital, had the opportunity to be independent. However, when property rights of private enterprises were clarified, these could conflict with the interests of local governments to the point of incompatibility. In the end, they would fight to the breaking point, and private capital was the one most likely to be knocked out. The founder of Jianlibao, Li Jingwei, crossed swords with the local government over differences in property rights. At the time, 90 percent of the officials declared that Jianlibao should be sold, but they would rather sell it to a foreign company and so refused to sell it to the highest bidder, which was the Li Jingwei team. Despite his various efforts, Li Jingwei was not able to pull out a victory. Li Jingwei was kicked out of Jianlibao, and the company was hastily sold. This was not even the worst news for Li Jingwei. The same year that Jianlibao was sold, Li Jingwei, who was already suffering from a brain hemorrhage, was given a notice that he, "being under the management of state agencies with the authority to operate state-owned property, disregarded national laws, and together with others, took advantage of his purchasing position in the form of life insurance, embezzling ¥3.3188 million in state-owned property."[13]

THE DISTANCE BETWEEN ENTREPRENEURS AND POWER

On the micro-level, politics are specific to government-business relations, and the relationship between entrepreneurs and power. In addition to experiencing the hot and cold running emotions of macroeconomic policy, private enterprises need to diligently define their relationship with administrative powers. Regarding micro-economic activities in China, the administrative powers possess extensive and in-depth powers of intervention, to the extent that the potential expansion of capital depends on how happy the administrative powers are.

Economist Zhang Wuchang considers human society to have created two kinds of basic economic systems. One kind uses a system of hierarchy and privilege to regulate and constrain people's behavior to prevent scarce resources from being thoroughly abused; the second kind is a property rights system that uses the definition of property rights to divide the free space where people engage in economic activities, using this to stimulate production, exchange, and the division of labor and cooperation. When the first kind of economic system transitions toward the second kind of economic system, it is easy to generate the price of renting power[14] that is institutionalized corruption.[15]

Power seeks company and often crosses boundaries of coveted capital, stretching out its hand from time to time to interfere with the normal movement of capital. If capital does not know how to read the facial expressions of power, thinking that it only needs to be open and aboveboard—who cares if any ghosts or immortals knock on the door in the middle of the night?—it would insist on acting in accordance with the laws of the market. Perpetually floating in the commercial arena, how could it avoid being backstabbed? If it does not watch out, it will incur a scourge and push itself forward on the road to ruin.

Some private entrepreneurs are even sleeker and more sophisticated. They are deeply afraid of power, and yet they are obsessed with power. They are well versed in the art of appeasing power and can obtain more resources and maneuvering space. They are determined to rely on the towering tree of political power, so they take risks in the form of capital bribery and flattery of the powers that be, willing to be reduced to being the tools and client of power. Over time, power and money blend together and continue to "encircle the area with a galloping horse." Many powers that had been sitting on the sidelines uninvolved will also be roped in to enjoy the camaraderie and benefit of connections, thus the net of crony capitalism grows larger. However, dependence on power that involves capital bribery is precisely the poison that private entrepreneurs drink in order to quench their thirst. As the trade of money and power increases, the black hole of disciplinary offenses also grows. There will eventually be a day when "the paper can no longer wrap around the fire." Once everything is unmasked, the seamless network of crony capitalism may also be destroyed. At that time, the private entrepreneurs who are besieged on all sides will turn around to look for the protective umbrella. However, they will discover that the smiling officials who had called them brothers before will either feel like the clay Buddha crossing the river, because they lack self-protection, or simply be so afraid that they avoid the entrepreneurs altogether.

If China's political system of reforms plateaus, the feet of power will easily step on the hands of capital, the institutional transfer of interests will be endless, and the market premium of deceptive practices will become the premium of power. Moreover, while lost in the field of power, the morality of entrepreneurs will be diluted, affecting the psychological and moral shape of private entrepreneurs overall.

It is necessary that Chinese business people understand politics as well as business strategy in order to build their businesses bigger and stronger.

Moderate relations with the government are essential. It is inappropriate to say "I will die before dealing with them," but it is also inappropriate to blindly flatter them. Maintain an appropriate distance, relate peacefully with the government, obtain reasonable and legitimate policies and resources of support from the government, and put the icing on the cake of government accomplishment. Maintain the bottom line, and develop an ethical and legal firewall in order to avoid disaster. Improve sensitivity toward the political environment in order to be perceptive of policy direction in a timely manner and capable of adjusting business strategy at any time; and avoid hitting the muzzle of regulation to avoid becoming the cannon fodder of system adjustments.

CHAPTER EIGHT

Why Do Housing Prices Keep Adjusting Higher and Higher?

Policy Punches Cannot Beat Stubborn Housing Rates

All of the people around you are talking about houses, flipping houses, hoarding houses. If you do not have a house, you will feel marginalized and suddenly fearful.

Love is the trickery of men lying to women. When a man loves a woman, he says nothing at first. First, he sends her a stack of money to give this woman a sense of security. Then he offers her a house. Although he ends up breaking her heart, she would at least have physical security.

Every day when I open my eyes, a string of numbers pops out: mortgage 6,000, food and clothing 2,500, socializing 600, transportation costs 580, property management fee 340, mobile phone fee 250, also utilities 200 . . . in other words, starting from my first breath upon waking, every day I have to use at least 400 of my credit, at minimum! This is my cost of living in this city. These figures have forced me not to slack off even for one day.

—LIU LIU[1]

JOYS AND SORROWS AFTER OWNING A HOME

As time goes by, within ordinary life's flickering flame, people are manipulated by different kinds of fate/luck.

In this world, no matter how prideful people are, no matter how they cynically squander their wealth while young, their bodies are slaves to fame and wealth—and they are in bondage to a thing that can lock up their fame and profit, and this thing is a house. No matter how many glamorous treasures people own, or how many achievements of fame they have won, when all of these things are combined like a kaleidoscope, people cannot escape the soft question, which is nightmarish: have you purchased a house yet?

In the world of reinforced concrete, this basic function of "shelter from the wind and rain" expresses multiple social symbols—fame, dignity, success or failure, and even the price of social stability. Shuttling back and forth in the spaces between buildings, a material civilization has been nurtured to become a spiritual civilization, and the economic drama has become the main event of the political stage.

Housing prices ebb and flow, determining the ups, downs, and setbacks of the properties of various groups. In particular, as housing prices continue to rise, people wear the mask of a blossoming smile when they are in front of people, but they bear their joys and sorrows in private when no one is looking. After buying a house, rising housing prices mean the family property increases in market value, and even if they only have a small apartment big enough for an entire family to have a humble abode, it is enough to squeeze them onto the list of millionaires in first and second tier cities. They cannot help but secretly wear a tall hat of "investing in the proper way." Those who haven't purchased a house or are preparing to buy a house, on the other hand, complain incessantly that their plans to buy a house within five years were forcibly lengthened to six years, seven years, and even longer. They listen to "experts" who swear by their personality, reputation, life, and even their "ancestors' peace under the ground" as gambling chips backing prophetic bargains. They keep on hoping and hoping, all the time enduring the suffering of housing prices being adjusted higher and higher. The number of square meters within the scope of what buyers can afford plummets from one hundred to eighty, seventy, or even fifty. They feel the pain of shrinking deposits more deeply than the complaints of disgruntled housewives carrying vegetable baskets. Some people have begun to stir trouble in the Internet arena, and fresh and graceful women have turned into hostile "destroyer teacher-mistresses" (fighting women). Forthright men become fickle and feminine. The smallest case of dissatisfaction will cause people to feel the need to vent their frustrations on the the Internet, as they roll up their sleeves, shouting abusively and implicating their eight generations of ancestors in the network violence.

Housing prices continue to rise, houses become a luxury item, and there are always people who rank themselves as those unable to buy a house. The loneliness and helplessness of houseless people hides and floats behind the hustling and bustling sounds of bulldozers, whether in new towns or in old towns. The feelings are involuntarily expressed on their faces and affect their self-esteem, happiness, and dreams for the future.

Self-frustration is aggravated when comparing oneself with the wealthy. This echoes particularly in a hatred and disgust of people who boast that they have "purchased half of an apartment building." They spend money freely, like water, in front of buyers, and this causes society to make negative moral judgments about them, such as calling them "opportunists," etc. Of course, developers are unavoidably stakeholders, and the public cannot tell if the developer's suddenly huge profits that "generate negative press" are genuine. This further aggravates society's collective ill feelings toward the developers, not to mention that some developers even presumptuously say that "houses are built for the wealthy." The murky relationship between local governments and developers is also listed as a culprit for the high housing prices, and especially because the demolition scandals continue to explode forth, people are more convinced that local governments are trapped in an official whirlpool where "political results come first, and people's livelihoods come second," from which they do not want to extricate themselves.

Of course, every coin has two sides. Not all developers are profiteers. Some of them have a conscience, and they will not hesitate to risk being derogatorily called an industry "black sheep," will adhere to contrarian prices, and will not accept bribes. A considerable part of local governments adhere to a naïve governing philosophy that "if officials do not serve the people, then they may as well go home to sell sweet potatoes." The demolition movement that was dismissed as a history of blood and tears is restaged from time to time as a flourishing and joyful drama. However, the negative emotions triggered by negative events spread extraordinarily quickly. People go through one, several, or countless periods of unhappy experiences and easily draw the conclusion that "this current situation is a little bastard."

HOUSING PRICES ARE ADJUSTED HIGHER AND HIGHER

The chess piece of housing falls squarely in the center of China's chessboard. It heralds the economy, politics, and the joy, anger, and sorrow of the people's livelihoods. The Chinese government cannot stand and watch from the sidelines. Real estate macro-regulation began in 2003 with Document No. 121.[2] The efforts and intensity of real estate regulation continued to increase, and the means of regulation trended toward the heavy-handed, from raising interest rates, to shrinking mortgages, limitations on land possession, and increasing protection of the entire process from housing construction to purchase. In addition, new versions of the policy were continually introduced. The direction of macro-regulation and control developed from the previous single policy approach of suppressing housing supply into the bipedal approach of increasing the supply of affordable housing and reducing the demand for real estate. However, despite being continuously tossed and turned by regulation policies, the housing market has an unexpected vitality. Its appetite is surprisingly good, and it is able to quietly swallow whatever that macroeconomic regulation throws into it. It has even learned how to be stubbornly antagonistic: the greater the regulation of housing prices, the higher the prices.

In 2007, the object of the people's zealous complaints in the streets was already not the unusually high price of real estate. Civilian property prices were extremely peculiar, with prices fluctuating monthly and even weekly or daily. Under the influence of the sweeping financial crisis, real estate lay dormant in 2008 for a short time, but the shoots of economic recovery soon began to show a little green, and housing rates began to soar again throughout the entire country in a retaliatory rebound. Housing prices rose faster than in any previously recorded growth rate. The China Land Surveying and Planning Institute's National Urban Land Price Monitoring Group (a subordinate of the Ministry of Land and Resources) released a telling report: "The 2009 national average of residential prices is ¥4,474 per square meter, an increase of 25.1 percent, and the highest level since 2001"—when the people endlessly clamored for a "cut" in prices, the data shrunk considerably.[3]

In January 2011, the National Bureau of Statistics (NBS) provided reference data indicating that as of December 2010, housing prices in seventy cities in the country had risen 6.4 percent over the same statistics in December 2009.[4] Most of the time, people classify the Bureau of Statistics' aggregate data of fluctuations in housing prices as only a baseline, and they consider it reasonable to double these numbers, repeat them, or move the decimal place over to the right. In short, the housing market is still projecting the "beauty of a flashing mix of colors," without the slightest fear that the cold mask of price regulation is continually changing its appearance.

Housing prices are being adjusted higher and higher, and the reason for that phenomenon is extremely strange. For a time, the chest of the housing industry was tightened, and the fuzzy feelings that they had desperately wanted to express had crystallized into clear speech. The widespread murmur that had attempted to push the housing market with a whispered sigh from an indistinguishable origin in the intricately intertwined issues of the past was now roaring everywhere . . .

The Real Estate Market Is a "Semi-False Proposition"

"Premier Zhu, how do you view the housing market?"

There was a moment of silence, and the Prime Minister asked in return, "If you cancel the welfare housing distribution system, could the real estate industry become a pillar industry?"

"It cannot."

"If the financial markets opened up, could the real estate industry not become a pillar industry?"

"It could not."

"If consumer credit were released, it still wouldn't work?"

Sensing that the Prime Minister was serious, I carefully worded, "Within two years, it would not."

"Within two years, I will certainly facilitate the housing industry to become a pillar industry," the Prime Minister categorically answered.

"Since the Prime Minister said it would work, then it certainly can work."

Audience laughs.

"Hey, you are a real estate expert. I hire you to be my real estate consultant. However, it would be an unpaid consultant."

I blushed on the spot, and with no mental preparation at all, I said with a bit of a stammer, "You do not . . . give me . . . wages, I will also feel extremely honored!"

—WANG SHI[5]

CHINA'S HOUSING MARKET MAKEOVER

The preceding excerpt was a November 1997 conversation between then First Deputy Prime Minister of the State Council Zhu Rongji (who was also governor of the People's Bank of China), and Vanke Group Chairman Wang Shi, at the Kylin Villa in Shenzhen. At the time, Wang Shi was undergoing a change in his appearance. His bald head was shaved until it shined and glowed, and he left behind an ambiguous impression for people who did not know what was going on. His "face beneath the bald head lacked kindness, had too much of the air of a robber, and was more like a warrior."[6]

However, in this report, the intelligent Wang Shi used the reform of the tax system, which Vice Premier Zhu Rongji had pushed since 1993, in his introduction. Zhu Rongji was therefore interested in Wang Shi's report and impressed by this bald-headed man who looked exceptionally unpleasant to the eye, and he wanted to talk one-on-one with him about the future direction of reform for China's real estate.

It now appears that Wang Shi and Zhu Rongji's conversation was meaningful. The measures that they referred to in this dialogue, to "cancel the welfare distribution system" and "open the financial markets" exerted their joint forces, and China's real estate industry rose rapidly.

The financial crisis that swept through Asia caused China's economy to fall into a tightening bottleneck, so China needed to activate the economy through domestic expansion. However, the central government that had just implemented the tax sharing system for three years was still not aggressive enough, and was unable to release the government-led investment plans on a large scale.[7] Some easily agitated blind spots in the market (e.g., real estate) stimulated domestic demand. Therefore, market orientation seemed all the more perfectly justified.

As a large-scale, durable consumer product, the space for growth of domestic demand for real estate is huge. It is not subject to the impact of the international market and is even able to stimulate investment—in particular, residential construction, which is an industry with a long supply chain. It can trigger expansion in construction materials, chemicals, iron and steel, and dozens of other industries; and its labor-intensive features can also attract a large quantity of labor, which is beneficial toward improving employment and helping the Chinese economy to come out of recession. Moreover, in 1998, China had more than ¥5 trillion in household savings accounts. This "caged tiger" of unlimited potential is still dormant and urgently needs the government to make an inventory of the changes in its purchasing power.

For nearly half a century before 1998, houses could not be completely linked to commodities, being separated by "seniority," "rank," and other narrow partitions. Leaders of government units controlled the ability for a complete family to obtain a house, and for the sake of having a house, they had to obey and even buckle under the unit and the leaders. Welfare housing and unit-financed housing, etc. also became a significant bottleneck that restricted real estate development.

On July 3, 1998, the State Council issued a "Notice Regarding Further Deepening of the Reform of the Urban Housing System and Accelerating Housing Construction." Through this notice, the State Council announced that it would "stop in-kind housing distribution, progressively implement the monetization of housing allocation, develop financing for housing, and cultivate and regulate the housing market." The system of in-kind housing distribution was officially abandoned, and the bottleneck in commodity housing development was broken. China's real estate industry stood on the starting line of the government-led economic growth policy, and the industry was full of high spirits.

Subsequently, in order to stimulate home purchases by the populace, the government also introduced various financial policies to guide the development of the real estate industry. The People's Bank of China issued the "Secured Loans for Personal Housing Management Approach" in order to allow commercial banks to provide housing mortgage loan services for home buyers, and the central bank arranged a ¥100 billion housing loan guidance plan. Various entities competed to launch homebuyer tax credits, encourage the purchase of high-rise residences, and push other preferential policies. Since then, the survival status of China's real estate industry has been thoroughly rewritten.

Under the encouragement of these policies, the once depressed real estate industry suddenly turned into a colorful feast. With various interest groups eager to please, or wearing heavy makeup, or acting gracefully, the industry had the appearance of a dense crowd of smiling faces making joyful sounds, overflowing the center of the stage. It seemed that the jubilant drama in the garden of sweet dreams was everlasting and would never end.

Before real estate became market-oriented, even if ordinary people had houses to live in, these belonged to the units. The people did not have discretionary power regarding houses, and moreover, did not have the ability to buy or sell. Those who had no homes had to clutch onto their length-of-service rank and professional titles as points for housing distribution, and also know how to use the "vertical and horizontal technique to interpersonal relationships (i.e., work all angles and connections in interpersonal relationships) in order to win over the leadership. Therefore, a single family residence was pinched in the palm of the unit or leadership. Even lofty, angry youths had to bend at the waists to bow to this.

The most obvious feature of the real estate market was that houses could be freely bought and sold. "As long as you have money, if you want to buy a house, you are able to buy a house; as long as you have a house, if you want to sell the house, you will be able to sell." After market-oriented housing reform, many people no longer had to live out their days watching the facial expressions of party leaders for the sake of a house, and among the propertied middle class, "Because the wealth of urban residents has been significantly improved, household savings suddenly increased from a few hundred or thousands of yuan, to tens of thousands of yuan in fixed assets. About 60 percent of urban households increased their wealth and improved their living conditions via housing reform."[8]

THE MARKET IS A RELUCTANT SCAPEGOAT

However, the hustle and bustle was destined for only a moment's pleasure, and the joyful occasion had dispersed in one day. The real estate party of leisure drinking and soft singing on stage was exchanged for some annoying circumstances. People suddenly discovered that housing prices were bolting like a wild, unbridled horse, surpassing even the extremes of many people's imagination.

Because the market has real estate's "ruffian" prefix, it has experienced scorn, contempt, and abuse, as well as the belief that business people are exceedingly unscrupulous, and the market is excessively greedy, which causes the market to be an uncontrollable, chaotic mess. Perhaps the market is only a reluctant scapegoat, and if the ornate gown of real estate were shaken, the lice that fell from it would not necessarily have market pedigrees.

It has become the consensus that the functioning of China's economy requires a complete, market-oriented system, and that a complete, healthy market economy is far more complicated than mere free trade. The premise of the healthy operation of the market economy is guaranteed by clear property boundaries, and the equality and freedoms of the subjects of market transactions. From the point of view of property boundaries, the subjects of market transactions, and other factors, China's real estate market is a "half-false proposition."

As a long supply-and-demand chain, the real estate industry includes land acquisition, construction, sales, property management, and other multiple linking factors. Among these, land is the first link of the real estate industry chain, and is a key factor in determining the ups and downs of real estate. The land market is also known as the primary market of real estate—i.e., the market for transactions regarding rights to land use.

The state-owned and collective nature of land has determined that the government is land's absolute owner and profiteer.

If we say that Article 41 of the 1986 edition of the "Land Management Law"—which includes the provisions that "urban residents may build residences on rural collective land, and shall pay the appropriate fees; building houses for sale on rural collective land is not limited by administrative departments"—may provide a glimmer of hope that the land market will begin to be free, then the deletion of the original Article 41 from the 1998 "People's Republic of China Land Management Law Implementation Regulations" has thoroughly broken the land market's desire for supply-side competition.

Farmers who have earned their livelihood from farming for generations are the primary patrons of land use. There is a sharp depreciation in economic value between the costly land in the cities and the countryside, where almost everyone has a homestead of some size. The real estate boom that is in full swing has also begun to sweep through the rural areas surrounding the cities, and numerous farmers have built bungalows or buildings on their homesteads to rent or sell to urban residents or foreign enterprises. These are "houses with limited property rights." From an economic sense, these houses with limited property rights are beneficial and harmless. Suburbs and rural residents rent and sell their surplus products—and the property earns an income. Urban residents and businesses get property in a poor location with relatively low investment value at prices that are lower than urban real estate.

However once the "houses with limited property rights" become available, they encounter the cynicism of the government. With their left hand, the administrative departments suppress these houses, using loud and stern voices to warn the farmers to reign in their horses at the edge of the cliff in order to avoid imminent disaster; and with their right hand, they guide public opinion, appealing to homebuyers not to be blinded by the cheap veil of houses with limited property rights. Houses with limited property rights belong to the wild road and are not the farmers' properties in the full sense of the word. There is no means of transferring the freedom to buy and sell them; they do not have legal protection; and in the case of disputes, it is likely that everything will be in vain, like drawing water with a bamboo sieve. If they were to call heaven, heaven would not respond, and if they were to call earth, neither would earth respond. Such appeals from the government weakened consumers' willingness to buy.

All levels of government have the right to land disposal and planning for land that is state-owned. The planning includes value-added planning (transportation, hospitals, schools, shopping malls, etc.) and devaluation planning (garbage station, chemical projects). It also includes planning for direct claiming of the land (government claiming land in exchange for cheap compensation, eviction, and demolition). Local governments and land collectives, with black-and-white evidence of being state-owned, and whose true purpose is to accelerate urbanization, obtain the land at low or no cost without even one "soldier" to seize it. They turn around and resell it to developers who fight for it until they are badly injured in order to obtain high profits. The local finance administration is thus rolling in financial resources. This has swept away the shadow of being a "poor place" that was brought on by tax sharing.

The strongest role in the real estate market should be that of developers. The profiteering "faces" that they reveal, which cause people to envy and hate them, have almost become their sealed, identified roles. Analytical data from the Chinese Academy of Social Sciences shows that the main reason public enterprises invest in real estate is that the industry's gross margin is higher. In 2009, the real estate industry's average gross margin was 55.72 percent.[9] Up to 50 percent of the average gross profit margin was still considered to have shrunk considerably, but some economists stated that real estate businesses had up to a 500 percent return on capital.

On the other hand, Mei Xinyu, who works at the International Trade and Economic Cooperation Research Institute of the Department of Commerce, gave a more straightforward and pragmatic method of measuring real estate profits:

China's real estate development industry is amazing people with its sudden and huge profits, and this has created the greatest hotbed of billionaires in mainland China, and real estate magnates always occupy prominent positions on the various kinds of lists of wealthy people in mainland China. In recent years, enterprises from many other industries, including Lenovo and other high-tech enterprises, have also joined this market one after the other. They have also seemed to provide evidence of "real estate profiteering."[10]

In July 2010, the *China Youth Daily* published the report "Real Estate Developers Expose the Industry's Unspoken Rules: Where the Huge Profits Come From," in which someone said, "Five years ago, I spent about ¥2 million to buy land; five years later, I sold the commercial building that I had built with a net profit of ¥200 million." And anonymous real estate business people revealed a bit of profiteering trickery:

Sometimes it is using planning loopholes, such as developing only 2,709 square meters of land out of a total of 7,539.5 square meters of land allotted for the project, Village A. The remaining land of 4,830.5 square meters is already being used by the government for the construction of housing for farmers. The actual construction area is only about 4,000 square meters, and the floor area ratio is about 0.82. And in fact, the initially planned floor area ratio was 1.6, and this way, the developer gives out an excess development space of a 0.78 floor area ratio.

I will also tell you two developers' means of profit gain. For example, our real estate projects have a total construction area of over 40,000 square meters. Among that, the residential area is 34,000 square meters, and the commercial area is over 3,000 square meters.

The first way that this made money is that the contract did not state more than 3,000 square meters of commercial area. This is the developer's bonus, which is worth at least ¥100 million.

The other way that this made money is that after the total construction area is subtracted from the commercial area (of which 10,000 square meters is returned to the farmers and 4,000 square meters given to the farmers' housing construction according to the contract), the developers still have about 30,000 square meters available for sale. According to the project, and counting according to the property's average price of ¥12,000 per square meter, one could sell at a total of nearly ¥400 million. The various costs per square meter are about ¥2,500, so the builder's total cost is around ¥1 billion. Finally, subtract the builder's profits and other costs of about ¥100 million, and the developers could benefit from a total of ¥200 million for the development of this real estate. In addition, there is still commercial land worth 100 million.[11]

Greed is walking with a swagger between the lines of the economic story. Expelling profits, the real estate business almost has a godlike ability, and all manner of false pretenses, for gaining favor with people. Using the easiest methods to eloquently gain huge amounts of profit, the real estate business and real estate agents have already been criticized severely in the court of morality. In 2011, Premier Wen Jiabao also used the Internet to remind the real estate developers, "I do not investigate the profits of each of your real estate businesses, but I think that the real estate industry and you as members of the society should do everything you can to fulfill your responsibility toward society. The blood of morality should flow inside your bodies." The real estate business immediately had an "innocent" response to the Premier's online admonishment, claiming that their bodies had "blood that is extremely moral," that they had a great love in their love of the motherland, their love of the people, and their love of their nationality. No one was a traitor. They also had a small love in their love of their families and their employees.

To borrow a sentence from real estate critic Niu Dao, "Talking ethics to capital is like talking chastity to a prostitute." And in terms of talking ethics with capital, it is not as good as talking about the market, rules, and order. A considerable part of the reason that the real estate business has been able to successfully drill loopholes into a variety of systems and rules lies in it gaining the acquiescence of relevant local power sectors, along with fact that regulations exist in name only.

Many real estate businesses have drifted outside the market. They flatter the powers, using their capital to buy power, gaining huge profits through crony capitalism—and they are not commodity providers of the real market in the true sense of the word. To them, doing a good job of public relations work for the relevant departments is more important than building a beautiful, strong house. Whether it is state-owned enterprises or private enterprises, most are inextricably linked to the power sector.

The end link of the housing industry chain: building sales have not yet been thoroughly market optimized. The property rights of immovable property that are involved in the transactions of the real estate market mainly include space ownership and property rights over architectural forms. Property rights law provides for residential living rights to have a term of seventy years, with fifty-year terms for commercial real estate. Even though there is automatic renewal for expired construction land use rights, some people cannot help but whisper in their hearts, "after all, these are not eternal property rights, and maybe if the policy changes, there will be another reshuffling of property."

Housing prices and regulation efforts rose in tandem, which also weakened the market-based nature of real estate. Especially the housing restriction policy, which was maligned in a carnival-like manner by the media as the "most evil policy in history," set up round after round of strong barriers to free market transactions.[12] And today's real estate arena no longer reflects the saying, "as long as you have money, if you want something, you will be able to purchase."

Local Governments and Land in a Fight to the Death

I had been putting what little money I had in ocean frontage, for
the sole reason that there was only so much of it and no more,
and that they wasn't making any more.

—WILL ROGERS[13]

THE TEMPTATION OF "LAND FINANCE"

These matters are as real as gold and silver. How could mere written words and some repeated injunctions stop them?

In order to defend her ancestral property, Rong Pan, a forty-three-year-old woman from Shanghai, threw homemade Molotov cocktails at an advancing excavator. At her side, her husband, Zhang Long, carried a crossbow, ready to shoot the "invaders" at any time. This was the image of the two frozen resisters in the cold of winter at the end of the year 2009.

Their "defending" actions did not change the outcome that the ancestral home was demolished. Also lost with the three-story building was the fact that Zhang Long was sentenced to lose eight months of personal freedom for the crime of obstruction of business.

Rong Pan, who returned to New Zealand, instantly became a news figure because she gained the concern of CCTV. This woman, who held Molotov cocktails in her hand, was called a "brave woman" by netizens.[14]

Some news stories were even more intense and tragic than the depiction of "throwing Molotov cocktails," such as the stories of self-immolation and hanging that were documented in local newspaper *Southern Weekend*. This information was reported to the authorities, as well as on forums, blogs, microblogs, and other forms. These were tenaciously pressed into our vision and living space like scars, splitting the placards of government credibility.

Rong Pan's husband shouted until he was hoarse, accusing:

"I personally saw my wife gang slapped in the face, her glasses went flying, she was pushed to the ground, she was dragged barefoot by the demolition crew, but I could not protect her."

"I fully did not expect to become a prisoner by protecting my legitimate property."

"The demolition actually had police and local government involvement. The country's laws are like words on paper that tease people to play with them."[15]

This extended to the emotional experiences of onlookers, and exaggerations such as "abominable behavior," "humiliation to human nature," "shameless," and "we have entrusted the most valuable of our nonrenewable resources to some of the most unreliable people." Public opinion of demolition rebounded to a white-hot stage—and a white-hot rage—but the bulldozers still have not stopped roaring, and incidents of bloodshed will still occur.

The government shouted that this was unjust—it was just one case, some local government's poor crisis management and failure. No matter what, the continuing violent demolition events have fed the extreme insinuation that the government is urgently promoting "land financing."

Amidst social transformation, local governments and land are battling to the death; and the "land financing dependency syndrome" is an intensifying trend. The Central Government repeatedly releases harsh proclamations and throws hard punches, requiring local governments to cooperate, and manage with high housing prices "as if catching a turtle in an urn" (i.e., to easily best one's cornered enemy). However, local governments are halfhearted and silently procrastinate, probably battling the high prices in the open while secretly and discreetly protecting the real estate industry.

Investigating thoroughly, some people have followed the vines of local finance administration to the melons of tax sharing, and they consider that these "disasters are all the fault of the tax sharing system." After the implementation of the tax sharing system in 1994, the central government and local governments used a 75:25 ratio split of the value-added taxes of all local enterprises. And at this time, after being subject to many years of games from central and local governments, land premiums had already become a fixed income from the local finance administrations to the local government. At the same time, the taxes that local government revenue was based on also transferred from value-added taxes to local basic exclusive business taxes, which mainly taxed the construction and tertiary industries. The enthusiasm of local government investments thus tilted toward the construction industry. In 2002, the central government included income tax within the range of the tax sharing reform, of which the central government received 60 percent, and local governments received 40 percent.[16] Hence local governments relied more on business taxes.

The financial powers of local governments continued to be weakened, and there was an urgent need to expand the source channels. Business taxes and land premiums that were not within the scope of central sharing became the lucky geomantic "green dragon on the left and white tiger on the right"[17] of local governments that were improving their financial powers. Among these, land premiums still belonged to nonbudgetary funds and extra-budgetary revenue, and there were mild to no restrictions on the sources of the income and expenses. A retired financial official pointed out something that he was not supposed to talk about even for a second—

> With regard to extrabudgetary funds (even though these needed to be reported through the layers of government), in general, the higher levels of government do not increase their restrictions on the distribution and use of this part of the fund. And with regard to nonbudgetary funds, the higher levels of government, on the other hand, are often not clear about even the specific amounts . . . there is quite a degree of freedom in the management and use of the net income of land development, and its scale is far greater than the corporate tax, and driven by such a huge interest that local governments are almost rushing toward, and flinging themselves at, urbanization that is based on land development.[18]

To cleanse the real estate businesses of the blot of "profiteering," during the sessions of the National People's Congress (NPC) and National Committee of the Chinese People's Political Consultative Conference (CPPCC), the China Federation of Industry and Commerce submitted a speech to the CPPCC titled, "Why Our Country's Housing Prices are High: Half of the Total Expenses of Real Estate Development Flow to the Government." In the speech, the Federation claimed that it would investigate the "development costs of the real estate business" in nine cities across the country. The costs that flowed to the government were 49.42 percent of the total expenses (land cost plus total tax revenue), and among those, the Shanghai development projects accounted for the highest share of expenditures to the government at more than 64.5 percent.

Real estate has the unique advantage of being "short, flat, and fast" when compared to the manufacturing and tertiary industries. If you buy a piece of land, there are several hundred million, more than a billion, or even billions in potential income.

Nie Meisheng, president of the China Real Estate Chamber of Commerce, and a standing committee member of the China National Federation of Industry and Commerce, said that in 2004, local government land revenue was ¥589.4 billion, and by 2010, it was ¥2.9397 trillion, accounting for 49.56 percent of local principal income in 2004 and rising to 71 percent in 2010.[19] Take for example the city of Hangzhou: in 2009 alone, the land transfer fees were over ¥120 billion, and when compared to 2008 (¥24.33 billion), these increased 393.22 percent, capturing first place in the country. For a ¥120 billion land transfer fee, how many small and medium-size enterprises will local governments require, and how much in taxes would these small and medium-size enterprises need to pay? The gap is self-evident; local governments are very willing to do lucrative business.

In addition to the land-transfer fee, there are many other real estate taxes. There are as many as twelve different kinds of real estate-related taxes that are actually collected, and among these, the main items are the business tax and surcharges, corporate income tax, and land value increment tax.[20] The business tax is 5 percent of sales revenue; and corporate income taxes are divided into the two sections of prepayments and liquidations. Estimating that corporate profits can account for 15 percent of the sales revenue, 3.75 percent of the estimated sales revenue is prepaid to the government. According to the various kinds of land items, the land appreciation tax is different, with an average of 4.5 percent of sales revenue. Adding together the numerous fees, the overall cost of the real estate taxes account for about 15 percent of sales revenue. If the government collects a few more pieces of land, and if it builds several more buildings, it will easily fill its purse. Even if other industries increase their capabilities, I'm afraid that none will be as generous as real estate.

In addition, some related departments and officials are even able to receive public relations fees from real estate businesses. These shady sources of income are also an important link of the interest-driven industry chain in the real estate market.

The tax sharing system, which at one time was considered "unique," was also subject to a period of attack and suspicion. Going around in circles, the tax sharing system, which once served as a stepping stone for Wang Shi, was once again "forced to be poor," and the local government made the tax sharing policy suffer and be disparaged as the "land finance dependency syndrome" in the shadows of public opinion. In May 2011, on the occasion of the centennial celebration of the founding of Tsinghua University, former State Council Premier Zhu Rongji correctly defined the tax sharing system during a discussion with teachers and students. He bluntly pointed out the serious mistake of including land-transfer revenue in nonbudgetary revenue:

We formulated one wrong policy, which was to collect all of the real estate money for local governments. Moreover, this was not included in the budget, which is terrible. This money is the plunder of the people's cream, and is the reason why land prices have risen so high. This is absolutely not the error of the tax sharing system.

The local governments did not collect any less money. The finance administration revenue totaled eight trillion, and after the back-and-forth collection of money, the local government collected a total of 7.3 trillion, and is that less money? Did they still have no money? What local governments now have is money. The roots of this real estate problem are the housing reform policy errors.

People who attack the tax sharing system and say that the tax sharing system has hollowed out local finance administrations, causing the farmers' poverty, are simply ignorant! Last year (2010), the national fiscal revenue was 8.3 trillion, and among that, the local governments' direct revenue was four trillion. The central taxes returned to local governments was 3.3 trillion, and the two added together is 7.3 trillion, so local governments took most of it.[21]

GDP DOCTRINE IS THE INITIATOR OF A BAD TREND

At the very least, if the tax sharing system is canceled, the illness of local government—i.e., the "land financing dependency syndrome"—will not be automatically eliminated. In the transfer of revenue from the land, the money was natural and unrestrained—fast and cheap, the mode of expenditure was much more arbitrary, and it was not within the scope of supervision of the local people's congresses, spreading a broad road for the GDP doctrine.

China's GDP doctrine originated a long time ago, and it has become increasingly trendy. Indeed, the growth of the GDP can bring the people a variety of tangible benefits such as the improvement of social security standards and generally increased affluence. However, if there is an overemphasis on the GDP, if everything revolves around the GDP as the center, it will cause GDP-ism.

Our country's current performance assessment system for officials is still a competitive system where everything lines up with GDP. Whether the GDP grows is always an important indicator for assessing the performance of local governments. The higher the GDP, the better officials are able to explain their achievements and capacity, and then the more likely they are to have a smooth and successful career. If the GDP is ordinary, then they might be labeled as having "poor capability," which would end their career. This is not the outcome that any government official would be willing to see.

From another perspective, as the saying goes, "iron barracks are permanent and do not change, but soldiers come and go." Government officials have a high level of mobility, specifically the main leadership. Today, they may still be managing the work of area A, and tomorrow, they might be going to area B to assume a new job because of a paper transfer order. Therefore, assessments of officials must be noncontinuous. As the saying goes, whichever mountain you go to, sing the song of that mountain. This has objectively created a concept of political achievements in officialdom that seeks quick success and instant benefits. Under the circumstances that real-time assessments are being implemented on their projects, some officials no longer concentrate their attention on reinforcing the groundwork, working for long-term benefits, or promoting development work. Instead, they turn and contemplate whether they will be able to make their projects bear fruit during their term of office, to gain political achievements. They light a fire and then leave; and as long as the GDP numbers look good during their term of office, everything is fine.

In the eyes of many government officials, "face projects"—projects to build a good image—are as important as the GDP. As the name suggests, these are specific and tangible projects that are presented in front of the public because they have the ability to help officials to better their image. Currently, most "projects to build a good image" manifest as regional landmark buildings and plazas, streetlamps, and other installations. In the ecosystem of officialdom, where an area has tall buildings, large plazas, and magnificent commercial districts, the official of that area feels that his image is adequately special.

Whether it be increasing the GDP, or constructing "projects to build a good image," these all require money, and what's more, a large quantity of money needs to be invested in a short period of time. Then where will the money come from? China has always had a demographic pattern of centralized wealth and poor areas that leaves the rural areas and small towns poor. It is unrealistic and also very difficult for local government officials to extend their hands and ask the central government for money. It is just as Former Prime Minister Zhu Rongji expressed, "The work of refunding taxes (transferring payments) is done poorly, and in order to rely on local governments to obtain funding, they have to run for the money and beg in order to obtain it."[22]

If this method does not work, local government officials can only turn to the business tycoons who control large funds, using industry to gain business and using business to gain money. This route is not bad. However, because their term of office is limited, and also because there are very few officials willing to "make a wedding dress for someone else" the ability to make money (GDP) in the shortest amount of time has become the first consideration for many government officials.

Enumerating the various industries, it is evident that since the manufacturing and tertiary industries produce results more slowly, these industries can barely catch up enough to set up their businesses. As soon as they begin to see the hint of results, the local government officials may need to be transferred elsewhere, which is absolutely not the most ideal option in the eyes of some officials. Because real estate involves a long industrial chain, with multiple routes of "making money fast," such as land transfers and occupation taxes, the GDP via real estate has been achieved with ferocious rapidity. So is that why many officials are rushing headlong at these things?

But standing on the summit of the big picture of socioeconomic development and looking at the long term, vigorously stimulating the real estate industry and maintaining high housing prices can indeed pull up the GDP and help local governments to earn a good image. However, overreliance on real estate such that the real estate industry is even allowed to go unchecked and dominate the economy as a single industry, to operate without a plan, or without guiding the progressive development of other industries, could ultimately damage local sustainable development. If we wait until the government runs out of saleable land to reflect upon and rectify this, it will clearly be too late.

In Eileen Chang's "A Chronicle of Changing Clothes," there is the following passage:

> People in the past went laboriously about their lives, but all their deeds are gradually coated in a thick layer of dust; when their descendants air these old clothes, that dust is shaken out and set dancing in the yellow sunlight. If memory has a smell, it is the scent of camphor, sweet and cozy like remembered happiness, sweet and forlorn like forgotten sorrow.[23]

Where local governments are concerned, what those forklifts destroyed were just dilapidated buildings, indicators to show that tasks had been completed, and political performance improved to another level. But to others, the diffuse dust has ruined their entire world. Such a memory accumulates day by day and month by month, until over time it comes down to a wound of public opinion that will be difficult to heal.

No Concerns about Housing Inflation

In the market economy, no one can control prices, and even a
stronger government cannot harness the market. Are share prices
controlled? Coal prices controlled? Vegetable prices controlled?
Drug prices controlled? Housing prices controlled? The market
does not even listen to the prices of the refined oil market, which
is monopolized by the government. From ancient times to the
modern day, there is only one way to manage prices: a comprehensive and thorough planned economy, which is the same as before
reform and opening up; the same as is seen in North Korea today.

—Economist XU XIAONIAN[24]

RED LINE LIMIT OF 1.8 BILLION *MU* OF ARABLE LAND—
"SPELL OF THE MONKEY KING'S INHIBITING GOLDEN RING"

Almost everyone considers that China's housing prices are outrageously high
and must fall. So, what price level should they fall to? From the perspective of
consumers, of course, there is "no minimum, only lower." One thousand per
square meter or even lower would be good; if it cannot fall to that price, then
one thousand per square meter is also not bad; if this still cannot be achieved,
then let it fall to the price of five years ago; and if the housing market still does
not agree, I can also accept it falling to the prices of the financial crisis.

The rational return of housing prices also has a bottom line, and it is closely
related to the current price level, the supply of land resources, and demand.

Raw materials prices rise, food prices rise, pork prices rise, clothing prices
rise, edible oil prices rise, gasoline prices rise— besides computers, color televi-
sions, and other high-tech durable products, almost all products that are closely
related to your life are rising—and housing prices have even less of a reason to
drop back to where they were five years ago.

China's housing prices have room to fall, but not too much. Moreover, from
the perspective of the long-term trends, housing prices will continue to rise.

People are used to attributing the reason for price increases of a particular
commodity to insufficient supply and excess demand, but production and
distribution factors can all cause a sharp rise in prices of certain essential
commodities. We are able to not watch television, not drive cars, and not use
cell phones, but we must drink water, eat food, and wear clothes. The essential
commodities of life lack substitutability. We cannot stop drinking water because
it is expensive or stop eating because rice is too costly. Products with small or no
elasticity in their demand have a limited supply, and their prices will go up. The

same is true of housing since we cannot simply camp out in the open because houses are expensive. Moreover, the supply of houses is also limited.

The red line of China's 1.8 billion *mu*[25] of arable land is a key factor in determining the highs and lows of housing prices in China. The reason for having the limit of 1.8 billion *mu* is that "if it is less than this figure, China's food security will be threatened, and there will be significant trouble." The red line of 1.8 billion *mu* of arable land has become a high-voltage line, and whoever proposes that the land be released from this line is a criminal for the ages. On December 24, 2008, at the Food Security and Protection of Farmland conference releasing the results of academic findings, Mao Yushi, as the chairman of the Beijing Institute of Economics, said that the concept of 1.8 billion *mu* of arable land in order to protect food security is wrong, even harmful. Because of this, the former director of the State Bureau of Grain Reserve, Gao Tiesheng, stormed out of the place. He rudely made scathing denouncements on the Internet, and these denouncements that described Mao Yushi as "betraying the country," and committing "crimes against the nation," became mainstream public opinion.

With the lesson learned at the expense of Mao Yushi,[26] very few people have bluntly questioned whether it is reasonable to have the red line of 1.8 billion *mu* of arable land. Of course, there are also economists and scholars who euphemistically point out that as long as the agricultural production rate or the utilization rate of a single area of arable land is increased to a certain degree, there is no need to worry about not having enough to eat. Per the point of view of "man-made" farmland proposed by economist Chen Zhiwu:

Modern agricultural technology is able to artificially imitate sunlight and any required climatic effects. Specifically because man-made climate and biological engineering has greatly accelerated the growth cycles of vegetables and crops, for example, many vegetables that originally had only two growing seasons per year in the south may now require only one or two weeks to grow. That is to say, an acre of land can now repeat a crop twenty-seven times in a year.

If we take an acre of land and build thirty floors on it, using workers on every floor to produce greenhouse vegetables, and complete twenty-seven growing seasons of vegetable production per floor per year, this year's production will be equivalent to 405 acres of previous production, which is equal to magnifying the supply of an acre of agricultural land 404 times![27]

However, increasing the agricultural production rate or the utilization rate of a single area of arable land seems to be very risky, and the government has not shown any indication of loosening the red line of arable land. The red line of 1.8 billion *mu* of arable land of real estate does not count for much, and the farmers' houses with limited property rights are also in the gray areas; and when it's all figured out, local governments continue to have the sole right to dispose of urban state-owned land and rural collective land, the scale of real estate land has been restricted, and real estate land has become a scarce resource. Land is not an inexhaustible, infinite resource, and when one piece is collected or purchased, there is one less piece.

In the era in which land is king, developers muster all of their strength to snatch land resources, and land prices rise in round after round of enclosure movements to the tune of hundreds of millions, more than a billion, or even billions in land prices. Land prices rise year after year, and this has determined that housing prices soar from the basis of the increase in prices of most basic materials used in housing construction. This is the "rare materials are expensive" phenomenon in economics. Whether it is the buyer or the seller, all expect the prices to rise, and higher consumer expectations will also push up housing prices.

China's scarce land resources have determined that China's housing prices cannot be too low. This is exactly the same as buying bread during a disaster. In a flood, everything in a house is swept away. However, it is good to be quick-witted and resourceful in an emergency, and to have stashed some money on your person in advance. When you go to the local store to buy bread, if you unfortunately encounter a bona fide price-cheater, he may take advantage of your misfortune and make a profit by selling you a ¥2 piece of bread for ¥20. Even though you are extremely dissatisfied, at least you have been able to buy bread. For high profits, unscrupulous business people will hoard a large quantity of bread. When they sell it at high prices, the customers will purchase with more caution. The bread that has been hoarded by the unscrupulous business people is not completely bought off the shelves by the customers in front of them, and the customers will have also received their lifesaving bread. Therefore, an evil price cheat will have saved your child. As Adam Smith said, "The food and drink that we require every day is not by the favor of the butcher, the winemaker or the baker, but it is due to their self-serving plans."

Though such prices are fraudulent, we cannot deny that charging of high prices for scarce resources can be seen as the protection of these resources. If we lived in a country where the citizens did not give aid to disaster victims, and if a store owner decided not to prevent people from looting, then his shop would quickly be looted. By the same token, if the land were cheap, then there would be an increased number of developers to hoard the land. When land prices drop sharply, land resources face the embarrassment of depletion. Of course, we cannot let land prices skyrocket. As in the example cited earlier, water worth ¥1 and sold for ¥20 is acceptable, but if it is sold for ¥100, ¥1,000, or even ¥10,000, then that is crazy.

"BUYING" LIKE THE TIDE

With the development of towns and urbanization, our demand for houses continues to increase. Compared to other commodities that can be produced in larger quantities and with higher efficiency, houses take longer to build. Land acquisition, construction, and decoration all take time; and when a longer construction period has been determined, even if the real estate business works around the clock to build the house, it will be very difficult to satisfy the exponentially increasing housing needs of the people. People not only have a demand for a first home, they will also have a demand for a second and even third house. Inadequate social security has caused people's insecurities to emerge from time to time. Therefore, people may buy a second house, using it to hedge against inflation, and to prepare for future retirement purposes through rental income. People buy their third house to give to their children, because their children's accumulation of wealth is still not enough to pay the room rate.

In the real estate market, there is a crucial link, which is a key factor in determining whether supply and demand can smoothly connect: purchasing power. From a macroeconomics point of view, currency release is a short-term factor that promotes the rising of housing prices. When a large volume of currency is released into the broad money supply, and this amount exceeds GDP growth in the same year, this will produce capital bubbles, which will be relieved in the form of loans with banks as intermediaries.

Additionally, in the thirty plus years of reform and opening up, the people have accumulated a large amount of private wealth that is not controlled by the banks, and it is circulating among the population in a gathered or scattered pattern. We can only use the most obscure numbers to measure the scale of private capital. Private capital and bank loans urgently require exports, and since industrial profits are relatively low (particularly in manufacturing), and domestic investment channels are narrow, neither private capital nor bank loans are pegging themselves to industry. Instead they turn and go after real estate, the stock market, and other lucrative industries. Via private capital—known for being "short," "flat," and "fast"—private capital and bank loans can rapidly come together in a short time to enter the real estate market, create shortages in housing listings, and raise housing prices. These are the "groups that flip houses," such as the Wenzhou Real Estate Group and the Inner Mongolia Real Estate Group.

From a social stratification angle, China's wealthy are the ones who "became wealthy first" in the reform and opening up: they are the upper layer of the wealth pyramid (such as the owners of private enterprises), the upper layers of state-owned enterprises, senior employees of private enterprises, and so on. They have strong financial resources, and it is easy for them to buy housing in general. Not to mention the fact that paying ¥10,000 or ¥20,000 per square meter, even ¥30,000 or ¥50,000 per square meter, would also be something they could withstand. They do not lack a house to live in. After having their house, they often still want to buy a second or even third home. Or they simply and specifically allocate funds to speculate in real estate.

Furthermore, since houses are related to dignity, honor, personal marriage, and most importantly, family happiness, the middle of the pyramid (the middle class) and even the lower layer (college students who just graduated, ordinary workers, and migrant workers), all strive to buy a house, toward which they struggle with a lifetime of efforts. Even if they had struggled in a "naked marriage" (unable to afford a proper wedding), as ant tribes in humble, "narrow dwellings" (cheap housing), they would mobilize the entire family to sell scrap metal to put together a down payment, become slaves of their house, and struggle lifelong for the house enterprise.

Regarding housing prices, in the final analysis, wants are greater than needs in terms of supply and demand. In today's housing market, the wants are greater than the needs, so there are no worries about housing inflation.

Are Real Estate and Regulation a World Apart?

I would not hesitate to say that I'm the "vested stakeholder" from the relationships and profiteering era, but starting from the enforced implementation date of the 2004 auction system (referred to as the "8.31 doomsday" in the industry), the "era of mythology" ended . . .

Although the age of mythology has ended, and although the market has standardized, the regulations and systems have matured, and the supply of land has opened and become transparent. Developers can no longer earn "evil money" by using underhanded means to cheat people via the "tricks of the trade."

But this does not mean that housing buyers would be able to earn less money!

This is a fact that sounds unusually harsh, and is also difficult for people to accept, but there is always someone who points out this fact. Just like the people who wholeheartedly hope for "revolution" in the writings of Lu Xun: the "revolution" finally happened, but they discovered business as usual post-"revolution." While some of the people that they customarily hated had become "unlucky," their own days had not improved at all.

Even though I am a developer, I will still not avoid saying that if it is really developers' insatiable greed and moral depravity that caused high housing prices with no declines, and made residents unable to obtain homes, then things would be all too easy to handle. The more that the market matures, and functions in accordance with its own laws to develop operations, the lower the dependence on the ethical standards of its members. The same is true of the real estate market.

—ZHANG BAOQUAN[28]

THE FALSE THEME OF EVERYONE IS HAPPY

The above passage is excerpted from an article entitled "Fifteen Years of Mood," written by Zhang Baoquan of Beijing, the chairman of the board of the Antaeus Group. The article contains his grievances and complaints along with the idea that he is at one with the victims of people's emotional violence. This causes readers to be unaware that he "reaped profits and boasted about it." The real fact is that, although the developer's story of "drinking wine from a large bowl and eating large pieces of meat" has had multiple interpretations—from the streets to the official authority of the media—until this profiteering persona has deeply penetrated peoples' hearts, there would be even more developers whose epic profiteering came to an abrupt end after 2004.

The real estate regulation that began in 2003 had become more intense by 2004. This included restrictions on the conversion of agricultural land to agricultural construction land, the controlling of real estate credit, as well as the introduction of the land bidding and auction system. In particular, the auction system has been referred to as the "8.31 doomsday" by the real estate business.[29]

Each magic spell that is aimed at manipulating the overheated real estate market is in fact the government administration forcefully reshuffling its participation in the market. Small and medium developers who have fewer pathways, a smaller scale, and limited inventory of land, become the vanguards of reshuffling and bear the brunt of its impact. At the same time, the pattern of real estate oligarchs, who have erected a high entrepreneurial threshold in the real estate industry, is more obvious, and they have improved the bargaining power of the real estate business in the housing market.

The purse of land is suddenly tightened, and the land auction system has also helped the real estate business to understand that "hoarding land is king." To grab land is to grab real money. Local governments are also pleased that their own small coffers have grown fat and sturdy from the land auction system. With developers and local governments working together, land prices are skyrocketing. When land prices bullishly increase, housing costs naturally increase. These punches and reregulation measures cannot push down the high housing prices, and it is necessary to restrict the supply of land, and necessary to raise land prices and also to allow housing prices to be cheap. Even if developers are willing to listen to the Party, they will not want to bear losses. They only want to be known as good businessman—i.e., "if they have to wear a flower, it must be a large red flower" (according to traditional Chinese customs, only the first wife can wear a red flower, while second wives must settle for pink flowers. In this context, a red flower signifies "a good name").

The regulation of supply and demand in the housing market appears upside down when it turns toward curbing demand. This demand then is a man-made scarcity, inhibiting consumers' willingness to buy, and with "purchase restriction orders" as the primary representative—if there is no one to buy a house, how long will the supply party be arrogant for? "Purchase restriction orders" are a strong medicine indeed, and as "purchase restriction orders" continue to be carried out, housing prices in many cities already have signs of loosening. However, when the potency of the medicine is too great, there are side effects, in that much of the normal demand for housing is also stifled. At the same time, it also gave birth to disguised prosperity of the rental market, making many people's lives more difficult: they cannot afford to buy a house or an apartment, rent is too expensive, and they must seriously consider where in the world to find shelter.

Moreover, even though purchase restriction orders have lethally stripped away a layer of skin from housing prices to the satisfaction of all, they are only an expediency measure. When the tide of the purchase order restrictions recedes, the local governments will still depend on land financing, housing buyers will still be like the tide, developers will still control the bargaining power, and business will be as usual. Will the farce repeat itself, and those days of buying houses at low prices flash by, causing people to think that it was a dream that ended too quickly?

Further, the government suppression of housing prices had the "mass response" of public opinion and the collective emotion, and it seemed that people were all "young warriors" trying to fight high housing prices, to force developers and speculators to change or to be defeated. However, people had mixed feelings toward the tidy slogan "lower housing prices, return livelihoods to the people." Developers, for the sake of survival and profit, and local governments, for financial revenue, naturally hope for housing prices and enterprises to be high and not to go down. Then there is the central government to openly protect the livelihoods of the people while local governments secretly maneuver in order to increase fiscal revenue, using both secret and open means with pushing-and-pulling, Tai Chi–like movements. When the strength and determination of central government policies pass through layer upon layer, and when they really fall upon the specific policies of housing price controls, they will become a spent force.

Towns have housing residents who, whether they own one or two houses, are unwilling to see a drop in housing prices that would cause their wealth to shrink. The psychology of some housing residents is like that of people who want to board a public bus. When the area in the front of the bus is full of people, and everyone wants to board the bus as soon as possible, they fight to squeeze in, mumbling to people already on the bus to "give way, free up some more space, if you have meat let everyone eat it." They will be relieved once they have squeezed onto the bus. But they will see that there are still people who were saying the same things, and these people continue to cling to the door and not let go, preventing the bus from moving. So the people who have just boarded the bus become impatient, saying "The bus is already full and overloaded. Wait for the next bus, and don't cause this entire bus full of people to be delayed because of you." The people on the bus echo, "Yes, yes, we're in a hurry, master driver, hurry and drive the bus!" accidentally becoming momentary "heroes" of the "battle of wits of the people on the crowded bus."

WHEN ECONOMIC ISSUES BECOME POLITICAL ISSUES

The situation looks very troublesome, and it seems that no matter the method employed, a win-win situation will not appear. The issue of housing prices has already gone from being an economic issue to becoming a political issue where the interests of all parties are thoroughly entangled.

The root cause of high housing prices is nothing more than an imbalance between high land prices and supply and demand. To unilaterally control the overheating of the supply side, and repress the demand side's willingness to buy, would be to treat the symptoms without affecting a permanent cure. The government should instead apply maximum effort on the supply end. The government-led protection of housing construction is proof of this. In the morning of November 21, 2007, after Premier Wen Jiabao inspected Singapore housing construction, he said,

> Home ownership is key. The most important duty of the government is to be effective regarding low-cost housing in order to allow both those who cannot afford to buy a house, and the migrant workers who enter the cities to work, to be able to afford to rent a room, and to have housing to live in. The second most important duty is to construct affordable housing for the middle class.[30]

Houses with limited property rights have brought another competitive factor into the real estate market. As long as the corresponding measures of the legal system are complete, houses with limited property rights that are beautiful and yet inexpensive will cause a catfish effect in the real estate market, which not only will increase the housing supply, it will also have the ability to increase farmers' incomes—and why not?

Furthermore, land finance administrations, as well as the GDP doctrine that caused the government to crazily pursue land finance administrations, also need to make a fresh start. In 2011, a smart and fierce microstory called "A cold joke" was much touted on the microblogs:

> If I were a representative of the National People's Congress, I would definitely propose: when it is time to pay taxes, use a promise payment method where one can fully withdraw or get a refund if it is undesirable. By waiting until the government has made political achievements or fulfilled its promises, we will confirm the payment, and otherwise we will get a full refund. At that time, government officials will be chasing our rear ends, shouting: Dear relative, give a good evaluation, dear relative! Dear relative, choose me, and the package will include People's Services, dear relative! Dear relative, the political achievements are here, please find it enclosed, dear relative![31]

The years are forcefully pushing ahead like a hurricane, and the era of splendor gave this world a beautiful, magnificent, and ornamental structure, but people could not escape the slavery of fame and wealth. The houses that we could have as large or as small as we desired caused us to feel as if we were living in a prehistoric, uncultivated land, depressed and unable to find peace. Only when the seemingly ordinary "seven emotions and six sensory pleasures" are satisfied—housing to live in, schools to attend, medical care, support for the elderly, and the ability to earn money—will people really live respectable and also dignified lives. We will also no longer be strangers in a large and wealthy country.

CHAPTER NINE

Why Is the Financial System Closer to Perfection, While Usury Is More Rampant?

Financial Light and Shadows

Just as the electricity of the whole atmosphere is concentrated in the tip of a lightning rod, an immeasurable number of events then come together in the narrowest span of time.

—STEFAN ZWEIG[1]

THE MAGINOT LINE OF STABLE FINANCE

Once, people thought that a fresh dawning was but a fleeting moment, while prudence lasted forever. However, destiny cannot be resisted, and it seems that no one can occupy a strategic position for all time. Every time a ring of light shines down, it always leaves a shadow, large or small.

China's financial system, which was always in the spotlight during the international financial crisis of 2008, has not enjoyed more applause and praise with the passage of time. On the contrary, it has been heavily criticized because a specific economic sector or territory has shown glaring confusion, such as informal private lending, which walks in the gray areas and is currently wearing a "mask of usury," perpetuating crimes in all directions.

In October 1979, Deng Xiaoping proposed that, "banks should be used for economic development, as leverage for innovative technologies; and banks should be made into real banks." The work of reconstructing China's financial organization system thus began.

After thirty years of development, China's financial system has improved day by day. Most of the time, the mainstream voices of public opinion that evaluate China's financial system display a high level of emotional consistency and verbal discretion:

> Under the party's leadership, our country's financial organization system has developed from the original, single system of the People's Bank of China with steady, step-by-step reform. So far, it has already established

new financial systems that function in a complementary way and coordi-
nate development. They are regulated by the People's Bank of China under
the separate supervision of the China Banking Regulatory Commission,
the China Insurance Regulatory Commission, and the China Securities
Regulatory Commission (CSRC). In the financial systems, the state-owned
commercial banks are the main body, with policy-oriented finance separated from commercial-oriented finance. There are a variety of financial
institutions, and multiple financing channels coexist.[2]

When the international financial crisis broke out in 2008, the financial
systems of many countries, including Western developed countries, were in a
disastrous state, even to the embarrassing point of collapse. China's financial
system, however, was the sole thriving and sound branch of that tree, and
reached the pinnacle of its prestige. In the financial crisis, China exhibited a
tranquil posture and once again confirmed that the fame it gained in 2007—the
"sudden rise of a great nation"—had not just been empty words. China walked
into various summits and international forums with the more descriptive
identity of "Kung Fu Panda." And people acted in one accord to recognize and
support the firm financial Maginot Line: the regulatory efforts of the China
Banking Regulatory Commission were much greater relative to the inactive
regulatory efforts of Western countries: for example, China's strict prevention
of risks brought on by the banking and securities businesses, and the system's
adherence to the relative independence of the banking system, avoiding the "if
one loses, all lose" situation with the capital markets. In addition, because China
had a financial system that did not entirely integrate with the world, it prevented
the financial bonds manufactured by Wall Street investors from advancing deep
into China unchecked, and China's financial system successfully escaped the
international fiscal disaster.

In February 2009, the global banking and financial systems still had not
freed themselves from the whirlpool of financial turmoil, and Liu Mingkang of
the China Banking Regulatory Commission gave a four-point summary full of
forced optimism. He used rational data to prove that China's financial system
was in the spotlight everywhere:

The first is that nonperforming loans are maintaining a "double down."
At the end of December 2008, the balance of commercial banks' nonperforming loans was ¥568.18 billion, a decrease of ¥700.24 billion from
the beginning of the year. The rate of nonperforming loans was 2.45
percent, which was a decrease of 3.71 percentage points compared to the

beginning of the year. The second is that the risk compensation capability further strengthened. At the end of 2008, the loan loss reserve adequacy ratio of state-owned commercial banks had reached 153 percent, a year-on-year rise of 122.2 percentage points. The loan loss reserve adequacy ratio of joint stock commercial banks reached 198.5 percent, a year-over-year increase of 28.3 percentage points. The third is that the number of cases and the amount of money involved continued to decline. In 2008, there were 309 cumulative incidences of various cases in the banking industry and financial institutions, and there were eighty-nine cases involving more than ¥1 million, which was a decline of 29 percent. The fourth is that the profitability of the banking industry was significantly enhanced. In 2008, under the circumstance where large-scale provisions were made for our country's banking industry and financial institutions, the rate of return on capital was still as high as 17.1 percent, which improved 0.4 and 2.0 percentage points compared to 2007 and 2006, respectively.[3]

Summaries from places of power that are joyful and take a broad and long-term kind of view are not enough to allow people to be deeply aware of the treacherousness of the continually changing financial system. People who come from the grassroots society may be more capable of reflecting on the financial system's powerful penetration into society. A contemporary financial system that is built on the foundation of the rule of law will free the carriers of financial transactions in traditional cultural systems—i.e., the people's instrumental function in economics—and people will gain a greater manifestation of values, rights, and freedom.

Meanwhile, the modern financial system has also broken through the interpersonal financial transactions that are linked by an internal kinship network, avoiding the phenomenon of free riding caused by traditional interpersonal financial transactions. Additionally, the validity of utilizing funds has greatly increased, so people have more opportunities to be self-reliant, which has stimulated people's desire and ability to create wealth.

USURY ATTACKS: BOAT CAPSIZED IN THE GUTTER?

However, time is a revolving door of unpredictable joys and sorrows. During the financial crisis, China's financial system, which had been called strongly fortified, withstood the storm of the financial crisis. But in the days after the crisis, it was difficult to dam the flow of usury.

In many people's eyes, usury has really become a scourge, and small to medium sized enterprises are drowning one after another. The entrepreneurial dream that was once everlasting, suddenly and unexpectedly seemed to be pulling away, bewitched, and the protagonist had no chance of survival.

Japanese writer Yasunari Kawabata gave us these beautiful words: "I thought I saw white-winged insects flying in the sky, but it turned out to be rain, spring rain."[4] In today's troubled financial world, is it ultimately white-winged insects flying in the sky or rain, spring rain?

Usury Nightmare

I cannot say whether financial markets have morality or not; they are just a type of system. The financial market does not belong to the area of morality; it is not immoral, but morality is simply not part of the equation, because financial operations have their own rules of the game. I am a participant in the financial market, and I will follow the given rules to play this game, I will not violate these rules, so I do not feel guilty nor feel that I need to be responsible. In terms of this matter of the Asian financial crisis, whether or not I speculate does not have any effect on what happens. If I do not speculate, it will still happen. I do not think that . . . there is anything immoral about speculation.

—GEORGE SOROS[5]

THE FLOOD OF CAPITAL

When a nightmare begins to develop and prepares to manifest itself, the people who see it are often unaware that it is a nightmare. Until the nightmare exposes its hideous face.

All along, because it lacks its rightful title and therefore cannot be implemented smoothly, informal private lending is frequently in the teeth of the storm; and this is especially true in 2011. If the words "informal private lending" are used, they evoke simple, plain, unofficial, and folksy feelings. But when people, as they often do, use the term "usury" rather than "informal private lending," they are bluntly expressing their abhorrence of the evil of usury that is masked as informal private lending.

What is usury? There is no clear definition. People subconsciously take the relationship between cost, profit, and interest to be a measure of the standard, so if the interest rates in informal private lending are higher, then it is usury. In people's subjective expectations, usury would be interest rates that are much higher than normal bank interest, more than double the bank rate or twice as much.

In 2010 and even in the first half of 2011, major media focused on bold words such as "small- and medium-size enterprises face starvation," "rampant usury," and "interest is so high that it's comparable to selling drugs."

The precariously situated small and medium-size enterprises activated the flood of usury. Trapped by rising costs, with money tightening and with their chain of capital on the verge of crumbling, they desperately seized every last straw in order to ride out the storm. At such a moment, banks will rarely extend aid to these enterprises, but active usury can actually manipulate financing. In order to survive, what they care about is not how high the interest rates are, or whether they have the capacity to repay the debt. Rather, what matters is that they are able to borrow money, and the level of the interest rates is already outside of the scope of consideration.

Private capital that is driven by its profiteering and greedy nature has unlimited expansion because "enterprises lack money to spend, and they only care about borrowing money to survive." The money shortage has led to a money famine, and people are stifled by an environment as heavy as a tropical rainforest, where the stiflingly hot and humid air is all-encompassing. In this environment, greed and ambition continually give birth to the ideals that "money produces more money" and "interest compounds." Since they have broken away from the normal system and legal pathway, those desires that once were suppressed by law, morality, and humanity are currently being incited by impulsive, agitated, simplistic, and paranoid herdlike emotions, which are crazy to the point of completely lacking taboos or restrictions. The scope is broad and the interest is high, with unprecedented public participation. Private capital in the city of Wenzhou alone soared to ¥40 billion in one year, and the speed was eye-popping.

Geographically, informal private lending is the most active and ostentatious in the economically developed coastal areas such as Jiangsu and Zhejiang, where it has almost reached a white-hot level. They delay to put on the hat of legalization. The underground banks with unlicensed operations are fearful that their illegal activity will be caught, so they place their advertisements inconspicuously, and rely mainly on word of mouth to attract business. When there is a surge in demand for informal private lending, the lenders then have the courage to display large and pointed advertisements, letting people look to them as saviors.

The range of borrowing continues to break through the limitations of the circle of acquaintances. What began as borrowing among acquaintances a few years ago has expanded to borrowing from strangers and from other districts and provinces. At the same time, the identities of those who now borrow are more diverse, ranging from entrepreneurs, civil servants, workers, and teachers, to even farmers . . . people from all strata of society want to take advantage of this "once in a lifetime opportunity" to fish (i.e., profit) relentlessly. This cannot help but cause people to remember 2007, and the stock market madness that set off the tide of "everyone is a player of stocks."

Southern Weekend once reported the story of a man from Hangzhou called He Jin. He Jin had been in the industry for three years, and ran tens of millions of dollars' worth of credit funds. When this man tasted his first piece of business, he tasted the sweetness of lending: he lent ¥6 million and made a profit of ¥72,000 in two months. What made him more obsessed was that he personally saw some entering the industry with ¥50,000 and having a net worth of 20 million three years later. Even with the constant upheaval in the industry, he still has a soft spot for this "earn money fast" industry, and has been quoted as saying that he "would not want to do anything else in this line of business. The money comes too quickly and too easily."[6] When the money comes too quickly, it inevitably causes people to go into a trancelike state; and the concealed "gambling nature" has also become more heavy-handed and strong. Like addicted gamblers, even having seen many, many stories of bankruptcy, ruin, and death, their eyes still shine when they see the gambling devices, and their gambling nature does not change.

The huge charm of the industry comes not just from profits, but also from the halo effect brought by the identity of certain lenders. No matter how haughty the borrower is, no matter how large his influence through the enterprise that he operates, he is still a poor peasant like "Yang Bailao," and, to borrow He Jin's words, "no matter how wealthy the boss is, when he meets with us, he swallows his pride."[7]

People have not stopped enthusiastically believing that "if there is money to be earned, everyone can earn it," and the informal private lending industry thus prospers in economically developed areas because it is the right climate, which is like "the wind that causes waters to rise." Other regions are waiting wistfully, and some areas of economic poverty in the central and western regions, and even remote areas, cannot help but surge into the large tide of speculation, otherwise known as "frying money."

Sihong County is one of the poorest counties in Jiangsu Province, but there is no shortage of all brands of luxury cars, including BMW, Mercedes-Benz, Infiniti, Cadillac, Hummer, Ferrari, Lamborghini, Maserati, . . . The number and types of these cars cause people not to dare underestimate this unattractive, poverty-stricken county. Also among this type of city is the town of Shiji, which is under the county's jurisdiction. It is even called "BMW Town." The root cause of these strange economics-lifestyle situations is the deluge of usury. Usury was once popular in Sihong County, as well as in the towns of Shiji, Qingyang, Chengtou, and others, where almost every household spent some savings on usury. The amounts are beyond tens of thousands of Chinese yuan, and the interest is high. For example, ¥50,000 gets ¥0.15 in interest. This interest rate is extremely high, and the intermediary lender "unscrupulously" retains funds, which gives birth to the phenomenon of abnormal overnight wealth accumulation.

In Erdos, a resource city in Inner Mongolia Autonomous Region, there is another "borrowing landscape." This city has rapidly accumulated wealth because of its endowment of natural resources. Erdos rapidly shot to fame and "mass-produced" a large number of wealthy people. These people, who rapidly gained their new wealth, are big spenders, obsessed with luxury cars and mansions, and keen to copy the "way to sudden wealth" of economically developed areas. The building of capital markets is still a blind spot, formal financial institutions are rare, and at the same time, private wealth is rapidly expanding, providing a breeding ground for the spread of informal lending. Locals have already been influenced by informal lending to the degree of turning their backs on their relatives. Even when a father is borrowing money from a son, he needs to pay high interest rates. According to the logic of finance, it is understandable that lending practices produce interest, but in Erdos, which is a blank slate compared to the rest of the capital markets, such "market rules" are unseemly.

Compared to Jiangsu and Zhejiang Provinces where informal lending has been developing all along, Erdos lacks a foundation and is "starting from scratch." Even though it has generated large-scale informal lending funds and much informal lending behavior, the informal lending structures lack credit protection. Therefore, the risks are greater, and it is more unreliable and much more of a gamble.

PROVOKING ECONOMIC CONTRADICTIONS

Stubborn craziness and greed are like children who are ignorant of the ways of the world and are becoming more frivolous and unscrupulous, provoking economic contradictions. These contradictions are just beginning to appear.

Informal capital, which entered the financial chain by bypassing the main economic arterials, still remains in the no-man's-land of financial macro-control. It is vulnerable to the unlimited downward spiral that is the risk of nonstandardized, high-risk operations, and it can easily initiate confusion in the financial system.

Informal lending has no official "status" and cannot obtain legal protection. Neither does it have interest limits set by policy and law, causing the interest rate moderation of informal lending to be weak and the rates to be generally higher. Since 2011, many small- and medium-size enterprises solicited money in order to survive; interest rates also increased several fold. Increases of six to eight points were common. In some short-term interest-bearing contracts, there were even interest rates of ¥0.1 to 0.15.

High interest rates also caused the tentacles of informal lending friendship to extend far beyond the "community of acquaintances." This caused the entire borrowing chain to be more fragile. In fact, lenders are well aware that informal lending drifts in an area between legality and illegality, and lacks legal protection. So they try every method to formulate some conventional unspoken rules to avoid lending risks. For example, a lender in Yiwu once formulated the "three rules for no lending." These are: do not lend to people who reside further than a radius of 100 km; do not lend to those who have never eaten a meal on a dinner table; and do not lend for factory machinery that is not on a full load operation. As informal lending becomes increasingly crazed, this prudent lender has unconsciously reduced the lending threshold, and the three standards have turned into ambiguous statements, where things may only "look reliable." In this crazy world, how can a person be able to determine who is reliable and who is unreliable at just one glance?

Medium- and small-size enterprises are the main entities that have borrowed money, and they seem unreliable. Because they are facing the plight of a broken capital chain, they have chosen their last battle, holding on to the psychology of trusting luck in borrowing, thinking that "if I don't borrow, I will die, but in borrowing, there is still a possibility that things will turn for the better." Rationally analyzing this, when usury interest rates far exceed operational profit margins, usury lending would be more like a gambling game where "compensation is a high-probability event." If an enterprise makes a slight mistake, such as repaying the loan too slowly, then it might not be able to repay the usury.

Another main purpose in borrowing is for stocks, real estate, and other quick money or usurious investments. However, the stock market is volatile and constantly carries covert deals. And real estate is in a prolonged bear market while going through menacing macro-regulation. Therefore, this is a gamble, where wins and losses are unpredictable.

There is a saying that kinship, regional relations, and pride do not last and are like dust in the wind, and winners must also decline. The liquidation era has begun . . .

The Liquidation Era

We are, all of us, hunter-gatherers lost in the big city. And therein, say the theorists, lie the roots of many of our bad habits. Our craving for sweets evolved in a world without ice cream; our interest in gossip evolved in a world without tabloids; our emotional response to music evolved in a world without Celine Dion. And we have investment instincts designed for hunting mammoths, not capital gains.

—PAUL KRUGMAN[8]

PREVALENCE OF "BEING ON THE RUN"

In this era of excess wealth creation hormones, life is no longer tranquil. Various lenders and borrowers hide a shocking intent to kill behind their façade of recklessness. Nevertheless, a single disaster can eliminate all of their excessive squandering of capital. In the second half of 2011, a flood of terms appeared which described usury "crimes," such as "on the run," "bankrupt," "suicide," and "debt claim."

There are still no definite figures on the business owners who have disappeared or the enterprises that have stopped their operations. The general public has been more focused on enterprises with a larger scale that are more well known. Some of the smaller enterprises are simply not included in the statistics. In short, wherever usury exists, people will hear the extremely negative words that go hand in hand with usury, and such terms are catalysts that instigate people's fear and blame of usury.

Jiangsu and Zhejiang Provinces were hit the hardest when the chains of usury debt broke. The names of many business owners involved in usury have appeared in the media. Phoenix Television reported the incident of a Zhejiang business owner involved in usury who had fled. The "escape path" continues and is far from ending.

FLEEING INCIDENTS OF ZHEJIANG BUSINESS OWNERS INVOLVED IN USURY[9]

DATE: Early April 2011
COMPANY: Jiangnan Leather Co., Ltd.
BOARD CHAIR: Huang He
DETAILS: He fled the country because of a huge gambling debt.

DATE: April 2011
COMPANY: Portman Coffee

BOARD CHAIR: Yan Qinwei

DETAILS: Yan fled. Because of poor management of his company, he informally borrowed high-yield funds, but ultimately the capital chain fractured.

DATE: April 2011
COMPANY: Three Flags Group
BOARD CHAIR: Chen Fucai
DETAILS: Chen fled the country because of a crisis in the company's capital chain and problems in corporate mutual insurance.

DATE: Early June 2011
COMPANY: Wenzhou Railway Electrical Alloy Co., Ltd.
BOARD CHAIR: no data
DETAILS: One of the shareholders of the Wenzhou Railway Electrical Alloy Co. fled because of involvement in ¥10 million worth of informal lending.

DATE: Mid-June 2011
COMPANY: Zhejiang Tianshi Electronics Corporation
BOARD CHAIR: Ye Jianle
DETAILS: Ye fled because he was unable to repay a huge debt of ¥70 million.

DATE: July 2011
COMPANY: Hengmao Footwear
BOARD CHAIR: Yu Zhenglin
DETAILS: Yu fled. The reasons and funds involved are unknown.

DATE: End of July 2011
COMPANY: Jubang Shoe Co., Ltd.
BOARD CHAIR: Wang Hexia
DETAILS: Wang fled because of problems with her shares that guaranteed her company, involving ¥100 million in funds.

DATE: August 24, 2011
COMPANY: Jinchao Electrical Appliance Co., Ltd.
BOARD CHAIR: Dai Liejun
DETAILS: Dai fled because of problems with his operation of a guarantee corporation.

DATE: August 29, 2011
COMPANY: Nai Dang Lao Shoe Materials, Ltd.
BOARD CHAIR: Dai Zhixiong
DETAILS: Dai fled because of owing a huge debt.

DATE: August 31, 2011
COMPANY: The Tribal God Footwear Co.
BOARD CHAIR: Wu Weihua
DETAILS: Wu fled. The reasons and funds involved are unknown.

DATE: August 31, 2011
COMPANY: Tang Ying Clothing
BOARD CHAIR: Hu Xuer
DETAILS: Hu fled with his wife and children. Hu had taken out loans from many commercial banks and had a total debt of about ¥200 million.

DATE: September 1, 2011
COMPANY: Butterfly Dream Shoe Factory
BOARD CHAIR: Huang Jie
DETAILS: Huang fled. The reasons and funds involved are unknown.

DATE: September 9, 2011
COMPANY: Bai Le Appliances
BOARD CHAIR: Zheng Zhuju
DETAILS: Zheng absconded with money and is being hunted down by the police. Zheng owes a total of ¥2.8 billion to creditors in cash loans, bankers' acceptances, and so on.

DATE: September 13, 2011
COMPANY: Ao Mi Fluid Equipment Technology Co., Ltd.
BOARD CHAIR: no data
DETAILS: The board chair, general manager, and other responsible persons have fled; tens of millions worth of precision machine equipment is missing.

DATE: During the Mid-Autumn Festival, 2011
COMPANY: New Naibao Footwear
BOARD CHAIR: no data
DETAILS: The board chair fled. The reasons and funds involved are unknown.

DATE: During the Mid-Autumn Festival, 2011
COMPANY: Tang Style Shoes
BOARD CHAIR: Huang Bohe
DETAILS: Huang fled. The reasons and funds involved are unknown.

DATE: During the Mid-Autumn Festival, 2011
COMPANY: Interstellar Footwear
BOARD CHAIR: no data
DETAILS: The board chair fled. The reasons and funds involved are unknown.

DATE: During the Mid-Autumn Festival, 2011
COMPANY: Europa Standard Parts Co., Ltd.
BOARD CHAIR: no data
DETAILS: The board chair fled. The reasons and funds involved are unknown.

DATE: September 15, 2011
COMPANY: Bao Hang Stainless Steel Products Co., Ltd.
BOARD CHAIR: Wu Baozhong
DETAILS: Wu has disappeared. He owes more than ¥200 million in bank loans, ¥80 million in informal loans, and ¥50 million in acceptance bills.

DATE: September 19, 2011
COMPANY: Fu Yan Brothers Industrial Co., Ltd.
BOARD CHAIR: no data
DETAILS: The board chair fled owing hundreds of millions in usury. After his funding chain broke, his property was resold by the bank.

DATE: September 22, 2011
COMPANY: Long Wan Blue Sky Pharmacy
BOARD CHAIR: no data
DETAILS: The board chair fled, owing 80 million in funds

DATE: September 21, 2011
COMPANY: Zhejiang Xintai Group
BOARD CHAIR: Hu Fulin
DETAILS: Hu fled with his wife and children. Hu had taken out loans from many commercial banks and owes up to ¥800 million, but insiders disclose that he actually owes more than ¥2 billion.

NO ONE IS IMMUNE

The nightmare has finally started. Once the usury capital chain starts to break, no participant can be spared.

In the usury chain, the debtors at the downstream end are often the first to fall. When lending interest rates are too high, it greatly increases the cost of capital to lending companies, causing the companies' already fragile capital chain to be further tightened, and making payment riskier. There is a popular saying in Jiangsu and Zhejiang Provinces: "Usurious interest is a bottomless pit. Real estate is the only lucrative industry that can fill up that pit other than selling drugs." The black hole of usurious funds grows deeper and deeper, and when people who are involved think they are powerless in the black hole, their final choice is fleeing, suicide, and other extreme methods of escape. They think that fleeing is not much better than suicide. To them, fleeing means that the credit they have accumulated over the years is doomed. They will be left with half of a lifetime of credit to reclaim. Moreover, some creditors have a Triad background, and once they are on the run, they are doomed to set foot on precarious roads.

In addition to borrowers left with a choice between outstanding debts or escape, middlemen such as loan sharks and guarantors are also implicated. He Jin, who was previously mentioned, also suffered the nightmare of a debtor escaping with unpaid debts. A clothing business owner borrowed ¥3.7 million in usury from He Jin as bridge financing. Four days later, after the owner borrowed another ¥5 million from the bank, all the money evaporated. The borrower had quietly transferred his money. He Jin went to the Ministry of Public Security for help, but because his loan interest rates had been more than four times the legal interest rate, the law could not protect him. He Jin had been "burned" by his debtor.

Many loan sharks are on the run. They are forced to be on the run because borrowers are on the run. When borrowers cannot repay their debts, loan sharks still need to keep up appearances—"robbing Peter to pay Paul." However, as more and more accounts "default," the loan sharks can no longer keep a lid on things. When creditors hear about the situation, they rush to make a "run on the bank," and the loan sharks also use their exit strategy to leave as soon as possible.

The front end of the debt chain has "fallen into enemy hands," and all is lost for creditors, who are the upstream of capital customers. They have done everything in vain, as if "collecting water with a sieve." Not only are high interest rates a "pipe dream," even the principal investment is altogether lost.

The case of the wise (and scheming) woman of Erdos has already provoked much discussion in the lending industry. This "entrepreneuse," who was an ordinary working girl, continually used usurious financing to expand her business. She involved beauty companies, hot pot restaurants, food and beverage companies, real estate, and more. She even knew how to use borrowed money to "enjoy life." She made several real estate investments, purchased villas and luxury cars, often visited high-end consumer areas, was obsessed with gambling, and enjoyed playing the lottery. Because of the grifter's "good reputation, high interest rates, and connections," more and more people wanted to be her creditor. People lent her money in order to obtain the interest, and this was not limited to locals, but also included people from nearby Tongliao, Henan, and other places. There are no exact figures on the exact amount of money this con artist borrowed. It is estimated to be between ¥830 million and ¥1 billion; and there are an estimated 4,000 victims.

More and more people have been drawn to the "bloodthirsty nature" of usury, and are constantly investing their money in this manner, disrupting the local financial order. Moreover, the business entities of many areas are taking on the risk of borrowing and lending just to survive. Lenders "add insult to injury" by raising interest rates and exploiting the real economy. In doing so, they cause greater distress to the real economy, which has been struggling already. In the end, many business owners may go on the lam, and many enterprises may go bankrupt. Thus the foundation of local enterprises, which had been painstakingly built, will be destroyed overnight.

One's lifetime is as short as a bird flying by, so things happen rapidly, and everything has cause and effect. These financial fluctuations of usury and confusion have been caused by a series of factors, including the increasingly thin profits of business entities, low bank interest rates, the currency policy loosening and then tightening, the openness of financing platforms, and a lack of transparency.

A Game of "Drinking Poison to Quench the Thirst"

There are only two subjects I'm interested in: zoology, and botany. Actually, I'm also interested in history, but not in the textbook that we study. . . .

. . . He always asks the students stupid questions. And stupid questions are far more difficult to answer than intelligent ones. . . .

Then it dawned on me that I'm not afraid of beggars. I'm just afraid of their hands. I'm not afraid of beggars who take something away from me, but I'm afraid of the hands that deprive me of things that I had.

—MIKHAIL ZOSHCHENKO[10]

THE STRUGGLE OF SMALL AND MEDIUM-SIZE ENTERPRISES (SMES)

Data from the Wenzhou Central Branch of the People's Bank of China shows that 35 percent of Wenzhou's informal lending funds are used for operating business enterprises.[11] Extremely high interest rate-based usury is a poison, and the borrowers—i.e., small and medium-size enterprises—drink it repeatedly. They are addicted.

During a time of peace and prosperity, it seems to be more difficult for small and medium-size enterprises to come to life. Many enterprises complain incessantly, putting on the sad faces of doomsday. For years, they are destitute, sometimes in chains and sometimes in self-confinement, but they usually end up seeing better days. However, today it looks like the bright private economy has been flipped upside down and is unrecognizable in its misery.

Business people have complained that 2011 was the year that they faced the greatest pressure to survive. Life had never been so tough, even compared to the time during which the financial crisis broke out.

Small and medium-size enterprises are ill-fated mainly in two areas: first, transitions faced at the low end of the industry chain, and second, monetary tightening and financing difficulties.

The market-oriented trend continues to strengthen the economic environment. In the short term, however, this trend may not be making things easy for independent small and medium-size enterprises; and the battle for the survival of the fittest might become more brutal. Markets which stick to the principle of "efficiency and fairness" have a cruelty that can be worse than the ideology of "speculation" and the unpredictability of policy. Maneuvering through the market is like crossing a river. When one begins to cross a river, even though he starts by feeling for stones, he may be able to stumble across because the water is shallow, and because he relies on vigor, courage, and hard work. However, as the water becomes deeper, crossing also requires skill. If he relies on vigor, courage, and recklessness alone, he is very likely to drown.

When multiple factors work together, such as when the demographic dividend disappears, the price of raw materials rises, and the renminbi appreciates, it causes many real economy practitioners to enter a stormy period of doom and gloom.

Using the "labor shortage" as an example: during a continuing "labor shortage," enterprises have to pull out all the stops in order to retain their employees, and pressures on business operations surge. Economist Zhang Wuchang gives some clues about salary increases in "The New Labor Law and the Erosion Theory," in which he says that:

China's minimum wage and the new labor law have come too early. Can't you see that the factories that have had to close down are almost all simple order-taking factories where there are no research departments, with no workers unions to force the boss to pay the workers higher wages, so even though the new minimum wage law requires the boss to pay the workers higher wages, the boss just gives up on the workers and disappears. The factory is then forced to shut down.[12]

But the "labor shortage" is getting worse, and if businesses maintain staff's original salary packages, no workers will be willing to show up, and the enterprise will be unable to survive.

Low wages and wasteful production modes have become a thing of the past. The general trend for economic development is renminbi appreciation and a disappearing demographic dividend. The transition away from low-end manufacturing is also consistent with market rules. These are key steps for China's economic structure to move further toward a positive direction. The best option for the enterprises is to adapt to changes in the economic structure. In order to cross the river, the only skills one must perfectly master are brand, technology, and talent.

Transformation is life or death for enterprises. The process is very uncomfortable, and it has determined the elimination of many enterprises. At the same time, many excellent small and medium-size enterprises have successfully broken the transition bottleneck, achieved nirvana, and are adapting to the development of the market economy with a better chance for survival.

However, the transition requires a more caring policy. The forced market regulations have caused small and medium-size enterprises to be bruised and beaten, so the government should provide a relatively moderate policy and financing environment for these enterprises so that they can complete the difficult transformation.

Regrettably, however, problems such as financing difficulties act in tandem with transformations to attack small and medium-size enterprises, weakening their defenses. The real return on investment continues to decrease, there are no sustainable development funds, and even survival of the company is a problem. Because they are in survival mode, to even talk about transforming their business would be a stretch. In many factories, the former day-and-night rumbling of machines is just a memory. Shifts have declined from three, to two, and then to one; workers get an unprecedented two days of rest per work week. In addition, some factories have closed their doors and suspended operations.

"MONEY FAMINE"

Many enterprise funding chains are falling apart. The primary reason for this is monetary tightening. The economy finally broke free from the high inflation that was the negative aftereffect of the massive release of credit to deal with the financial crisis. The government began to tighten credit beginning in the second half of 2010. To some extent, this gave a glimmer of hope about the government's regulatory plans. The government carried out macroeconomic controls aimed at the capital markets with a preference to quantity over pricing, and the market stepped aside, embarrassed. Even though the central government emphasized credit control, that process was disrupted by distressed large enterprises and by local government financing. The moment that the government raised interest rates, these large consumers of credit would predictably complain, but since the government had not tested the effect of leveraging the exchange rate appreciation, the government thought that bringing credit control onto the stage was the logical thing to do. As a result, banking credit lines shrunk dramatically; and the banks were also able to recover their reported daily loan-to-deposit ratio, as well as credit rights.

During a credit crunch, many projects face crises akin to running out of food, and enterprises and local governments scramble for money. In this environment, financing discrimination becomes more obvious, where state-owned enterprises and local governments, which are rationing their funds, are given priority. Private enterprises, especially small and medium-size enterprises, are the most vulnerable to discrimination. Therefore, the all-important allocation of resources—represented by finance—is still completely dysfunctional.

During the good years, small and medium-size enterprises are able to obtain some loans from formal financial institutions. However, when there's a "money famine," bank doors suddenly shut on them, and it becomes more difficult to take out a loan. The legitimate forms of informal financing that go hand in hand with developing small and medium-size enterprises has not been fully established. Take the "New 36 Clauses" as an example: the State Council's "Several Opinions on Encouraging and Guiding the Healthy Development of Private Investment," known as the "New 36 Clauses," encourages informal investment to be drawn into the financial sector by setting forth the following:

> [The government will] allow nonstate domestic investors to set up financial institutions. Under the prerequisite of strengthening effective supervision, promoting standardized operations, and preventing financial risks, [the government will] relax the equity ratio restrictions on financial institutions. It will support nonstate domestic investors to buy shares to

participate in the capital increase and share expansion of commercial banks and to participate in the restructuring of rural and urban credit co-ops. It will encourage nonstate domestic investors to initiate or participate in establishing village banks, loan companies and rural mutual co-ops (credit unions) and other financial institutions. It will loosen the restrictions on the minimum contribution ratio in village banks, corporate banks, or community banks. It will implement full tax deductions for loss reserve policies on loans for small and medium-sized enterprises and simplify audit procedures for small and medium-sized write-offs by financial institutions. It will appropriately relax the single investor stake limit on small loan companies. It will implement financial subsidy policies toward agricultural-related business of small loan companies, which are equivalent to village banks. It will encourage nonstate domestic investors to start credit guarantee companies and to perfect the risk compensation mechanisms and risk-sharing mechanisms of the same. It will encourage nonstate domestic investors to start financial intermediary service organizations, and to participate in the restructuring and reorganization of securities, insurance, and other financial institutions.[13]

The policy is a good policy, and we look forward to seeing better results from it. Yet the policy is transitioning with great difficulty from being just a document to bringing about practical results. When many nonstate domestic investors notice the policy liberalizing in their favor, they submit a plan to the government; but who would have thought, after endlessly waiting for their plan to be approved, the approval would never materialize? Thus the policy was simply all thunder and no rain. This indicates that some government departments simply did not trust nonstate domestic investors. The departments adopted a wait-and-see attitude, worried that once the tiger is set free, it will return to the wild. It would then be difficult to control the wild investors, and everything could very well end up in ruin. So they waver in their resolve to lend to the investors.

The "small" loan companies that were so happily successful a few years ago have been somewhat fettered by the severe constraints. And because they generally handled such small quantities of money, they have been unable to provide "timely rain" during borrowers' hour of need in the recent "money famine." Because they are driven by their own interests, they will probably become involved in lending, becoming complicit in usury.

The manufacturing industry, which represents small and medium-size enterprises, survives only with extreme difficulty because they face the "wolf" of diluted profits on one end, and the "tiger" of monetary tightening on the other.

However, these manufacturers are unwilling to allow years of blood and tears to be destroyed all at once. They refuse to initiate defeat, so they do everything they can to persevere, waiting for things to dramatically turn in their favor. If things become too rocky, they will consider "gambling"—i.e., borrowing from a loan shark. The loan shark is a delaying tactic in order to remit the failure of their business by maintaining normal operations or repaying maturing loans.

Small and medium-size enterprises have a greater flexibility and faster turn-over rate. If they receive a certain amount of deposits from incoming orders, take out a loan for production, and use the annual rate to repay the loan interest, they might manage to scrape by. But business as usual cannot cope with the skyrocketing interest on a usurious loan. If a business owner is ultimately unable to pay off the loan, then s/he is forced to walk away from the business.

Many enterprises take usurious loans to pay off matured debt, since outstanding balances in matured debt will not only provoke bank claims but also affect the credit rating of the business. To deal with such critical situations, enterprises will first attempt to dismantle their usurious loans and carry out a rollover in order to pay off the matured debt. Then they will take out another loan from the bank in order to pay off the usurious debt. Using a usurious loan to pay off debt is the same as using smoke and mirrors to hide the true problem of the business: liquidity. The quality of bank loans severely drops, and a local financial earthquake hits as soon as crisis embroils the enterprise. Furthermore, not all banks keep their commitment to tighten credit when there is a tight monetary policy: as long as a previous loan can be repaid, the bank will provide another loan. Some enterprises take out usurious loans as a last resort to repay debt, and yet banks can change their previous policies or break their promises and deny further loans to the small businesses, thereby causing the business owner's wishful calculations to fall short. The enterprises put on an obsequious smile in front of the banks to hide their gloomy, sullen faces, but there is not enough money to go around. The bank that controls the purse strings is the god who calls all the shots, so businesses are helpless.

"Money" Falls from Heaven?

State-owned banks and securities markets carry too many moral hazards and distorted interests, and although the financial backing of national credit can provide expedient solutions to these problems, it will stifle innovation in the financial industry and hinder institutional changes needed by the industry. This will inevitably cause resources to be misallocated with an excessive amount of resources wasted in image-building projects. Without the room to freely develop and without the rule of law, nonstate domestic finance cannot be modern finance.

—CHEN ZHIWU[14]

THE REAL GLASS DOOR

In this particular scenario, informal lending seems to be the volcanic crater of the era, with greed and madness rising up like thermal heat, and profit-driven smoke curling up, enveloping the nonstate domestic financial sector like fog.

Profit and risk make deadly strikes in turn, and although a lot of people are well aware that these are irrational capitalistic games played with worldly favors as collateral, many people still rush to gamble with the fatalistic attitude that they are letting fate take its course. It is a mystery exactly where the rapidly assembled and expanded capital originated, and why it remains in the area of lending, but it will unhesitatingly crush one into powder.

In thirty years of reform and opening up, the nonstate domestic sector has accumulated large amounts of capital, and while specific numbers are unavailable, it is known to be "vast and mighty." Nonstate domestic capital has many options, and it looks for opportunities everywhere to achieve its purpose of money producing money. However, in the long run, the pathways for nonstate domestic capital are becoming narrower, not wider.

The term "Made in China" used to describe a nonstop production machine for nonstate domestic capital, which gave birth to the "Made in China" glory, making us wonder which came first, the chicken or the egg. Nowadays, the phrase "Made in China" is losing its allure. Its former glory and dreams are diminished, and the term is as diluted as water. Placing bulk orders for mass-manufactured products in specific quantities, producing commodities quickly and inexpensively, overdrawing the market's resources, etc., are defective genes in the survival-of-the-fittest market economy. These defective genes cause the industries associated with "Made in China" to slide toward the low end of the industrial chain, and be trapped in the downhill mode of meager profits, unable to extricate themselves. With capital fleeing manufacturing en masse because it is unprofitable, some owners of small and medium-size enterprises simply sell their plant with the single-minded intention to become creditors.

In contrast with this attitude toward the manufacturing industry, private capital "covets" the consistently lush land of financial resources, and relatively abundant profits to be found in energy, minerals, finance, and other sectors.

Nonetheless, these sectors are terrified of private capital, so the glass door of reality remains a huge barrier. One aspect of the fear is derived from inadequate clarity and refinement in policy posture. In electricity, telecommunications, rail, civil aviation, petroleum, and other industries and areas, policy clauses have welcomed the entry of nonstate domestic capital, but have not introduced additional measures or further details about the entry conditions for such capital. Thanks to a lack of detailed rules, the original obstacles remain, private capital has no access to those industries, and it can only hover around the "gristle."

On the other hand, even if private capital is given access and has comprehensive and considerate rules to guide it, it may not be able to enter successfully enter. The industry sectors, where repeated orders and injunctions banned the entry of private capital, are now the domain of state-owned enterprises, which form a conglomerated monopoly. If private capital is permitted to enter, private enterprises could compete for resources, funds, and technology, causing the pampered state-owned enterprises to naturally be unhappy with the situation. Therefore, state-owned enterprises would inevitably suppress and cause the marginalization of private capital at its first opportunity.

Just as people ceased to pay attention in "The Boy Who Cried Wolf," if government policies have too many instances of "all thunder and no rain," then the nonstate domestic capital will also lose patience. Nonstate domestic capital no longer has the authority to rally a mass response in many policy-guided sectors. They fear that policy is hardly to be trusted, is inept once introduced to reality, or would flip-flop between loosening and tightening of restrictions. The bottom line is that they would bear the losses of macroeconomic regulation and control.

Policies are fickle, and the nonstate domestic investors who have struggled along for many years are still unable to find their way. They fear that an unspeakably painful and large wave of macro-control will come their way. At the same time, their investments are being blocked in many sectors, and thus informal lending—with its high profits, low thresholds and lack of restrictions on thinking outside the box—gives them a "Peach Blossom Spring" utopia.[15]

CONTINUOUSLY EXPANDING PROFIT-DRIVEN NATURE

Capital has a profit-driven nature, and if you force it to put on various hats of moralities and denounce it for its greediness, you would be forcing it to do something entirely unnatural, like "forcing a duck onto a perch." Nonprofit-driven capital is charitable, rather than economic. The key is in whether society has provided reasonable channels and found more reasonable, safe, and healthy methods of making a profit.

The snowball of informal lending is growing larger as it rolls with astonishing speed. The reason for its massive growth is the infusion of new blood in the form of banks, listed companies, individuals, and so on, in addition to the nonstate domestic capital that extends from the real economy.

When quoting bourgeois writer T.J. Dunning, Marx emphasized that:

> With adequate profit, capital is very bold. A certain 10 percent will ensure its employment anywhere; 20 percent will certainly produce eagerness; 50 percent, positive audacity; 100 percent will make it ready to trample all human laws; 300 percent, and there is not a crime at which it will scruple nor risk it will not run, even to the chance of its owner being hanged.[16]

Profit is the best bait. Even banks are unable to withstand the temptation of usury and covet its benefits. In China, financial institutions are subject to strict control of their interest rates, and financial institutions themselves do not have too many interest rate decision rights. It fluctuates only within a relatively small range, but the interest rate is not greatly impacted by the supply and demand of funds, rather it is a disguised form of price control. By market logic, during a credit crunch, corporate demand for funds soar, and interest rates increase correspondingly.

However, being constrained by the confining spell of interest rates controls, interest could only seesaw on a small scale. In contrast to the tepid bank interest rates, the informal lending momentum is fierce, and its excessively rich profits have invited the "envy and jealous hatred" of banking institutions. Some banks have begun to consider usury. Bank funds have used various undercover approaches to enter the usury chain: banks deduct money from short-term deposits and join hands with guarantee companies to carry out usury; the bank's high interest rates are absorbed by the guarantee companies, and after completing one quarter's "loan-to-deposit ratio" task, the other party removes the deposited money the next quarter, while at the same time, the banks provide low-interest loans to the guarantee companies; or the bank staff become usury shareholders of the company and engage in covered-up lending under false pretenses.

Furthermore, listed companies, state-owned enterprises, and some other enterprises that do not lack money are quietly joining the ranks of lenders. According to statistics published by the *People's Daily Online* statistics, as of September 1, 2011, a cumulative total of 117 listed companies released entrusted loan announcements, involving sixty-four listed companies, among which thirty-five exceeded bank loans in the same period. The total loans amounted to ¥16.935 billion, and the year-on-year growth was 38.2 percent. Most of these listed companies with entrusted loans were state-owned holding companies, such as China Railway Group, COFCO Property, Hangzhou Jiebai, Modern Pharmaceutical, and so on.[17] Part of the entrusted loans of listed companies were related loans: capital flows to their holding companies, mainly for emergency, with low interest rates, generally subject to the benchmark interest rate, in order to ensure the unobstructed flow of the capital chain of affiliated companies. For nonrelated transactions, interest rates were higher, with most borrowers having guarantees or mortgages—e.g., such as the loans from Eastern Communications to Dynamic Group of Jiangsu, which used 50 million outstanding shares of Jianghuai Engine as loan guarantees.

More of the prevalent entrusted loans of listed companies were driven by high interest. Moreover, entrusted loans could bring lucrative profits to listed companies and whitewash their financial statements. For instance, Jingshan Light Machine announced that it would provide public investors with an annual interest rate of 15 percent of the entrusted loan of ¥60 million, with a six-month loan period. Jingshan Light Machine could have earned ¥4.5 million in interest income, but its first-quarter net profit was only ¥1.74 million; Ningbo Bird Company released its 2011 mid-year report showing that shareholders of listed companies earned a net profit of ¥35.1458 million, and among that, entrusted loans to the public had a benefit of ¥17.7383, accounting for 50.47 percent of the proportion of profits.

The entrusted loans of listed companies were suspected of violations pertaining to the China Securities Regulatory Commission (CSRC), which had issued Article Ten, "Listed Companies' Issued Securities Management Approach," and the Shenzhen Stock Exchange, which had issued Article Ten, "Small and Medium-Size Listed Companies Fundraising Management Regulations." Article Eleven provided that the amount of funds raised by listed companies could not exceed the actual requirements of the project, that the funds should be in special savings accounts (except for those of financial enterprises), and the funds should not be used for financial transactions and investments.

Listed companies' entrusted loans led to further misallocation of China's financial resources with further deterioration of the financial ecology. Meanwhile, the listed companies were sitting idly by, and reaping a "lending interest," creating a dependence on lending to create value, while on the contrary, its own growth was weakened.

Charles Kindleberger writes, "Manias and panics, I contend, are associated on occasion with general irrationality or mob psychology."[18]

In addition to original underground banks, guarantee companies, pawn shops, and small loan companies also act as fund brokers, drawing in capital from all around. People of various classes and occupations successively enter into usury, heightening its "enthusiastic" atmosphere. Among these, Wenzhou is especially notable.[19] So the media euphemistically called them the "Nationwide Money Speculation Carnival"; civil servant lenders have tacit, unspoken rules, which gave rise to the term "official's money"; individual business owners sell their business, but they give up real estate speculation and stocks and minerals speculation, going directly to "speculative money"; bank staff use the convenience of their employee identity to conduct underground bank lending; and there are even more ordinary citizens—such as teachers, corporate executives, white-collar workers or even migrant workers—who took out some or all of their savings to become creditors.

The beautiful "Peach Blossom Spring" is only a brief moment, described as "Petals of the dazzling and fragrant blossoms . . . falling everywhere in profusion."[20] A financial crash lies on the other side of irrational prosperity. China's nonstate domestic financial sector is facing tragedy too difficult to avert.

Where Does the Road Lead?

It is too windy,
Wind,
Behind me,
A stretch of gray sand
Has yellowed the snow-white clouds.
I have sown the seed of my heart,
Will it sprout?
It will! It is entirely possible!

—GU CHENG[21]

GIVING INFORMAL LENDING A "LEGAL" PATHWAY

The Yangtze River has always flowed to the east, and its original intention seems to be gone. Anxiety is like wild weeds—countless crazy stories are made ambiguous by the dim light—and for the time being, the future is unpredictable for the small and medium-size enterprises that rose from their boundless grassroots origins, as well as for informal lending.

Dawn inevitably always squeezes into the door. The greatest expectations for a government policy "life preserver" came from Premier Wen Jiabao's visit to Wenzhou, Guangzhou, and other places in October 2011. He called for the government to support and assist small and medium-size enterprises to ride out the storm. Hereafter, a series of sunshine policies were introduced, such as a 50 percent reduction in income taxes. However, the timely policy was only an expediency measure. It did not fundamentally solve the "food shortage" of small and medium-size enterprises, and usury continued to spread unchecked as it seized the perfect opportunities to barbarically resurface.

Looking ahead, it is clear that changing the current development of the present nonstate domestic capital, giving input channels and more reasonable space in which to survive, will be more conducive to China's financial ecology, and give small and medium-size enterprises a healthier financing environment.

All along, the entity of nonstate domestic capital has been a feature on China's financial stage. It constantly walks on the fringes and in the gray areas, steadily providing a stream of development funds for a large number of private enterprises. A significant portion of private enterprises have obtained varying amounts of nonstate domestic credit in varying stages of development. It is difficult for small and medium-size enterprises (especially micro-enterprises), to obtain loans from formal banks, so the booming informal lending industry has become the natural and effective financing channel.

Economist Chen Zhiwu interprets informal lending by laying out the financial distress caused by current financial regulation:

> Our prior conception of lenders was that they were good, honest people, but the very behavior of lending is very poor, and their hearts are very dark, so we need government to intervene and prevent them from exploiting those who need to borrow. Perhaps this way of thinking is right, but after the government departments ban nonstate domestic financing, they must have a better way of solving the issue of ordinary people's demand for capital. State-owned banks and formal local credit cooperatives are only able to absorb deposits from ordinary people, but they don't give loans to them. This has forced the common citizen to look for underground banks, pay higher interest rates for access to capital, and be without options apart from this.[22]

Nonstate domestic investors are like soldier ants—many and scattered, able to quickly assemble. Nothing is impossible for them, and they invade many unexpected corners, eventually accumulating in number as "many grains of sand accumulate to form a pagoda"—they have an enormous influence on the local economy. However, since they have drifted outside of the law for so long, their capital chain is relatively hidden, and relevant government departments have difficulty regulating them effectively. Hence, many regulatory authorities tacitly manage lenders in an effort to "maintain the status quo in informal lending, but if someone excessively stands out, then the remedy is to 'punish the culprit as a warning to others.'"

The relevant departments regulate ineffectively, because of a blank slate of relevant laws and other factors, allowing the problematic, invincible Lulin Army[23] of nonstate domestic investors to arise. These are vigorous, wild, and high-risk, managed with confusion, and relying on force to make debtors settle, which causes the government and society to be more fearful of informal lending.

However, it is unwise to simply "defeat these lender exploiters," rudely banning the development of nonstate domestic finance. On one hand, if the formal financial institutions' lending hole grows bigger, it will be difficult to meet the needs of nonstate domestic capital. Moreover, banks have always liked the icing on the cake, and if they are forced to offer their timely assistance to small and medium-size enterprises as "fuel in snowy weather," they may be unwilling, and might even raise the financial risks imposed upon those enterprises. On the other hand, the quantity of nonstate domestic capital is huge and cannot be blocked. If you beat it to death, forcefully suppressing it, it will only grow more rampant, and more underground banks will emerge.

THE LOGIC OF FINANCE: DEREGULATION

Instead of encircling and obstructing informal lending, it would be better to give it a pathway, allowing it to operate in the open and coexist with private enterprises. Meanwhile, it is crucially important to guide private enterprises down the appropriate road on which they ought to travel.

Economist Fred Hu pointed out one of the means to counter China's financial "preference for foreign capital," noting that:

> China has nonstate domestic investors with the international experience and reputation of HSBC, Citigroup, and Goldman Sachs. The advantages of these institutions are readily apparent. They can immediately bring the product technology and management experience of commercial banks, which conforms to the traditional Chinese cultural concept of the "perfect match."

Compared to the experienced and more professional overseas capital, nonstate domestic capital is mainly characterized by idleness, and is more suitable for smaller scale financial institutions, such as micro-credit banking companies, village banks, and so on.

In the process of allowing informal lending to operate in the open, government should play the role of guide and regulator: guide and encourage more and more organizations to conduct informal lending, and include nonstate domestic capital in standardized and legal channels, while at the same time strengthening the regulation of informal lending to ensure the legalization of the business, and avoid the occurrence of problems such as interest deformity, entanglement in underground society violence, and financing fraud.

In fact, other unknown aspects of China's financial reform are hiding behind the monumental drama of increasingly rampant usury, and do not know which course to follow.

The seemingly robust financial system is not fully adapting to China's stalwart and resolute style of economic growth. This has imposed higher standards on financial innovation and less stringent intervention in the national financial system by the government. In China, the government is the banks' main owner and manager, and this will, of course, expand the government's efforts to control funds. But this will also weaken the supervision and restraint of judicial and market mechanisms over banking operations. Moreover, the power-dominated financial system is a rent-seeking hotbed, which causes financial resources to be allocated according to the "theory of personal relationships," where entities or individuals with more intimate relationships with government power brokers have easier access to resources. Establishing a nonstate-based domestic financial system that adapts to developments in the private economy would precisely mean loosening financial control, implementing the important display of financial reform, and helping to weaken the monopoly of the financial sector, thereby creating a more reasonable and equitable financial environment.

NEW MYSTERY: CHINA'S ECONOMY IS NO LONGER SUBMISSIVE

The story that has been thrust to the foreground by history is not following the wishful thinking and carefully planned script consented to by the people and government. Since the beginning of 2010, the Eastern entity of the Chinese economy, that was "brilliant when given a bit of sun" and constantly created miracles under strong governmental guidance, is no longer submissive: inflation is high, the stock market is depressed and not easily improved, and small and medium-size enterprises continue to drown while shouting, "I can't live any longer!" Once again, people are impatiently awaiting the policy market (government using policy to influence the ups and downs of the stock market index). However, when the policy market hammer smashes down, it does not necessarily produce the immediate, beautiful results that the government desires—those outcomes that make a big splash everywhere. People cannot help panicking a little over the question: what has become of China's economy?

With "China's Economy is No Longer Submissive," Jin Qi, editor-in-chief of the *Financial Times*, at once named and mercilessly pierced the issue of the confusion that China's economic development has encountered:

> If Beijing hopes to introduce a new stimulus plan, it may find itself pow-erless to mobilize the rapid and resolute response in the way that they achieved in 2009. Of course, Beijing still has a few weapons. It can issue government bonds, or it can launch investment companies' relief toward banks and local governments, and for this, it might draw on a portion of the $3.2 trillion in foreign exchange reserves. But these methods would not produce the kind of immediate effects on economic growth as in 2009, and would be unable to solve another real problem: *if* the government merely provides the hint of high yields but allows the financial system to continue to exist, funds would flow from state-owned banks to shadow banks, and the funds that could be mobilized by the government-led stimulus plan will be further reduced.[24]

Since the rise of China's economy, it has been a constant source of debate in which no one can provide a conclusively correct answer, just as there was debate about whether a river was shallow or deep in the children's story "The Little Horse and The River." Throughout the path of development, and along with the ups and downs of the economy, China continuously throws out various riddles, one after another, then changes course and takes a 180-degree turn, which no one really understands. China's economy, sharpened by the financial crisis, became more dynamic but seemed to encounter even greater challenges in the days after economic recovery. And various problems caused pro-market factions and pro-centralized economic planning factions to debate endlessly about the solutions.

"The hour for action is come. Heaven's wonders brook not man's delay. . . . The god himself gives us the fire and the will."[25] The mystery of China continues, and we have no choice but to use indomitable courage and strength to blaze through the thorny trail and continually uncover new answers to the riddles!

Preface

1. Tang Degang, *Wanqing qishinian* [Seventy years in the late Qing dynasty] (Changsha: Yuelu Bookstore, 1999).

Chapter 1

1. Lu Xun, *Lu Xun quanji* (Complete works of Lu Xun), 16 vols. (Beijing: People's Literature Publishing House, 1981), 3:325–28.

2. Joseph Needham, *The Grand Titration: Science and Society in East and West* (Toronto: University of Toronto Press, 1969), 16.

3. Ronald I. McKinnon, *The Order of Economic Liberalization: Financial Control in the Transition to a Market Economy*, 2nd ed. (Baltimore: Johns Hopkins University Press, 1993), 192.

4. James M. Buchanan and Thomas L. Friedman statements from CCTV *China Memorandum* project team writings, *China Memorandum* (Shengyang: Volumes Publishing Company, 2010). The documentary series *China Memorandum*, directed by Jiang Shiming, began airing in 2009 on the financial channel CCTV-2; Gao Qiang is head writer for the show.

5. Joseph Alois Schumpeter, *Capitalism, Socialism, and Democracy* (London: Harper and Row, 1943); trans. Wu Liangjian (Beijing: Commercial Printing Press, 1999).

6. John and Doris Naisbitt, *China's Megatrends: The 8 Pillars of a New Society* (New York: HarperBusiness, 2010), 42.

7. Érik Izraelewicz, *Quand la Chine change le monde* [When China changes the world] (Paris: Grasset & Fasquelle, 2005); trans. Yao Haixing (Beijing: CITIC Press, 2005).

8. When China and Italy reestablished diplomatic relations in July 1971, the Italian state television station issued a letter to the Chinese Foreign Ministry Information Department, hoping to shoot a documentary in China and commissioning Michelangelo Antonioni as the director. The resulting film, *Chung Kuo, Cina* (1972), was said by Bernardo Bertolucci to "really depict the poetry of China's cities and countryside." Antonioni called it "not a movie about the country of China, but rather a movie about the Chinese people."

9. Hou Yujing, "China is far away: together we return to China" [in Chinese], *Life Magazine* (November 2006).

10. Ibid.

11. Huang Yasheng, *"Zhongguo mo shi" dao di you duo du te?* [Just how unique is the "China model"?] (Beijing: CITIC Press, 2011).

12. Zhou Qiren, *What Did China Do Right: Look Back to the Reform, Look Forward to the Future* [in Chinese] (Beijing: Peking University Press, 2010).

13. Zhang Weiwei, *Zhingguo zhen-han: Yige "wenming xing guojia" de jueqi* [China shock: the rise of a "civilization-state"] (Shanghai: Renmin chubanshe, 2011) was revised and translated into English by the author as *The China Wave: Rise of a Civilizational State* (Hackensack, NJ: World Century Publishing Corporation, 2012). Zhang is a professor at the Geneva School of Diplomacy and International Relations and Senior Fellow at the University of Geneva Center for Asian Studies, as well as a news commentator in *Global Times* and *People's Daily.*

14. Zhang Weiwei, quoted in "Society needs to be viewed with a type of mature mentality" [in Chinese], *First Financial Daily*, June 3, 2011, http://finance.ifeng.com/opinion/xzsuibi/20110603/4106882.shtml.

15. Huang, *"Zhongguo mo shi" dao di you duo du te?*

16. Huang Yasheng, "There is no unique China model" [in Chinese], *Business (Review)* (November 2011).

17. Jerry Dennerline, *Qian Mu and the World of Seven Mansions* (New Haven: Yale University Press, 1989), as quoted in Xu Zhiyuan, *Zu guo de mo sheng ren* [motherland stranger; in Chinese] (Beijing: CITIC Press, 2010).

18. Alexis de Tocqueville, *Democracy in America*, trans. Henry Reeve and Francis Bowen, 2nd ed. (Cambridge: Sever and Francis, 1863), 1:559.

19. Dani Rodrik, *One Economics, Many Recipes: Globalization, Institutions, and Economic Growth* (Princeton, NJ: Princeton University Press, 2007), 15–16; trans. Zhang Junkuo and Hou Yong-zhi (Beijing: CITIC Press, 2009).

20. Ren Zhongyi, quoted in "The revolution has not yet been successful; comrades must persevere" [in Chinese], *South Reviews* (November 15, 2005); the line is a quotation from Sun Yat-Sen.

21. The song "A Wolf in Sheep's Clothing," with music, lyrics, and performance by Dao Lang, became an online sensation in 2006.

22. Siqin Gaoli, vocal performance of "Siqin Gaoli's Sadness," by Qin Tian, recorded in Beijing, 2007, on *Siqin Gaoli's Sadness.*

23. Rosa Luxemburg to Sophie Liebknecht, July 20, 1917, in *Letters from Prison, with a Portrait and a Facsimile*, trans. Eden and Cedar Paul (Berlin: Publishing House of the Young International, 1923), 43.

24. Xu Zhiyuan, "Flowing Destiny" [in Chinese], *Life Magazine* (March 2006).

Chapter 2

1. Zhang Wuchang (Steven N.S. Cheung), *The Economic System of China* [in Chinese] (Beijing: CITIC Press, 2009).

2. Jeffrey Sachs, quoted in Fareed Zakaria, *The Post-American World* (New York: W.W. Norton & Company, 2008), 89; trans. Zhao Guangcheng and Lin Minwang (Beijing: CITIC Press, 2009).

3. Zhang Wuchang (Steven N.S. Cheung), *Thirty Years of China's Economic Reforms* (Beijing: CITIC Press, 2009).

4. Arthur H. Smith, *Chinese Characteristics* (Shanghai: "North China Herald" Office, 1890), 185, http://archive.org/stream/cu31924023247160#page/n195/mode/2up/; trans. Qin Yue (Shanghai: Xuelin Publishing House, 2001).

5. Constantine P. Cavafy, "Thermopylae," in *The Complete Poems of Cavafy*, trans. Rae Dalven (New York: Harcourt, Brace, & World, Inc., 1961), 9.

6. Martin Jacques, *When China Rules the World: The End of the Western World and the Birth of a New Global Order* (New York: The Penguin Press, 2009), 173; [in Chinese] (Beijing: CITIC Press, 2010).

7. Cui Jian was born in 1961 to an ethnic Korean family and is known as "the father of Chinese rock." He became famous with the 1986 song "Nothing to My Name": "The ground beneath my feet is moving, the water around me is flowing, but you always laugh at me, that I have nothing to my name . . ."

8. Peter Hessler, *Country Driving: A Chinese Road Trip* (New York: Harper Perennial, 2011), 284; trans. Li Xueshun (Shanghai: Shanghai Translation Publishing House, 2011).

9. Gary Becker, "Interview with Nobel Laureate in Economics" [in Chinese] by Gao Xiaoyong, 1994; sponsored by *Economics News*; published by China Press, July 2005.

10. Friedrich Hayek, *Fatal Conceit: The Errors of Socialism* (London: Routledge, 1988), as trans. by Feng Keli (China Social Sciences Press, 2000).

11. The 14th National Congress of the Chinese Communist Party, convened in 1992, held that the goal of China's economic system reforms would be to establish a socialist market economic system, which would enrich and develop the theory of socialism with Chinese characteristics. The establishment of a socialist market economy involves many areas including the economic base and superstructure. There must be a series of corresponding institutional reforms and policy adjustments, close attention must be paid to developing the master plan, and implementation must be systematic.

12. The 15th National Congress of the Chinese Communist Party, convened in 1997, confirmed Deng Xiaoping Theory as the guiding ideology of the party and confirmed governing the country according to law as the basic strategy for governing the country. It had upholding the public ownership as the mainstay and diverse forms of ownership developing side by side. It adhered to distribution in accordance with work and the coexistence of diverse modes of distribution and confirmed this as the basic economic system and distribution system for China's primary stage of socialism.

13. Zhou Qiren, [The path to redefining property rights], address delivered at the 10th Annual Guanghua New Year Forum (January 2008), Beijing University, revised and expanded by the author, http://www.cenet.org.cn/article.asp?articleid=30173.

14. Ling Zhijun, *1978, Li shi bu zai pai huai* [1978, history is no longer wandering: the rise and fall of communes in China] (Beijing: People's Press, 2008).

15. Ibid.

16. Translated for this book from Zhang Wuchang (Steven N.S. Cheung), *Zhongguo hui zou xiang "zi ben zhu yi" de dao lu ma?* (1982); this work has been previously published in English as *Will China Go "Capitalist"? An Economic Analysis of Property Rights and Institutional Change*, Hobart Paper 94 (London: Institute of Economic Affairs, 1982).

17. Chen Guang, quoted in Wu Xiaobo, *Jidang sanshi nian* [A turbulent thirty years], vol. 1, *Zhongguo qi ye, 1870–1977* [Chinese enterprises, 1870–1977] (Beijing: CITIC Press, 2007).

18. The Third Plenary Session of the 14th Central Committee of the CCP was convened on November 11–14, 1993. The Plenary Session adopted the *Decision on Certain Issues in Establishing the Socialist Market Economic System.* The Plenary Session pointed out that the socialist market economic system is fused with the basic socialist system. The socialist market economic system was established to allow the market, under national macroeconomic controls, to play a fundamental role in resource allocation. It was established to further transform the state-owned enterprise operating mechanism and to establish a modern enterprise system adapted to market economy requirements and with clear property rights, clarified powers and responsibilities, government functions separated from enterprise management, and scientific management.

19. This concept is named after Italian economist Vilfredo Pareto. Vilfredo Pareto proposed the idea of Pareto optimality, which is also called Pareto efficiency, an important concept in game theory. Pareto optimization refers to a state of resource allocation. Under the conditions of making no individual worse off, it is not possible to make the situation of some individuals change for the better; it is the "ideal kingdom" of fairness and efficiency.

20. CCTV, *The Power of Corporations,* documentary, 2009.

21. Smith, *Chinese Characteristics,* 395–6, http://archive.org/stream/cu31924023247160#page/n405/mode/2up.

22. Ibid, 329, http://archive.org/stream/cu31924023247160#page/n409/mode/2up/.

23. Alvin Toffler, *The Third Wave* (New York: William Morrow, 1980), 11; trans. Huang Mingjian (Beijing: CITIC Press, 2006).

24. Liyan Jie, "Zijin buzu cheng zhongguo qiye zou chuqu zuida ruanle" [Lack of funding for Chinese enterprises is greatest weakness], *China Business Network* (May 5, 2011), http://www.cb.com.cn/1634427/20110505/205640.html.

25. Thomas Murphy as quoted in Li Lanqing, *Tu wei : guo men chu kai de sui yue* [Breakthrough: opened the door early years; in Chinese] (Beijing: Central Literature Publishing House, 2008).

26. Deng Xiaoping as quoted in Li Zhenghua, "Zhunbei gaige kaifang de yici zhongyao huiyi" [ready to reform and opening up an important meeting], *Guoshi yanjiu canyue ziliao* [National history research], 214.

27. Ma Licheng, *Crossing Swords for Thirty Years: A Personal Account of Four Great Debates in Reform and Opening Up* [in Chinese] (Nanjing: Jiangsu People's Press, 2008).

28. Zheng Xiaoying quotation from CCTV *China Memorandum* project team writings, *China Memorandum* (Shengyang: Volumes Publishing Company, January 2010).

Chapter 3

1. John Kenneth Galbraith, *The Age of Uncertainty* (Boston: Houghton Mifflin, 1977), chapter 6.

2. "Beijing Normal University professor says a 10 million yuan pension may not be enough" [in Chinese], *People's Daily* (April 7, 2010), http://news.163.com/10/0407/03/63KURQPL0001124J.html.

3. Ernest Hemingway, "Notes on the Next War: A Serious Topical Letter," *Esquire*, September 1935.

4. Milton Friedman, *Money Mishief: Episodes in Monetary History* (New York: Harcourt Brace Jovanovich, 1992), 193.

5. John F. Kennedy, "Message to the Congress Presenting the President's First Economic Report," January 22, 1962, *The American Presidency Project*, http://www.presidency.ucsb.edu/ws/?pid=8621.

6. Lytton Strachey, as quoted in Yao Deng, *Huangjin zhengduo zhan* [The war for gold; in Chinese] (Hangzhou: Zhejiang People's Publishing House, 2012).

7. Zhu Rongji, quoted in Henry Yuhuai He, *Dictionary of the Political Thought of the People's Republic of China* (Armonk, NY: M.E. Sharpe, 2001), 215.

8. On April 1, 1994, Zhao Jingrong, president of the Agricultural Bank of China's Hengshui Branch, abused his authority by having his staff issue two hundred letters of credit, which are transferable and irrevocable, worth $10 billion total. Those letters of credit were then given to two swindlers who registered a company in the United States.

9. At the beginning of 1993, Shen Taifu, president of the Great Wall Machinery and Electronics Company, launched a fundraising spree on the promise of new energy-saving technology. More than 20 subsidiary companies and 100 branches were set up all over China, more than 3,000 people were hired, and more than $1 billion was amassed. This whirlwind of activity finally attracted the attention of Premier Zhu Rongji, who was incensed. Zhu felt that it disrupted the financial order as well as resulting in the corruption of party cadres. On April 8 of the following year, Shen was executed by firing squad.

10. Zhu Rongji at the National Financial Work Conference, China, 1993.

11. The *Decision Concerning Reforms of the Financial System* promulgated by the State Council in December 1993 stated that "the tools for monetary policies are mandatory reserve requirement ratio, central bank loans, the rediscount rate, open-market operation, foreign exchange operation by the central bank, credit limits, and the deposit and loan interest rate of the central bank."

12. John Maynard Keynes, *The Economic Consequences of the Peace* (London: MacMillan & Co., 1919), 220.

13. Website of the People's Bank of China.

14. Keynes, *Economic Consequences*, 220.

15. Zhou Qiren, "Currency like honey" [in Chinese], *The Economics of the Real World* (blog), June 19, 2009, http://zhouqiren.org/archives/839.html.

16. David Wessel, "A Lesson from the Blackout: Free Markets Also Need Rules," *Wall Street Journal*, August 28, 2003, A1.

17. "All-China Federation of Industry and Commerce: 90 Percent of Small and Medium Enterprises are Facing a Credit Crunch, and the Business Environment is Deteriorating."

18. Wu Jinglian, "China's Investment-Driven Model Causes Allocation Inequality, with the Poor Getting Poorer" [in Chinese], *China Radio Network* (March 20, 2011), http://finance.ifeng.com/news/20110320/3704636.shtml.

19. Zhang Wuchang (Steven N.S. Cheung), "Herijun zailai?" [Come again?], *Steven N.S. Cheung* (blog), December 19, 2008, http://blog.sina.com.cn/s/blog_47841af70100bwlp.html.

Chapter 4

1. André Kostelany, loosely translated from a 1961 address; in the recording at https://www .youtube.com/watch?v=GomcMKBIjMA, the analogy begins at 1:50.

2. The "August 10" stock market unrest in the Shenzhen stock market: On August 7, 1992, the Shenzhen Stock Exchange made a public announcement of the balloting for the subscription of new shares for 1992, saying that it would issue 500 million public shares in 1992 and sell five million shares subscription forms, with the subscription success rate at ten percent. This announcement attracted more than 1.5 million people all over China to Shenzhen for the shares subscription. On August 10th, the officials announced that all five million new shares forms had been sold out after just three days of sale. Those who were still queuing for the subscription forms were angry and frustrated. Being "mobilized" and "incited" by the various media channels with differing viewpoints and perspectives, a large number of people descended on the Shenzhen government office to protest, and police, armed officers and even water cannons had to be employed to quell the unrest. In the early morning of August 11, the Shenzhen government announced the issue of another five million shares of subscription forms and the people "dispersed immediately and went back to queuing." After that, Vice Premier Zhu Rongji gave this incident a name—"a technical out-of-control incident."

3. The "327" Treasury Bond Futures Incident: "327" treasury bonds refer to the three-year state treasury bonds issued in 1992. A total of ¥2.4 billion worth of bonds were issued with the maturity date in June 1995. The interest rate was 9.5 percent of the coupon rate plus the inflation subsidy rate, and the Ministry of Finance did not state if the interest subsidy would be included. Key short-sellers, represented by Wanguo Securities Company, deemed that there would be no interest subsidy and decided to short-sell. On February 23, 1995, Liaoning Guofa (Group) Co., Ltd., one of the allies of Wanguo Securities, suddenly changed position and started going long. The situation reversed and the stock price rose by ¥3.77 within ten minutes, meaning that Wanguo Securities would take a loss of billions of yuan. With seven minutes before the closure of the Treasury bond trading, Wanguo Securities, in desperation, suddenly dumped 1.056 million sell orders worth ¥211.2 billion after 16:22:13, and made a profit of ¥4.2 billion. The change in situation struck everyone dumb and caused chaos in the stock exchange. That night, the Shanghai Stock Exchange announced that all transactions made after 4:22:13 p.m. had been invalidated. Wanguo Securities took a loss of ¥1.3 billion, and had to merge with Shenyin Securities on July 16, 1996. Guan Jinsheng, the boss of Wanguo Securities, was sentenced to seventeen years of imprisonment.

4. Shi Jianxun, "As the Stock Market Continues to Fall, Why Is the Economic Barometer not Working?" [in Chinese], *People's Daily Overseas Edition* (December 29, 2010), http://finance .people.com.cn/GB/13606328.html.

5. "Liu Hongru: For the Sake of a Solemn Promise" [in Chinese], *China Securities News / Xinhua Wang* (October 9, 2004), http://news.xinhuanet.com/fortune/2004-10/09/content _2068059.htm.

6. Wang An, *The World of Stock Investors: Record of 30 Years of China's Securities Market* (Beijing: CITIC Press, 2011).

7. Xu Xiaonian, "How can one talk about saving the market with no crisis in the A share market?" [in Chinese], *Xinkuai Paper* (March 31, 2008).

8. Yuan Jian, *Zhongguo zhengquan shichang pipan* [Critique of the Chinese securities market] (Beijing: China Social Sciences Press, December 2004).

9. The split-share structure, also known as equity division, refers to the system in which only a portion of a listed company's shares are floated on the market. These shares are known as tradable shares, are public shares and take up about one-third of the total shares in the stock market; the other type of shares is not floated on the market and they are known as nontradable shares. These shares are mainly state-owned shares and corporate shares, and take up about two-thirds of the total shares in the stock market. As of the end of 2004, the total equity of listed companies was worth ¥714.9 billion, and the number of nontradable shares was 454.3 billion shares, taking up 64 percent of the total equity. Of these, state-owned shares took up 74 percent of the nontradable shares.

10. Cai Shen Kun, "The Chinese stock market, approaching the brink of death, is in urgent need of reinvention" [in Chinese], *Securities Review*, January 31, 2005, http://blog.ifeng.com/article/15285816.html.

11. "The Key Turning Point of the Chinese Stock Market: China Securities Regulatory Commission Chairman Shang Fulin Accepts Exclusive Interview with Xinhua News Agency Reporter on the Focus of the 'Split-Share Reforms'" [in Chinese], *Xinhua News Daily*, May 15, 2005, http://news.xinhuanet.com/zhengfu/2005-05/16/content_2962035.htm.

12. Ai Jingwei, "Twenty Years of Taking and Returning of Listed Companies: Financing is 2.27 Times of Dividends" [in Chinese], *First Financial Daily* (November 27, 2010), http://finance.sina.com.cn/stock/s/20101127/01269018159.shtml.

13. "Resignations of Senior Management of Small and Medium Enterprise Board, Growth Enterprise Board Increased Many Times, Reason May Be to Reduce Holdings and Cash Out," *China Securities Journal* (September 20, 2011).

14. Wu Jinglian, television interview on CCTV *Economic Half-Hour*, January 14, 2001; Chinese transcript at http://www.cctv.com/financial/jingji/sanji/toutiao/200102/toutiao08.html.

15. Julius Fuchik, *Notes from the Gallows* (New York: New Century Publishers, 1948), 112; original Julius Fučík, *Reportáž psaná na oprátce* (Prague: Nakladatelství Svoboda, 1945).

16. Matt. 7:13–14 (New International Version).

17. "Wu Jinglian: State-owned assets should be transferred to workers to narrow the wealth gap" [in Chinese], *West China City Daily*, February 15, 2005, http://news.xinhuanet.com/fortune/2005-02/15/content_2579257.htm.

18. Daniel Kahneman and Amos Tversky, "Prospect Theory: An Analysis of Decision under Risk," *Econometrica*, 47, no. 2 (March 1979): 263–91.

19. Yuan, [Critique of the Chinese securities market].

20. Wang, *The World of Stock Investors*.

21. Chen Zhiwu, "Shui lai jianguan jianguan weiyuanhui" [Who will supervise the monitoring committee?], *Economic Observer*, November 21, 2004, http://finance.sina.com.cn/g/20041121/15401169680.shtml

22. "Reform of the Split Share Structure: The Final Battle Will Come in 2006," *Xinhua Daily Telegraph* (January 8, 2006), http://news.xinhuanet.com/stock/2006-01/08/content_4024470.htm.

23. Lu Yuan, "Securities and Futures Work Conference Convenes, Nine Key Points in Shang Fulin's Overall Arrangement" [in Chinese], *First Financial Daily* (January 22, 2007), http://finance.sina.com.cn/stock/t/20070122/03373267689.shtml.

24. Deng Xiaoping, "Excerpts from Talks Given in Wuchang, Shenzhen, Zhuhai and Shanghai, January 18–February 21, 1992" in *Selected Works of Deng Xiaoping* Vol. 3 (Beijing: Foreign Languages Press, 1994), 241, http://archive.org/stream/SelectedWorksOfDeng XiaopingVol.3/Deng03#page/n241/mode/1up.

Chapter 5

1. Adam Smith, *An Inquiry into the Nature and Causes of the Wealth of Nations, Volume 2,* (London: W. Strahan and T. Cadell, 1778), 2: 316.

2. "Urban and rural residents move from poverty towards overall prosperity" [in Chinese], National Bureau of Statistics of China (October 31, 2008), http://www.stats.gov .cn/tjfx/ztfx/jnggkf3on/t20081031_402513470.htm.

3. "More effective fiscal policy for expanding domestic demand," *China Economic Weekly* (November 24, 2008).

4. Qu Jing, Qin Yazhou, and Yao Runfeng, "Scholastic research claims the gap between different income groups in China is up to 23 times," *Xinhua* (December 28, 2009), http://news.163.com /09/1228/15/5RKMRMP4000120GU.html.

5. Yao Yang, "The End of the Beijing Consensus: Can China's Model of Authoritarian Growth Survive?" [in Chinese], *Foreign Affairs* (February 2, 2010), http://www.foreignaffairs.com /articles/65947/the-end-of-the-beijing-consensus.

6. Gerard Manley Hopkins, "Pied Beauty" in *Gerard Manley Hopkins: The Major Works*, ed. Catherine Phillips (New York: Oxford University Press, 1986), 132.

7. Arthur Okun, *Equality and Efficiency: The Big Tradeoff* (Washington, DC: Brookings Institution, 1975), 2.

8. Chen Zhiwu, *Why Are the Chinese Industrious and Yet Not Rich?* [in Chinese] (Beijing: CITIC Press, 2008).

9. Zheng Gongcheng, "Such Things in China," in *22 Degrees Observation Column*, Chinese Business Association Press, Beijing (January 2010).

10. Zhou Bapi is a despotic landlord character created by the famous writer Gao Yubao, and is a famous male villain role. So that long-term hired hands could work more, Zhou Bapi learned how to crow like a rooster late at night (the text of the indenture contract expressly provided that when the rooster crows, you must wake up and work). Because there were no clocks or other timekeeping tools back then, long-term laborers would get up for work when the rooster crowed and then call it a day at sunset. Zhou Bapi crowing like a rooster at midnight made those long-term hired hands get up earlier and work for him day and night. (*Baidu Encyclopedia*)

11. Liang Xiaosheng, *Zhongguo shehui ge jieceng fenxi* [Analysis of the various strata in Chinese society] (Beijing: Hunan Literature & Art Publishing House, 2011).

12. John Maynard Keynes, *The General Theory of Employment, Interest, and Money* (New York: Harcourt, Brace and Co., 1991), 372.

13. Cui Xiaohong, "Fiscal revenue of 8 trillion yuan: too much or too little" [in Chinese], *Yahoo! Financial Review* (September 2, 2010), http://biz.cn.yahoo.com/10-09-/149/y8k9.html.

14. Wen Jibao on March 5, 2010, quoted indirectly in "Bao Xilai: Jinzhi gaodang zhangxiu bangong lou fandui puzhang langfei" [Bo Xilai: ban upscale office building renovation, oppose extravagance], *People*, March 6, 2010, http://news.sina.com.cn/c/2010-03-06/012219800198 .shtml; transcript at http://bbs1.people.com.cn/postDetail.do?id=98112216.

15. Liu Guangfu, quoted indirectly in Wan Koa, "Gongche xiaofei jiejin guofang kaizhi daibiao weiyuan huyu jian jieyue jiguan" [Consumer representative members call for reduced spending . . .], *China Youth Daily*, March 13, 2006, http://news.sina.com.cn/c/2006-03 -13/06299334758.shtml.

16. Zhong Wei, "1000 Wan weibi gou yanglao?" [Is ¥10 million enough for retirement?], *Talents*, March 1, 2010, http://www.talentsmag.com/article.aspx/2353.

17. CCTV *China Memorandum* project team writings, *China Memorandum* (Shengyang: Volumes Publishing Company, 2010).

18. Dai Xianglong, quoted in Wang Guoqiang, "Zhong ru qianjin de minsheng chengnuo" [Your daughter's livelihood pledged], *China Youth Daily*, December 27, 2009, http://zqb .cyol.com/content/2009-12/27/content_3002216.htm.

19. Zhou Qiren, "Bing you suo yi dang wen shui" [Medical services and whom you turn to], op-ed, *Economic Observer*, September 9, 2008, http://www.eeo.com.cn/observer/special/2008 /09/09/113094.html.

20. Department of Health website.

21. Wu Mingjiang, quoted in Guoxiang He, "Zhengxie weiyuan Wu Mingjiang: Gongli yiyuan bingfei zhenzheng gongli" [CPPCC member Wu Mingjiang: public hospitals are not really public], *Morning News*, March 10, 2009, http://old.jfdaily.com/xwzt/news/2009/z1r_60069 /15_60088/200903/t20090310_564651.htm.

22. William Wilson as quoted in Paul A. Samuelson and William D. Nordhaus, *Jing ji xue*, trans. by Chen Xiao (Beijing: Posts & Telecom Press, 2008), chapter 19; originally published as *Economics* (Boston: McGraw-Hill, 2001).

23. [Ralph Waldo?] Emerson as quoted in Xiaosheng Liang, *Zhongguo she hui ge jie ceng fen xi* [Analysis of all sectors of Chinese society] (Beijing: Economic Daily Press, 1997).

24. "Situational Analysis of the Implementation of National Education Expenditure from 2004 to 2008," *China Education Daily*.

25. Li Xiaoliang, "Youth Assault Incident Becomes Target Again, How Sad" [in Chinese], *China City Daily, September 9, 2011*, http://www.wccdaily.com.cn/epaper/hxdsb/html/2011-09 /09/content_378626.htm.

Chapter 6

1. Ye Tan, *What Can Save the Chinese Economy?* [in Chinese] (Beijing: CITIC Press, 2009).

2. "Sinopec collects 30 billion yuan capital from domestic banking group to build Fujian refinery project" [in Chinese], *China Securities Journal* (September 7, 2007).

3. Listing indicators: This term is a Chinese characteristic and the product of a planned economy; the government-issued allocation can also be interpreted as a market-listing permit, that is, the certificate that allows companies to list on the market. Only by possessing

market-listing indicators do enterprises have the possibility of listing on the market (*Summary of the Accumulation of Knowledge According to Finance*).

4. "Zhejiang business funds remain stagnant, private enterprises wait for detailed guidelines after new private investment policy introduced" [in Chinese], *China Newsweek* (June 2010).

5. "Gangtie chanye tiaozheng he zhenxing guihua" [Steel industry restructuring and revitalization plan], March 20, 2009, http://www.gov.cn/zwgk/2009-03/20/content_1264318.htm.

6. Zhou Yaoting, quoted in Wu Xiaobo, *Jidang sanshi nian* [A turbulent thirty years], vol. 2, *Zhongguo qi ye, 1978–2008* [Chinese enterprises, 1978–2008] (Beijing: CITIC Press, 2007), 262–3.

7. Masahiko Aoki, as quoted in Xue'an Ren, *Gong si de li liang* [The power of corporations] (Taiyuan: Shanxi Education Press, 2010).

8. "Regarding the State Council of the CPC Central Committee's Decision to Combat Serious Criminal Activities in the Economic Sphere," 1982.

9. Feng Lun, *Wild Growth* [in Chinese] (Beijing: CITIC Press, 2007), 148–9.

10. Shi Yuzhu, quoted in Xu Jin, "Shi Yuzhu: Shehui dui wo de yaoqiu bi dui chen tianqiao dinglei gao" [interview with Shi Yuzhu], *China Business News*, January 27, 2008, http://tech.sina.com.cn/i/2008-01-27/10131999390.shtml

11. Harry M. Markowitz, as quoted in *Interview series: Nobel laureates on Chinese economy and economics* [in Chinese], Economics News newspaper series (Beijing: China Planning Press, 1995), 4.

12. The "catfish effect" is the idea that strong competition rallies weak businesses or sectors to improve. For more on the catfish effect and the private sector of China's economy, see Zhang Youzhuo et al., "The 'Catfish Effect' of the Private Sector on the Economy of the People's Republic of China," *J. Enterprising Culture* 4:331 (1996). DOI: 10.1142/S0218495896000198.

13. Ye, *What Can Save the Chinese Economy?*.

14. Adam Smith, *An Inquiry into the Nature and Causes of the Wealth of Nations, Volume 2*, (London: W. Strahan and T. Cadell, 1778), 2: 35.

15. Ling Zhijun, *1978, Li shi bu zai pai huai* [1978, history is no longer wandering: the rise and fall of communes in China] (Beijing: People's Press, 2008).

16. Friedrich von Hayek, *The Road to Serfdom* (London: Routledge, 1944); trans. Wang Mingyi (Beijing: China Social Sciences Publishing House, 1997).

17. Liu Chuanzhi, "I am the one who has starved and also ate roast pork" [in Chinese], speech given at the Tenth China "Future Star" annual meeting, June 25, 2010; full text at http://it.sohu.com/20100625/n273075673.shtml. Liu Chuanzi, senior engineer, is the chairman of the board of Legend Holdings Limited, chairman of the board of Lenovo Group Limited, and vice-chairman of the All-China Federation of Industry and Commerce. He has been named "Model Worker" and "Man of Reform in China," the "2000 CCTV China Economic Person of the Year," "Outstanding Individual Contribution to Promoting US—China Relations," "Asia's Best Business Person," and "Business Leader of China's Economic Decade," and was selected by *Time* magazine as one of the "25 Most Influential Global Executives," among other honors (*Chinese Times*, November 1, 2011).

Chapter 7

1. Will Durant, in Will and Ariel Durant, *The Lessons of History* (New York: Simon and Schuster, 1968), 102.

2. John King Fairbank, *The Cambridge History of China*, vol. 14, *The People's Republic* (Cambridge: Cambridge University Press, 1978). Fairbank was a Harvard University tenured professor, famous historian, America's most prestigious China observer, dean of the field of research of recent contemporary history of the United States and China, the "number one China hand," and founder of the Center for East Asian Research at Harvard. During his lifetime, he served as vice-chairman of the Far Eastern Association of the United States, Chairman of the Asia Society, President of the Historical Society and other important roles. Fairbank was dedicated to China research for fifty years, from the time he entered Oxford until his death in 1991. The vast majority of his works are discourses on issues in China. (*Chinese Times*, November 1, 2011).

3. Chen Xulu, *The metabolism of modern Chinese Society* [in Chinese] (Shanghai: Shanghai Academy of Social Sciences Press, 2006).

4. Sam Walton, *Made in America: My Story* (New York: Random House, 1993), 45.

5. Guo Jiaxue, quoted in Zhang Rui, "Dongsheng jituan dongshi zhang Guo jiaxue: Hen bu she de chushou bai jia hei" [Dongsheng Group chairman Guo Jiaxue: far from willing to sell white and black], *Beijing News*, April 16, 2008, http://news.hexun.com/2008-04-16/105285223.html.

6. Xu Zhiyuan, Huang Jixin, and Kenichi Ohmae, "China Has Awakened" [in Chinese], *The Economic Observer* (December 2003).

7. David Packard, cofounder of Hewlett-Packard, as quoted on "HP huipu zhi dao" [The HP Way], November 11, 2008, http://www.chinahp.net/article/anoutHP/2008-11-11/67.html.

8. William R. Hewlett, interview by Jim Collins and Jerry I. Porras, November 19, 1990, quoted in *Built to Last: Successful Habits of Visionary Companies* (New York: HarperBusiness, 1994), 1.

9. Zhou Hong quoted in "Cracking the Chinese Internet Jungle Genes" [in Chinese], *Chinese Entrepreneur*, November 22, 2010, http://www.iceo.com.cn/renwu/35/2010/1122/204179_7.shtml.

10. Feng Lun, *Wild Growth* [in Chinese] (Beijing: CITIC Press, 2007), 12–13.

11. Gao Mengling, quoted in "'Fengyu ma shengli' zuozhe Gao Mengling: Ma shengli chongpo di shi fanlong" [Gao Mengling's "Ma Shengli storm"], *Dazhong-Qilu Evening News*, November 13, 2008, http://news.sina.com.cn/c/2008-11-13/110216646609.shtml.

12. Wu Jinglian, *Calling for a Rule of Law Market Economy* (Beijing: SDX Joint Publishing Company, 2007).

13. Wang Qi Guang, "Jianlibao 3 laochen zai zao jubu beihou: Yi she 7 nian qian zhuanyi ju zi" [Jianlibao 3 behind veteran arrest], *Oriental Outlook Weekly*, July 20, 2009, http://news.sina.com.cn/c/sd/2009-07-20/142818258213.shtml.

14. In early times, rent was just rent on land. Later, it referred to the excess revenue brought about by all the scarce factors of production. Modern research has discovered that government policy intervention and administrative controls—such as import quotas, production licenses, price controls, and even industry-specific special controls that include restrictions on the number of employees, etc.—can all create an artificial scarcity, thereby also forming excess revenue. Therefore, the rental concept used now has been further expanded to

include excess returns formed by the intervention of public authority in economic activities or controls. (*Baidu Encyclopedia*)

15. Zhang Wuchang (Steven N.S. Cheung), "The Future of China" [in Chinese], *Hong Kong Economic Journal* (August 1985).

Chapter 8

1. Liu Liu, *Dwelling Narrowness* (Wuhan: Changjiang Literature and Art Publishing House, 2007). The novel *Dwelling Narrowness*, also known literally as "Snail House," is the most realistic depiction of the various kinds of craziness and bleakness staged every day under the backdrop of high housing prices in China (*Chinese Times*, November 1, 2011).

2. On June 5, 2003, the People's Bank of China issued Document No. 121, titled "Notice on Further Strengthening the Management of Real Estate Credit Business." This document provided a provision that loans should focus support in accordance with residential projects in order to bolster the purchasing power of low- and middle-income families. These should be appropriate on large houses, large acreages, high-end real estate, villas and other projects; and in regards to mortgage loans for land reserve institutions, the loan amount shall not exceed seventy percent of the appraised value of land acquired, and the maximum loan period shall not exceed two years. When a borrower applying for an individual housing loan is buying his first owner-occupied house, banks should continue to enforce the twenty percent rule on the proportion of the down payment; and for those buying beyond the second house (including the second home), the proportion of the down payment should be appropriately increased.

3. The Ministry of Land and Resources, *2009 Analysis Report of Land Price Situation in Major Cities Nationwide* [in Chinese].

4. "National Bureau of Statistics 2010 Annual [Housing Prices] Rate Chart" [graph, in Chinese], *China Economic Net* (February 28, 2011), http://house.ifeng.com/news/detail_2011 _02/28/4890716_0.shtml.

5. Wang Shi and Mou Chuan, *Roads and Dreams* [in Chinese] (Beijing: CITIC Press, 2006).

6. Ibid., 163.

7. In the early 1990s, there were constraints on Central Finance. At the national financial meeting on July 23, 1993, when he was the Vice Premier of the State Council, Zhu Rongji adopted the proposals of economist Dong Fu and others, formally proposing a recommendation for the tax sharing system for the first time. That same year, at the convening of the Third Plenary Session of the 14th CPC Central Committee, The Plenary adopted the "Decisions on Issues about the Establishment of the Socialist Market Economic System," proposing three tasks for financial system reform. One of the reform tasks was to implement tax sharing between the two levels of government (i.e., the central government and the local governments). On January 1, 1994, the tax sharing management system was officially implemented.

8. Ye Tan, *What Can Save the Chinese Economy?* [in Chinese] (Beijing: CITIC Press, 2010).

9. Chinese Academy of Social Sciences, *Housing Green Paper: China Housing Development Report (2010–2011)* [in Chinese].

10. Mei Xinyu, "Real Estate Profits Amaze People, Opposing Huge Sudden Profits Urgent Essay" [in Chinese], *China News Network* (April 27, 2011), http://news.xinhuanet.com /house/2011-04/27/c_121352463.htm.

11. Juju Wang, "Real estate developers expose the industry's unspoken rules: Where the huge profits come from" [in Chinese], *China Youth Daily* (July 2, 2010), http://finance.qq.com /a/20100702/003557.htm.

12. April 30, 2010, in "Ten National Implementation Conditions," it was clearly stated that starting May 1, a Beijing family can only buy one new item of commodity housing, and when purchasing housing, buyers also need to truthfully fill out a "Family Members Situation Declaration Form." If they are found to have provided false information and fraudulently purchased housing, a real estate license transaction will not be conducted. This was the country's first proposed "housing restriction policy" on the set number of families purchasing houses. Since then, urban housing restriction policies on each of the first and second tiers were introduced close together.

13. Will Rogers, in his column of April 13, 1930, which was syndicated in papers across the United States.

14. Huang Xiu, "Rong Pan: The 'brave woman' holding the Molotov cocktails" [in Chinese], *Southern Weekend* (December 3, 2009), http://news.qq.com/a/20091203/001695_1.htm.

15. Ibid.

16. On December 31, 2001, the State Council issued the "Notice of the State Council, Regarding the Issuing of the Income Tax Revenue Sharing Program," requiring the implementation of the income tax revenue sharing reform from January 1, 2002. The specific elements of the program were: the State Council decided to reform the current method of obtaining income tax revenue according to the divisions of corporate affiliation and relations, and to implement the central and local government pro-rata share of corporate income taxes and personal income taxes. Besides a few special industries and enterprises, the central and local pro-rata share would be implemented toward revenue from other enterprises' income taxes and personal income taxes. In 2002, the central share of the income tax revenue was 50 percent and the local share was 50 percent; in 2003, the central share of the income tax revenue was 60 percent and the local share was 40 percent. The sharing ratio after 2003 will be reconsidered according to actual income situations.

17. Green Dragon on the Left, White Tiger on the Right: Ancient Chinese versed in the five elements matched the North, South, East, West, and Center with five colors according to the five elements of yin and yang, and each color was then also accompanied by a holy animal and a deity. The East was green and was matched with the dragon, the West was white and was matched with the tiger, the South was red and was matched with the phoenix, the North was black and matched up with the turtle, and yellow was the pure color in the center. When the feng shui master was exploring burial sites, the land forms that were protruding out on both sides at the front of the terrain could be used as the site of the graves. They all had unique names: some called it the Green Dragon on the left, or the White Tiger on the right, whichever had the meaning of guardians, and in a courtroom there were also the same decorations. On the pillars in the left and right chambers, green dragons and white tigers were painted, to suppress evil spirits. Later, "Green Dragon on the left, White Tiger on the right" acquired an extended meaning of being a very important advisor position or role. (*Baidu Encyclopedia*)

18. "Restart Fiscal Reforms," *Outlook Newsweek* (February 2011).

19. Nie Meisheng, "Analysis of the real estate market and regulation policies" [in Chinese], *Sina Real Estate* (April 19. 2011), http://h.house.sina.com.cn/n/2011-04-19/141143772 _8.shtml.

20. There are a total of fourteen kinds of real estate industry–related taxes, and they are, respectively, the business tax, corporate income tax, deed tax, personal income tax, fixed assets investment orientation regulation tax, urban maintenance and construction tax (urban construction tax), arable land occupation tax, property tax, urban real estate tax, stamp duty, land use tax (urban land use tax), land appreciation tax, resources tax, and the education surtax. Among these, the urban real estate tax that was levied on foreign companies was abolished in 2009, and the fixed assets investment tax was also suspended from 2010 onward.

21. "Zhu Rongji and alumni discuss current events" [in Chinese], *Phoenix Weekly* (2011, Period 15).

22. Zhu Rongji, quoted in "Zhu Rongji tong pi tudi caizheng shi sougua min gao" [Zhu Rhonji on land finance] China Research Intelligence Corporation, n.d., http://criic.com/zsgl/xqkanwu .aspx?nid=1517&Swittitle=2011%C4%EA%B5%DA6%C6%DA.

23. In 1942, Zhang Ailing published the essay "Chinese Life and Fashions" in the English-language monthly magazine *Twentieth Century*. Later, the essay was rewritten in Chinese and published under the title "A Chronicle of Changing Clothes" in the December 1943 issue of *Past and Present*. In 1945, the essay was then put into a collection of essays by Zhang Ailing titled *Liu Yan/Written on Water* (Beijing: October Arts and Literature Publishing House, 2012).

24. Xu Xiaonian, "Hutoushewei" [Anticlimax], *Xu Xiaonian* (blog), July 4, 2010, http://xuxiaonian .blog.sohu.com/155913019.html.

25. A *mu* is a unit of land area in the Chinese measurement system; 1 *mu* is approximately 666.67 sq. meters/797.33 sq. yards; 15 *mu* equals 1 hectare).

26. Mao Yushi, one of China's economists, is an expert on the U.S. and Chinese economies. He has published views such as "Affordable housing is the biggest corruption sweeping the nation," and "Housing prices are elevated by the buyers themselves." His father was Mao Yixin, a famous railway machinery expert who returned to China from studying abroad in his earlier days. His uncle, Mao Yisheng, was a famous bridge engineer. (*Chinese Times*, November 1, 2011)

27. Chen Zhiwu, *Why Are the Chinese Industrious and Yet Not Rich?* [in Chinese] (Beijing: CITIC Press, 2008).

28. Zhang Baoquan, quoted in Daidui Feng and Zhang We, "Focus of 2006: The 2006 housing price puzzle" [in Chinese], *Southern Weekend*, December 28, 2006, http://www.southcn.com /weekend/economic/200612280099.htm.

29. On March 30, 2004, the Ministry of Land and Resources and the Ministry of Supervision jointly issued "Regarding the Notice of Continuing to Carry Out Law Enforcement Work of Bidding and Auction of Commercial Land Use Rights and Listing for Sale," providing that after August 31, 2004, the issue of historical legacy can no longer be used as an agreement method to grant commercial land use rights, and state-owned land use rights must be carried out in the granting method of public tender listing.

30. Wen Jibao, quoted in "Ju zhe you qi wu [qushi]" [Home Ownership Scheme (trend)], *Southern Weekend*, July 14, 2006, http://www.southcn.com/weekend/economic/200607140033.htm.

31. See, for example, "Zhuan xiaohua yi ze: Nashui de shihou caiyong zhifubao" [Turn a joke: Tax time using Paypal], *Liu Xiaowei Tax studio* (blog), http://blog.sina.com.cn/s/blog_ 4c310b540100s4m7.html.

Chapter 9

1. Stefan Zweig, *Decisive Moments in History: Twelve Historical Miniatures*, trans. Lowell A. Bangerter (Riverside, CA: Ariadne Press, 1999), 5; originally published as *Sternstunden der Menschheit: Fünf Historische Miniaturen* (Frankfurt: Insel-Verlag, 1927).

2. "China's Financial Reform: The History and Development Trends of 30 Years of Reform and Opening Up," *China Economic Net*.

3. "Record of the report by Liu Ming Kang explaining how financial regulation is strengthened in the current situation, etc." [in Chinese], *Sina Finance* (February 26, 2009), http://finance .sina.com.cn/g/20090226/15365905780.shtml.

4. Yasunari Kawabata, "Hot Springs Communications" in *Sleepless: Selected Essays* [in Chinese], trans. Ye Weiqu (Guangxi Normal University Press, 2002).

5. George Soros, interview at environmental NGO Friends of Nature on September 17, 2001, quoted in Sun Danping, "Suo luosi: Wo bu chaozuo yazhou jinrong fengbao yiyang hui fasheng!" [Soros: If I do not speculate, the Asian financial crisis will still happen!], *Beijing Youth Daily*, September 18, 2001, http://finance.sina.com.cn/j/20010919/109013.html.

6. Feng Yu Ding, "The runaway Zhejiang 'speculation group,' usury 'on the run' becoming a trend, small- and medium-sized enterprises approach danger" [in Chinese], *Southern Weekend* (September 23, 2011), http://www.infzm.com/content/63368.

7. Ibid.

8. Paul Krugman, "The Ice Age Cometh," *Fortune*, May 25, 1998 http://money.cnn.com /magazines/fortune/fortune_archive/1998/05/25/242802/.

9. "Which CEOs have been forced to flee private enterprises in Wenzhou?" [in Chinese], special finance section, *Phoenix* (December 2011), http://finance.ifeng.com/news/special /ceobuguilu/.

10. Mikhail Zoshchenko, *The Key to Happiness* [in Chinese] (Shanghai: Shanghai Joint Publishing Company, 2009); published English translations use the title "Before Sunrise."

11. "Troubled industry: Wenzhou game of money producing money" [in Chinese], *Economic Observer* (October 15, 2011).

12. Zhang Wuchang (Steven N.S. Cheung), "The New Labor Law and the Erosion Theory" [in Chinese], *Steven N.S. Cheung* (blog), November 25, 2008, http://blog.sina.com.cn/s/blog_ 47841af70100bomd.html.

13. State Department (China), "Several Opinions on Encouraging and Guiding the Healthy Development of Private Investment," December 3, 2012, http://www.shaowu.gov.cn/showGgfwpt. aspx?id=736148826325&ctlgid=739622.

14. Chen Zhiwu, *Jin rong de luo ji* [The logic of finance] (Beijing: China International Culture Press, 2009). Chen Zhiwu is a famous economist of China's 1960s generation, and tenured professor of finance at Yale University School of Management. His areas of expertise include stocks, bonds, the futures and options markets, and macroeconomics. (*Chinese Times*, November 1, 2011)

15. "Peach Blossom Spring," written by Tao Yuanming in in 421, is a tale about a fisherman who chances upon a utopian land whose woods consist entirely of peach trees in bloom.

16. Karl Marx, *Capital: A Critique of Political Economy*, vol. 1, *The process of capitalist production*,

ed. Frederick Engels, trans. Samuel Moore and Edward Aveling (Chicago: Charles H. Kerr & Company, 1915), 834n2.

17. Zhang Bin, "According to Times Publishing, 64 listed companies put 17 billion in 'loan-sharking,' up to 24.5 percent per year," *People's Daily* (September 2, 2011), http://finance.people.com.cn/stock/GB/15572303.html.

18. Charles P. Kindleberger, *Manias, Panics, and Crashes: A History of Financial Crises*, 4th ed. (Hoboken: John Wiley & Sons, 2001), 26.

19. In 2011, the Wenzhou Central Branch of People's Bank of China released "The Most Cost-Effective Way to Invest." The survey shows that in Wenzhou, about 89 percent of families and individuals, and nearly 60 percent of the enterprises are involved in informal lending, with a total financing amount of about ¥110 billion.

20. Tao Yuanming, "Peach Blossom Shangri-la (Tao Hua Yuan Ji)," trans. Rick Davis and David Steelman (Project Gutenberg, 2008), http://www.gutenberg.org/catalog/world/readfile?fk_files=919539&pageno=2.

21. Gu Cheng, "I Cultivate" (1982).

22. Chen, *Jin rong de luo ji*.

23. The Lulin Army is one of the famous peasant insurgent armies in Chinese history. The end of the Xin Dynasty was a period of chaos, and heroes rose up in revolt one after another in an area of Lulin Mountain of Jing Province (Jingzhou, which is now modern Hubei, Hunan and southern Henan). The army was called the "Lulin Army" because it was stationed on Lulin [green forest] Mountain. Liu Xuan began his first year as emperor of the Han Dynasty, choosing the name General of the New Beginning (Gengshi Jiangjun), and the Lulin Army invaded Chang An and defeated the Xin Dynasty. Gengshi reigned for three years. However, the Lulin Army was attacked on two fronts by the Red Eyebrows Army and by the Liu Xiu Army (Liu Xiu became the Emperor Guangwu). It finally surrendered to the Red Eyebrows Army, and the Lulin Army was destroyed. Although the Lulin uprising failed, the words "Lulin" became synonymous with "hero" in future generations. (*Chinese Times*, November 1, 2011)

24. James Kynge, "Cracks in Beijing's financial edifice," *Financial Times* Chinese Network (October 11, 2011), http://www.ftchinese.com/ story/001041085/en; trans. Ho Li, http://www.ftchinese.com/story/001041085.

25. *The Aeneid of Virgil*, trans. John Conington (New York: Macmillan, 1917), 114, lines 29–32.

REFERENCES

Friedman, Milton. *Money Mischief: Episodes in Monetary History*. New York: Harcourt Brace Jovanovich, 1992. Translated as *Huo bi de huo hai: Huo bi shi pian duan* (Beijing: The Commercial Press, 2006).

Hessler, Peter. *Country Driving: A Chinese Road Trip*. New York: Harper Perennial, 2011. Translated by Li Xueshun as *Xun lu Zhongguo: Cong xiang cun dao gong chang de zi jia zhi lu* (Shanghai: Shanghai Translation Publishing House, 2011).

Jacques, Martin, *When China Rules the World: The End of the Western World and the Birth of a New Global Order*. New York: The Penguin Press, 2009. Translated by Zhang Li and Liu Qu as *Dang dai Zhongguo tong zhi shi jie: Zhongguo de jue qi he xi fang shi jie de shuai luo* (Beijing: CITIC Press, 2010).

Liang Xiaosheng. *Zhongguo shehui ge jieceng fenxi* [Analysis of the various strata in Chinese society]. Beijing: Hunan Literature & Art Publishing House, 2011.

Ling Zhijun. *1978, Li shi bu zai pai huai* [1978, history is no longer wandering: the rise and fall of communes in China]. Beijing: People's Press, 2008.

Ma Licheng. *Crossing Swords for Thirty Years: A Personal Account of Four Great Debates in Reform and Opening Up*. Nanjing: Jiangsu People's Press, 2008.

Rodrik, Dani. *One Economics, Many Recipes: Globalization, Institutions, and Economic Growth*. Princeton, NJ: Princeton University Press, 2007. Translated by Zhang Junkuo and Hou Yongzhi as *Xiang tong de jing ji xue bu tong de zheng ce chu fang* (Beijing: CITIC Press, 2009).

Smith, Arthur Henderson. *Chinese Characteristics*. Shanghai: "North China Herald" Office, 1890). https://openlibrary.org/books/OL24150565M/Chinese_characteristics. Translated by Qin Yue as *Zhongguo ren de su zhi* (Shanghai: Xuelin Publishing House, 2001).

Tang Degang. *Wanqing qishinian* [Seventy years in the late Qing dynasty]. Changsha: Yuelu Bookstore, 1999.

Toffler, Alvin. *The Third Wave.* New York: William Morrow, 1980. Translated by Huang Mingjian as *Di san bo* (Beijing: CITIC Press, 2006).

Wang An. *The World of Stock Investors: Record of 30 Years of China's Securities Market.* Beijing: CITIC Press, 2011.

Zhou Qiren. *What Did China Do Right: Look Back to the Reform, Look Forward to the Future.* Beijing: Peking University Press, 2010.

Zhang Wuchang (Steven N.S. Cheung). *Thirty Years of China's Economic Reforms.* Beijing: CITIC Press, 2009.

INDEX

A

allocation, 14

Annual Report on China's Enterprises Competitiveness: Blue Book of China's Enterprises, 92

Antonioni, Michelangelo, 7

Aoki, Masahiko, 115

B

Becker, Gary, 25

Beijing, 23, 37

"black hole effect," 43–45, 53–54

Bo Yibo, 123

BOE Technology Group Co., Ltd, 112–13

bubbles
    stock market, 71, 72, 79, 80, 82
    asset, 55, 62
    housing price, 54
    capital, 168

Buchanan, James M., 3

"butterfly effect" theory (Lorenz), 33

C

Capitalism with Chinese Characteristics (Huang), 8

catfish effect, 120–21, 211n12

Cavafy, Constantine P., 20

centralized enterprises, 111–15

Chang, Eileen, 164

Chen Guang, 30

Chen Guilin, 87

Chen Xulu, 131

Chen Zhiwu, 84, 166, 193–94, 199

Cheung, Steven N.S. (Zhang Wuchang), 8, 17, 29, 37, 63, 145, 189

China. *See also* Monetary wealth in China; "Wealthy nation, poor citizens"
    captivating "rebel," 18–20

under Deng Xiaoping leadership, 7

economic growth, 5–6
    decision-making powers for, 26
    drivers of, 54
    education costs, 107–8
    first-order principles, 11
    GDP growth, 17–18, 20, 44
    with investments, 62
    market liberalization, 9
    reduction in institutional costs, 8

facing differences in natural resources, 18–19

fractured commercial DNA, 129–34

globalization and national systems
    foreign investment, 36–38
    Third Wave, The, 33–34
    world civilizations, regulations of, 35

"go abroad" strategy, 35

Guangzhou, bustling scene of, 20–21

harm of hating the wealthy, 131–32

human capital, natural endowment of, 38–40

incentives to creating wealth, 27–32

industrialization in, 18–19

institutional deregulations, series of, 26–27

Third Plenary Session, 26, 31

moving toward great wealth, 87–88

mysteries of, 1–4
    Eastern perspective, 8–10
    expansion of freedoms, to creating wealth, 13–14
    Western scholars grievances, 5–8

powers and responsibilities, establishment of society with, 25–26

private enterprises, 143